Can You Be
GAY AND
CHRISTIAN?

Can You Be
GAY AND
CHRISTIAN?

MICHAEL L. BROWN, PhD

Most CHARISMA HOUSE BOOK GROUP products are available at special quantity discounts for bulk purchase for sales promotions, premiums, fundraising, and educational needs. For details, write Charisma House Book Group, 600 Rinehart Road, Lake Mary, Florida 32746, or telephone (407) 333-0600.

CAN YOU BE GAY AND CHRISTIAN? by Michael L. Brown, PhD
Published by FrontLine
Charisma Media/Charisma House Book Group
600 Rinehart Road
Lake Mary, Florida 32746
www.charismahouse.com

Cover design by Justin Evans
Design Director: Bill Johnson

Visit the author's website at www.AskDrBrown.org.

Library of Congress Cataloging-in-Publication Data:
Brown, Michael L., 1955-
  Can you be gay and Christian? / Michael L. Brown, PhD. -- First edition.
    pages cm
  Includes bibliographical references.
  ISBN 978-1-62136-593-8 (trade paper) -- ISBN 978-1-62136-594-5 (e-book)
 1. Homosexuality--Biblical teaching. 2. Homosexuality--Religious aspects--
Christianity. I. Title.
  BS680.H67B75 2014
  261.8'35766--dc23
                        2014002789

14 15 16 17 18 — 9 8 7 6 5 4 3 2
Printed in the United States of America

Dedicated to all those who identify
as LGBT or same-sex attracted
and who desire to love and
serve the Lord and to know the
fullness of His love in Jesus

CONTENTS

PREFACE

CAN YOU BE gay and Christian? How we answer that question has a lot to do with our definition of terms. Does "gay" simply mean having same-sex attractions? Does it mean practicing homosexuality romantically and sexually? Does it mean having a "gay" identity? And what about "Christian"? Does it mean going to a Christian church? Being born into a Christian family? Being a true follower of Jesus?

This book intends to answer the question of whether you can truly follow Jesus and practice homosexuality at one and the same time—and it has not been written lightly. For many of you reading, this is the biggest (and most urgent and painful) question in your life. Perhaps you grew up in a Christian home and, as long as you can remember, you were attracted to members of the same sex. Did this mean that God rejected you? That He preordained you to damnation? That you could never be married or have a family of your own?

Perhaps you deeply prized biblical morality and sexual purity, but you found no legitimate outlet for your romantic and sexual desires—a God-blessed outlet for the love you felt for someone—and so you went for counseling, for therapy, maybe even for some kind of deliverance and exorcism, only to find your desires unchanged. And perhaps you contemplated (or attempted) suicide.

Or perhaps you simply lost your faith, being unable to reconcile your romantic and sexual desires, which for you were not merely something you did but rather an essential part of who you are to the core of your being. Or perhaps you decided to study the theological issues afresh, coming to the conclusion that the Bible was not against loving, monogamous, same-sex relationships but rather against abusive relationships involving rape or pederasty or prostitution, or it was against homosexual acts in the context of idolatry.

If I'm describing you here, then this book is for you.

Perhaps you're on the other side of the spectrum. Perhaps you're a committed follower of Jesus and you're quite sure that the Scriptures, which reflect God's heart and will, forbid homosexual practice. Perhaps you're concerned with the pervasive effects of gay activism in our culture, and you are convinced that they are a real threat to our freedoms of speech, conscience, and religion. And perhaps you know people who claim to be "ex-gay"—in other words, former homosexuals or people who simply no longer identify and live as homosexuals—and you're quite sure that Jesus can set us free from anything.

This book is for you as well. In fact, this book is for all readers who are simply interested in what the Scriptures teach about this very important subject or in how we are to respond to the issue of homosexuality (for ourselves or for those to whom we minister).

As a happily married heterosexual man, I do not claim to be able to relate in full to the challenges faced by those who identify as gay or lesbian (or, for that matter, bisexual or transgender), but I can honestly say that I have taken these issues to the Lord in tears, that I have listened carefully to the stories of LGBT people (both those who identify as Christian and those who do not), that I have reviewed the relevant scriptural arguments in depth, and that every word of this book was written with a heart for God and a heart for people.

Although this book is written in a popular as opposed to academic style, it is based on decades of serious academic scholarship and makes reference to the most important studies on the subject. And although this book is written with a pastoral heart, it is not a counseling manual, nor is it a guide for helping those with unwanted same-sex attractions, although I believe it will prove helpful for pastors, counselors, and individual believers (or even nonbelievers) of all backgrounds.

The bibliography is meant to be selective rather than exhaustive, listing only directly relevant books (rather than articles) and excluding biblical commentaries and lexicons along with general works on homosexuality and relevant websites. I have also included a new book by Matthew Vines, scheduled to be released about the same time at this one. I did not have access to his manuscript, but because his lecture on the Bible and homosexuality went viral, I wanted to reference his book. (To be frank, I found nothing new or persuasive in his talk, despite its popularity.)

In the spirit of Isaiah 1:18, then, let us come before the Lord and reason together, embracing His will with confidence and joy, with our eyes fixed on Jesus, the author and perfecter of our faith (Heb. 12:2), knowing that whatever God has for His people is best.

—Dr. Michael Brown

A note about terminology: Last year, I began calling for teachers, preachers, professors, and Bible translators to stop using the name "James" in place of "Jacob" (which is what the Greek says throughout the New Testament),[1] even encouraging the recovery of "Judah" for "Jude" as well (yes, this certainly makes a difference). So, throughout the book, I use Jacob with James in parentheses (the same with Judah-Jude).

Chapter 1

LOVE DOES NO HARM
to ITS NEIGHBOR

The "gay Christian" argument: Love is the fulfillment of the Law and does no harm to its neighbor. But the church's teaching that homosexual practice is sin has done tremendous harm to many fine LGBT people and is therefore not loving. If we are to love our neighbor as our self, then we must affirm our LGBT brothers and sisters.

The biblical answer: While it is true that many "gay Christians" have been wounded by the church, and while the church has often failed miserably in reaching out with compassion to LGBT people, the greatest possible expression of love is to tell people God's truth, knowing that His ways are best.

JUSTIN LEE IS the founder of the Gay Christian Network. In his important book *Torn* he shares his life story in painful, heart-rending detail.[1] Called "Godboy" as a teenager because of his devotion to Jesus, he was shocked to discover that he was not attracted to the opposite sex, as were all his friends and peers. More shocking still was the discovery that he was attracted to the same sex!

Like many others who have lived through this spiritual and emotional trauma, he often cried himself to sleep, pleading with God to change him, only to find his romantic and sexual desires unchanged. What was he to do?

He knew he could not act on these desires—after all, he was single and Christian, and so acting on his sexual urges was forbidden—but he had his whole life ahead of him. Would he never be able to marry and have kids? Was he consigned to celibacy unless God changed him?

As he tells the story, in agony of heart and out of devotion to the Lord, he promised to be celibate for the rest of his life if that what was his heavenly Father required. But was it? What did the Scriptures say?

He gave himself to intensive study of the relevant biblical passages in Genesis, Leviticus, Romans, and 1 Corinthians, wrestling with the Word, wanting to find the truth, only to conclude that he was still not sure.

But the uncertainty was more than he could bear, and he was afraid of talking himself into something that wasn't right in God's sight, and he decided that he would have to commit to being celibate unless God somehow changed his thinking—but even this didn't sit right with him.[2]

And then the light went on. He concluded that there was a higher principle, an undeniable principle, based on which it would be perfectly right in God's sight for two gay men or two gay women to make a lifelong, monogamous commitment to one another—in other words, to enter into same-sex "marriage." It was the law of love, the Golden Rule.

As stated by Jesus, "So in everything, do to others what you would have them do to you, for this sums up the Law and the Prophets" (Matt. 7:12, NIV; see also Matt. 22:37–39). Or in the words of Paul:

> Let no debt remain outstanding, except the continuing debt to love one another, for he who loves his fellowman has fulfilled the law. The commandments, "Do not commit adultery," "Do not murder," "Do not steal," "Do not covet," and whatever other commandment there may be, are summed up in this one rule: "Love your neighbor as yourself." Love does no harm to its neighbor. Therefore love is the fulfillment of the law.
> —ROMANS 13:8–10, NIV; SEE ALSO GALATIANS 5:14

Lee explains the evolution of his thinking:

> With these standards in mind, it became much easier to interpret Scripture's difficult passages consistently. Yes, there were slaves in Bible times, but doesn't selfless *agape* love demand their freedom? Rules about head coverings and hair length had a purpose in Paul's culture [see 1 Corinthians 11], but if they have no ultimate bearing on our commission to selflessly love God and our neighbors, then, led by the Spirit, we can safely set them aside today.[3]

Lee then sought to apply "these standards" to the question of homosexuality," recognizing, of course, that there were "many types of homosexual behavior" that were clearly selfish, driven by the flesh and not by true love, including things like rape and prostitution and the exploitation of children. He wrote:

> But suppose two people loved each other with all their hearts, and they wanted to commit themselves to each other in the sight of God—to love, honor, and cherish; to selflessly serve and encourage one another; to serve God together; to be faithful for the rest of their lives. If they were of opposite sexes, we would call that holy and beautiful and something to celebrate. But if we changed only one thing—the gender of one of those individuals—while still keeping the same love and selflessness and commitment, suddenly many Christians would call it abominable and condemned to hell.[4]

President Barack Obama evoked a similar approach to Scripture when he famously stated on May 9, 2012:

> At a certain point, I've just concluded that for me personally it is important for me to go ahead and affirm that I think same-sex couples should be able to get married.... The thing at root that we think about is, not only Christ sacrificing himself on our behalf, but it's also the golden rule—you know, treat others the way you would want to be treated.[5]

This, in fact, has become one of the most forceful arguments in the "gay Christian" debate: the law of love requires us to embrace same-sex couples. Indeed, common humanity calls for it. In fact, to deny these committed same-sex couples the right to marry and be together is not only to violate the law of love. It is to deny *them* the right to love. Anthropologist Patrick Chapman expresses this in the title and subtitle of his wide-ranging book *"Thou Shalt Not Love": What Evangelicals Really Say to Gays*.[6]

What fair-minded, compassionate Christian would want to say to his gay brothers and sisters in the Lord, "Thou shalt not love"? Is this, then, what we are really saying to them as evangelical followers of Jesus? Journalist John Shore, himself a professing Christian, states that the answer is emphatically (and tragically) yes. He writes:

Here is that Big Difference between homosexuality and other sins: There is no sin I can commit that, by virtue of committing it, renders me incapable of loving or being loved. I can commit murder. I can steal. I can rob. I can rape. I can drink myself to death. I can do any terrible thing at all—and no one would ever claim that intrinsic to the condition that gave rise to my doing that terrible thing is that I am, by *nature*, simply incapable of giving or receiving love.

No one tells the chronic drinker, or glutton, or adulterer, or any other kind of sinner, to stop experiencing love. Yet that's exactly what so many Christians are insisting that gay people do.[7]

Is this really so? Shore continues:

When you tell a gay person to "resist" being gay, what you are really telling them—what you really *mean*—is for them to be celibate.

What you are truly and actually saying is that you want them to condemn themselves to a life devoid of the kind of enduring, romantic, partner-to-partner love that all people, Christians included, understand as just about the best part of being alive.[8]

What, then, are we telling a gay person who wants to follow Jesus? According to Shore, this is our message:

Be alone, you're demanding. Live alone. Don't hold anyone's hand. Don't snuggle on your couch with anyone. Don't cuddle up with anyone at night before you fall asleep. Don't have anyone to chat with over coffee in the morning.

Do not bind your life to that of another. Live your whole life without knowing that joy, that sharing, that peace.

Just say "no" to love.

Be alone. Live alone. Die alone.

The "sinful temptation" that Christians are forever urging LGBT people to resist is love.

Now isn't that funny, given that love is the *one thing* that Jesus was most clear about wanting his followers to extend to others? It's just so funny it makes you laugh until you want to cry. [In the first edition of this book, Shore called this position "cruel idiocy."][9]

"CRUEL IDIOCY"?

Is it, then, "cruel idiocy" to deny a gay person the right to love another person, especially if we do so in Jesus's name? Is this a matter of the church practicing "hate thy neighbor" rather than "love thy neighbor"? This is the thesis of Linda Patterson, a former heterosexual Christian, now a lesbian agnostic and civil litigations attorney, who authored the book *Hate Thy Neighbor: How the Bible Is Misused to Condemn Homosexuality*.[10] Is she right?

Jewish author Dr. Jay Michaelson, who has taught at both Boston University Law School and Harvard Divinity School, echoes the position of Justin Lee in his important book *God vs. Gay? The Religious Case for Equality*.[11] After adapting biblical language (from Genesis 2) to argue that, "It is not good for a person to be alone,"[12] Michaelson quotes the words of Jesus (Himself quoting from Leviticus 19:18), calling us to "love your neighbor as yourself" (Matt. 22:39).[13]

Basing his argument on Jesus's teaching, Michaelson writes:

> One New Testament scholar has written that "any interpretation of scripture that hurts people, oppresses people, or destroys people cannot be the right interpretation, no matter how traditional, historical, or exegetically respectable." This is a crucial point. If we approach "the question of homosexuality" as a legal, academic, or hermeneutical enterprise, we will get nowhere religiously. All the arguments work, and the anti-gay ones are just as clever as the pro-gay. No—to be responsible members of a faith tradition, we must first open our hearts, allow them to be broken by the heartrending stories of gays who have suffered from exclusion, plague, and self-loathing, and uplifted by inspiring stories of integration, love, and celebration. This is the evidence that we must admit in our deliberations—and if it is not immediately available, then we must seek it out. Any pretense of theological disposition that does not include in its procedure a long period of listening is morally bankrupt and borders on the blasphemous.[14]

Those are certainly strong words. Michaelson claims that we are "morally bankrupt" and "border[ing] on the blasphemous" if we don't hear these arguments out.

Simply stated, we are told that rejecting gays and lesbians has caused them pain and destruction; embracing them as brothers and sisters has brought them life and liberation. Surely there is only one way the church can go from here.

Michaelson continues:

> No religious tradition tells us to close our eyes, harden our hearts, and steel ourselves against the demands of love. Though it may occasionally offer us shelter in an uncertain world, rigidity of spirit is not the way to salvation. On the contrary, our diverse religious traditions demand that we be compassionate, loving, and caring toward others, even others whom we may not understand. The Golden Rule demands reciprocity and compassion, and basic equality. Do unto others as you would have them do unto you; give them the same privileges, civilly and religiously, that you would want for yourself. These are core religious principles, found over and over again in the Bible and in thousands of years of religious teaching. Compassion demands that we inquire into the lives of gay people, and discover if the "other" is like us or not. Look for the truth, and you will find it. Indeed, it will find you.[15]

Yes, this is the central argument being raised by gays and straights alike: love requires, even demands, that we recognize, embrace, sanction, and even celebrate committed same-sex unions.

Gene Robinson, the first openly gay bishop ordained by the Episcopal Church, says it all in the title of his 2012 book, endorsed by President Obama: *God Believes in Love: Straight Talk About Gay Marriage.*[16] Who can argue with love? As gay pastor Romell Weekly states on his JudahFirst .org website: "We are committed to championing God's word of truth, rightly applied through the lens of love....Scripture is the strongest opponent of oppression, marginalization, and disenfranchisement."[17]

Answering the question "What Would Jesus Do?", Robinson writes:

> No one can say for sure what Jesus would think and do in response to twenty-first century development. But for me, it is hard to imagine that Jesus wouldn't take a kindly, supportive attitude toward the love felt for each other by two people of the same gender. Can anyone imagine that Jesus would denounce and decry

two men or two women who have fallen in love, having promised to live in a faithful, monogamous, lifelong-intentioned relationship, and now seek the civil state and the Church's sacrament of marriage? I cannot.[18]

Princeton Theological Seminary professor William Stacy Johnson, a married heterosexual, makes a similar case in his 2006 volume *A Time to Embrace: Same-Gender Relationships in Religion, Law, and Politics*.[19] He concludes his book with these words:

> The time for the full consecration of exclusively committed same-gender love is coming. There are compelling theological, political, and legal reasons for us to do all we can to hasten its coming. Indeed, it is time for us to embrace those who for so many years have earnestly longed to be treated as equal and valued parts of the human family.[20]

Presbyterian pastor Jack Rogers writes even more passionately in his book *Jesus, the Bible, and Homosexuality: Explode the Myths, Heal the Church*,[21] and he too is a straight ally of the LGBT community. According to Rogers, we "are not living according to the ideals of our Savior and Sovereign, Jesus Christ, when we discriminate unjustly against any group of people in our midst."[22] Indeed, he states, "To act unjustly weakens our witness to Christ in the world. I believe that we will be one holy and whole church only when all our members are treated equally."[23]

Yes, for Rogers and Johnson and Robinson and Michaelson and Chapman and Lee and all those who agree with them, this is hardly an abstract theological issue. This is about real people—often kindly and devoted and caring and prayerful people—living real lives. Doesn't the law of love compel us to embrace them fully? Surely love would not condemn them and drive them away, would it?

Rogers recounts how he and his wife, Sharon, spent an evening at the home of a gay couple, meeting with other gay and lesbian couples sometime in 2001–2002:

> We met two elderly gentlemen, Dick and Jim, who at that time had been together for forty-seven years. One of them told me that he

lived every day of his life in fear that they would be "outed" and that he would lose his job. Yet they persisted in caring for one another. Many of the couples there had been together twenty years or more, and all of them ten years or more. I remember a heterosexual friend telling me that in her circle of friends anyone who had stayed married for more than five years was an exceptional case. The people I met [that night] were just ordinary, faithful Christians who displayed a profound commitment to each other.[24]

Would Jesus cast these people aside? Would He call them sodomites and vile sinners, worthy of condemnation? What would love do? What would Jesus call *us* to do? A comment on a Christian website offers this simple response: "Christ's Law is simple: Love God, love each other as God loves you. From this all current law flows and people can accept God's Grace regardless of sexual orientation."[25]

In her book *This We Believe: The Christian Case for Gay Civil Rights*, C. S. Pearce, herself a married heterosexual, writes that, "By claiming that name, Christian, we aspire to be Christ-like, to live in goodness and mercy, with compassion and kindness toward all."[26] She appeals to her readers "In the name of the God of love" and reminds us that "We have the opportunity to use our faith to demonstrate compassion and courage, empathy and justice." And she closes the Preface with this prayer: "May the love of Christ prevail."[27]

Pearce begins chapter 2, "Stop the Hurt," with these words: "No one should be separated from the love of God. That is the wonderful message of the entire New Testament. By requiring that LGBT people change their very essence to be connected to that love, however, we're putting huge barriers between them and God."[28] And she warns traditional Christians that the stakes are high, noting that "if the traditional Christian position on homosexuality is not supportable on biblical, intellectual, or compassionate grounds, and you continue to hold to it, you share in the responsibility of the consequences," which include LGBT people leaving the church and, worse still, committing suicide.[29]

In support of her position she argues that:

There are more than 2,000 Bible verses that describe God's immense concern and love for the poor and the oppressed, and very few that deal with homosexuality. But in a world full of poverty, disasters, and injustice, some Christians focus instead on lobbying for laws that legalize discrimination against gay people—many of whom surely fit into the category of oppressed. This flies in the face of the gospel love for our neighbors that Jesus preached.[30]

Do these arguments strike you as weighty? Do they appeal to your love for God and your love for all His creation? They certainly feel weighty to me!

M. W. Sphero, a passionate proponent of "gay Christianity," is more forceful still:

> Therefore if it is true that you try your best to love your neighbor as yourself by your *actions* (as sentiment has nothing to do with it); would you not accept, affirm, support, and *defend* your gay neighbor as you would want—and *need*—to be treated *yourself* in the same manner…especially if you *had*—hypothetically at least—been born gay? Would not homophobia, intolerances, excommunications, exclusions, unjustified condemnations, incitements to violence, work and church discriminations, and ostracisms against gays and lesbians seem very much *against* God's own will from that viewpoint?[31]

He asks:

> Do we not *want* to be loved by others as they love *themselves?* Would we not want to be loved by others as God *Himself* loves us…unconditionally and without strings attached? This *alone* should be sufficient reason for organized religion to begin to not only accept, but to in addition actively *defend* and *protect* its gay and lesbian neighbors as a matter of universal "Christian" policy.[32]

Sphero sums up his position with 1 John 4:8, which he quotes with emphasis: "For God *is* love, and he who does not love does not *know* God."[33] Therefore, he argues, to claim that the Bible is against homosexual practice "is simply nothing more than a diabolical hijacking of the Gospel by self-seeking homophobic modern-day Pharisees."[34]

Are Christians Terrorizing and Oppressing Homosexuals?

In keeping with these sentiments, Rod Brannum-Harris, in his self-proclaimed "attack piece," claims it is only false Christians—"The Pharisees Amongst Us," to use the title of his book[35]—who would reject "LGBT Christians." He calls conservative evangelicals "Biblical Contortionists" and "Christian Pretenders," and while his tone and rhetoric may be different from some of those just quoted, he expresses the sentiments of many others:

> It is time for Christians to turn over—metaphorically speaking—the tables of those who abuse the Bible to terrorize and oppress others, who promote fear and hate in the name of God. I challenge Christians to stand up to blasphemy as relates to the denial of God's assignment of variant sexual orientations, to end the widespread, senseless damage inflicted by such blasphemy.[36]

Are conservative Christians really using the Bible "to terrorize and oppress others"? Are we truly promoting "fear and hate in the name of God"? Are we guilty of "blasphemy"? Are we inflicting "widespread, senseless damage" on beloved children of the Lord, simply to their divinely assigned "variant sexual orientations"?

Even Dr. Mel White, a pioneer in the "gay Christian" movement and the founder and leader of Soulforce, has engaged in similar rhetoric. His writings have moved from his biographical account, *Stranger at the Gate: To Be Gay and Christian in America*,[37] to the openly confrontational *Religion Gone Bad: The Hidden Dangers of the Christian Right*.[38] In fact, in the second, virtually unchanged edition of this book, the title was changed from *Religion Gone Bad* to *Holy Terror: Lies the Christian Right Tells Us to Deny Gay Equality*.[39] Is the Christian Right actually guilty of "holy terror"?

Things have gotten to the point that, when the Southern Baptist Convention reaffirmed that same-sex "marriage" was not a civil right (as they were fully expected to do), White wrote an article titled, "Resist Southern Baptist 'Terrorism.'" While not calling for physical violence, he did reiterate the call for another type of aggressive resistance:

I'm a tired old activist from the 20th century. You are 21st-century activists with Internet tools that could be used to launch a powerful new resistance movement. Just don't wait for someone else to do it. Please, for the sake of millions of our sisters and brothers who are victims of holy terrorism, *resist!*[40]

The battle lines, then, have been clearly drawn, and this truly is the great question confronting the church at the beginning of the twenty-first century. What is God's heart on this issue? What is His mind? What is His Spirit saying? What is written in the Word? What would Jesus have us do?

Chapter 2

TO JUDGE or NOT to JUDGE?

The "gay Christian" argument: The church has become judgmental and homophobic to the point that many LGBT young people have actually killed themselves. Jesus taught us not to judge.

The biblical response: Some Christians may be judgmental and even hateful, which is wrong and inexcusable, but as followers of Jesus we are called to recognize the difference between right and wrong, to make proper moral judgments rather than be judgmental and condemning. As for the message that we preach, the gospel brings life, not death, and kids who commit suicide normally have other emotional problems. If we really love them, we will try to address those problems rather than just affirm their sexual and romantic desires.

Did you ever hear of the movie *Prayers for Bobby*, based on the book of the same name? The subtitle of the book is *A Mother's Coming to Terms With the Suicide of Her Gay Son*, and it tells the story of Bobby Griffith, who was his "mother's favorite son, the perfect all-American boy growing up under deeply religious influences in Walnut Creek, California." But "Bobby was also gay."[1]

This is how the movie is described on the film's website.

Struggling with a conflict no one knew of much less understood Bobby finally came out to his family. Despite the tentative support of his father, two sisters, and older brother, Bobby's mother, Mary…turned to the fundamentalist teachings of her church to rescue her son from what she felt was an irredeemable sin. As Mary came closer to the realization that Bobby could not be "healed," she rejected him, denying him a mother's unconditional love, and driving her favorite son to suicide.[2]

After her son's tragic suicide Mary had a radical change of heart, and through the book and the movie she has done her best to expose what she deeply believes to be the error of her ways, calling on parents to embrace and affirm their gay kids. (For the record, you can still embrace and affirm your kids, even if you disagree with them.) If only she could turn the clock back!

But as tragic as this story is, there is something even more tragic. It is actually not that uncommon, and so, we are told, Mary Griffith is not the only parent to lose a gay child to suicide due to the parents' religious convictions, convictions that drove the children to such despair that they ultimately took their own lives. This is a parent's worst nightmare.

Could it be, then, that well-meaning parents and religious leaders are driving gay kids to suicide by their religious dogmatism? Could it be that they are using the Bible, which is supposed to bring life and hope, to bring death and despair?

The 2007 DVD *For the Bible Tells Me So* affirms this same narrative, telling the story of the terrible struggles that gay and lesbian young people endure because of the Christian fundamentalism of their families, a fundamentalism, the video tells us, that is inspired by ministries like Dr. James Dobson's Focus on the Family. It also tells the story of how these families learned to embrace their children's homosexuality, calling on others to follow in their footsteps.

As a conservative Christian reader you might say, "You can't fool me with these emotional tricks. I'm going with the Bible, and if the Bible says it, I believe it, and that settles it."

Actually, I share that same conviction—God's Word is the final authority—but I do so understanding how weighty these issues are. As I've said already in this book, we're talking about people's lives here. And we're also talking about the Word *of God*—the God of compassion, the Father of the Lord Jesus, the God of mercy and forgiveness and grace, as well as the God of holiness and truth—not just some religious manual. All of which means that we should tread carefully and prayerfully when dealing with such sensitive, life-and-death issues.

An article attacking me on RightWingWatch.org stated:

> The Suicide Prevention Resource Center reported in 2008 that lesbian, gay, and bisexual youth "are nearly one and a half to three times more likely to have reported suicidal ideation" and "nearly one and a half to seven times more likely than non-LGB youth to have reported attempting suicide," noting that "stigma and discrimination are directly tied to risk factors for suicide."[3]

Of course, RightWingWatch.org, along with scores of other gay and gay-affirming websites, lays much of the blame for that alleged "stigma and discrimination" at the foot of the church—at least the conservative, Bible-believing church. It's not surprising, then, that commenters responding to some of my online articles have made the claim that I have the blood of many young gay people on my hands because I teach that God does not endorse or bless homosexual practice. In keeping with this mentality, when a large Christian ministry claimed that it helped gays become straight, it was accused of being responsible for many suicides among gays who tried to change.

Similarly, when I reached out to the LGBT community in my home city, inviting them to visit our church services or have a meal together or even invite me (or my friends) to one of their services, I received a response from a local "gay Christian" that ended with these words:

> Yes you do contribute to the harm of many in the gay community through your short sided [sic] views. Just because you are "polite" or have good intentions does not mean what you say is not damaging. When we have kids not taking their own lives because they are gay then we can sit down and have a friendly debate about this subject. Until then you may want to shut up and do more listening than talking.[4]

There you have it again: you are harming people with your views, and gay kids are killing themselves because of it.

Some even make more extreme charges, like this, posted in response to a comment I made in a TV interview in which I said that you can't fairly compare the black civil rights movement with today's gay rights movement, recognizing, however, the suffering many LGBT people have endured:

> What do you plan to do? Put all gay and lesbian teenagers in the gas chambers when their sexual orientation emerges in puberty? Would you do that once, or would you do that for the rest of human history? Sick.[5]

This is the kind of rhetoric we have to deal with simply because we say that God does not endorse homosexual practice and that change is possible, and this is the caricature of the church that many gays and lesbians have. And such views are commonplace, even if not always this extreme.

In their well-known book *unChristian* authors David Kinnaman and Gabe Lyons describe the results of their Barna Research study, which asked how young people in America view the church today:

> In our research, the perception that Christians are "against" gays and lesbians...has reached critical mass. The gay issue has become the "big one," the negative image most likely to be intertwined with Christianity's reputation. It is also the dimension that most clearly demonstrates the unChristian faith to young people today, surfacing a spate of negative perceptions: judgmental, bigoted, sheltered, right-wingers, hypocritical, insincere, and uncaring. Outsiders say our hostility toward gays—not just opposition to homosexual politics and behaviors but disdain for gay individuals— has become virtually synonymous with the Christian faith.[6]

The full title of the book is *unChristian: What a New Generation Really Thinks About Christianity...and Why It Matters,* and chapter 5 of the book is titled "Antihomosexual." How in the world did we get this reputation? And what does being "antihomosexual" have to do with the gospel?

Pointing to this same data, "gay Christian" leader Justin Lee noted that the sixteen- to nineteen-year-old respondents were given several choices to describe modern-day Christians, positive phrases such as "offers hope" and "has good values" as well as negative ones such as "judgmental" and "hypocritical." The most popular choice was "antihomosexual." Lee observed that, "Not only did 91 percent of the non-Christians describe the church this way, but 80 percent of *churchgoers* did as well."[7]

Is that what we have become? With all our claims to love Jesus and His Word, have we become judgmental, hypocritical, and antihomosexual (or even "homophobic")?

On May 6, 2006, in the same public park in Charlotte, North Carolina, where the annual gay pride event normally took place, I read a statement to Charlotte's gay and lesbian community after their gay pride event had been canceled. It began with these words:

> As a church leader in the greater Charlotte area, I want to take a moment to address the homosexual community of this city. As most of you know, for the last four years, Christian groups have protested the gay pride events that have taken place here in Marshall Park. You know that we have objected to the public displays of lewdness and to the obscene speeches and entertainment, and we have stated clearly that such things—be they heterosexual or homosexual—do not belong in our city parks.
>
> Most of you know that, as followers of Jesus, we have nonnegotiable moral convictions, based on God's Word and His natural laws, and we make no apology for those convictions. We believe that God's ways are best, and we believe that homosexual behavior is contrary to His ways, just as we believe that all sexual activity outside of the bonds of male-female marriage is contrary to His ways.
>
> We are not ashamed to take these stands, even if you consider us to be hateful and bigoted. We say again: God's ways are best, and we make no apology for our Lord and for His Word. We love Jesus, our Savior and Friend, and we are not ashamed to be identified with Him.
>
> But there is something else we want you to hear. We recognize that we have sometimes failed to reach out to you with grace and compassion, that we have often been insensitive to your struggles, that we have driven some of you away rather than drawn you in, that we have added to your sense of rejection. For these failings of ours, we ask you to forgive us. By God's grace, we intend to be models of His love.[8]

On more than one occasion, and on behalf of other Christians, I have apologized publicly to those who identify as LGBT, acknowledging the sins of the church against them, and I have done so for one reason only—love. Love for God and love for people. Nothing more and nothing less.

And it is that same love that compelled me to share something else in my statement to Charlotte's LGBT community back in May 2006:

> We understand, of course, that in your eyes, our biblical convictions constitute hate, and it is hurtful to us that you feel that way. The fact is that we really do love you—more than you realize or understand—and because we love you, we will continue to speak the truth, convinced that it is the truth that sets us free. Love does what is right, even when it is scorned and mocked and ridiculed....
>
> And so we will not stop loving you, even if you call us bigots, even if you claim we are depriving you of your civil rights, even if you mock us and call us Bible-bashers. We will pray for you and fast for you and reach out to you and suffer alongside of you. Whether you understand it or not, we are here to help.
>
> We do not look down on you or despise you, since for us, the ultimate issue is not homosexuality or heterosexuality. All human beings fall short of God's standards in many ways, and all of us—heterosexual and homosexual alike—need God's mercy through the blood of Jesus. All of us need forgiveness, and all of us need to turn from our sins and ask God for grace to lead a holy and virtuous life.
>
> You can reject our message, but we will still love you. You can question our motivation, but we will still love you. You can consider us hateful and intolerant, but we will still love you, and we hope that our actions will speak louder than our words. We personally extend an invitation to sit down and talk with us face to face. It is true that we have some profound and deep differences, but we need not differ in a mean-spirited and destructive way.
>
> We extend to you afresh the message of God's transforming love through Jesus.[9]

It is that same love, just deeper now with the passage of time, that compels me to write and to speak even today, and if you will allow me, I'd like to challenge some sacred cows and rock some politically correct boats. It's a difficult minefield to navigate. (How can we love the Lord, love the Word, and love gays and lesbians without compromising scriptural standards or hurting people we love?) But it can be done. No, it must be done.

You see, I am convinced that the message of Jesus brings life, not death; hope, not despair; liberation, not bondage.[10] The message of Jesus delivers people from suicide rather than driving them to commit suicide. And just as I have agonized over the stories of the Bobby Griffiths of this world, I have rejoiced over the stories of those who were once suicidal *because* they were living gay lifestyles—including "gay Christian" lifestyles—but who were delivered from suicide when they acknowledged their sin and turned to the Lord for forgiveness.

The same month I was writing this chapter—September 2013—I received an e-mail from some friends, telling me about a man who once worked with a ministry I knew. At that time I thought he was a happily married husband and father, so I was totally shocked when I learned some years back that he had left his wife and was living with another man, claiming that both of them were "gay Christians." They attended a gay-affirming church, and he was convinced that people like me were living in the spiritual dark ages, not understanding what the Word of God really said.

Then, just a few weeks ago, I received the e-mail I just mentioned from my friends. They told me that this man had driven six hours to see them, that he was in absolute spiritual and emotional torment because of his homosexual lifestyle, and that if he didn't break up with his partner and get right with God, he would kill himself. After hours of prayer together and many tears, he knew the course he had to take, and for the first time in years his hope was restored. Yes, it was turning *from* homosexuality that was the path of deliverance for him—including deliverance from suicide.

And remember: he wasn't living some wild, drug-fueled lifestyle. He wasn't sleeping with hundreds of different men. He had long since been divorced from his wife and was attending a gay-affirming church. Yet he was ready to take his own life if he couldn't get right with God again; he knew the way he was living was sinful in His sight.

This was the result of the Holy Spirit at work in his life, not the result of a homophobic, judgmental society and church, and his story is not unique. I have personally heard many other similar accounts, powerful stories of men and women, young and old alike, who were suicidal and depressed *because of their homosexual lifestyle* (by which I mean living out and affirming their homosexuality), and they experienced life and peace and joy and freedom when they turned to Jesus in repentance. That means that my friends who e-mailed me about this man could have had blood on *their* hands if they affirmed him in his gay lifestyle and gay faith. (Bear in mind that he was involved in a gay-affirming church and yet was still suicidal.)

So it's important that Bible-believing Christians draw a line in the sand and make this determination: *I will not let threats of suicide stop me from doing what is right, with compassion and with courage.* And if someone wants to hang this over my head, telling me that a book like this will lead to gay suicides, I could just as well say in reply, "If you encourage gays and lesbians *not* to read it, you could be contributing to their suicides."

GETTING TO THE HEART OF THE MATTER

Do you see how wrong this is and how it ultimately trivializes the lives of those we want to help? In fact, there are sociologists who believe that talk like this—telling society that gay teens will kill themselves if we don't affirm their homosexuality—actually contributes to their high suicidal rates by planting seeds of instability, hopelessness, and self-destruction in their hearts.[11]

But please allow me to get more controversial still. During the days of harsh segregation here in America, when blacks were treated far worse than gays were treated one generation ago, did you hear about an epidemic of black suicides? Did you hear about all the young blacks in the schools who were robbed of hope and dignity and were taking their own lives? And did you hear black leaders raise the scepter of the suicide of black youths over the nation, warning them that if America didn't change its racist ways these kids would take their own lives?

Obviously not. Why? Because these young African Americans were encouraged to be strong, to take a stand, to refuse to be intimidated, to make a determination that they would live with dignity even when society degraded them, and to work toward a better and brighter future.

Yet today, when we have an aggressively pro-gay president and an unashamedly pro-gay media, when we have any number of popular gay public figures (such as Ellen DeGeneres, Anderson Cooper, or Rachel Maddow), when we have pro-gay curricula in many of our schools and antidiscrimination laws (which include "sexual orientation") in most of our states, when the Supreme Court has overturned the Defense of Marriage Act as unconstitutional, we are constantly warned that if we don't affirm homosexuality, gay kids will be killing themselves. Can you see that something is very wrong with this picture?

Appearing on my radio show on May 8, 2012, and discussing the marriage bill that our state was about to vote on, gay activist Mitchell Gold claimed that if the people of North Carolina voted to affirm that marriage was the union of one man and woman, it would lead to gay suicides:

> For a 14-year-old kid trying to understand their sexuality, to have an amendment in the public discourse in this big public discussion to have people saying gays are sinners and an abomination, that they are not entitled, that it's not God's plan to have it this way.... This is why kids jump off bridges. This is why kids hang themselves.[12]

Actually, in the vast majority of cases, as suicide experts will verify, kids jump off bridges and hang themselves because they have other deep emotional or social problems.[13] Otherwise they would not take their own lives. And yet rather than trying to get the root of these issues and really help these young people find wholeness, we are held hostage with the fear that our biblical values will lead kids to kill themselves. If we really care about these young people and if we really want to help them, this guilt tripping must stop.

In fact, when you consider all the efforts being put into the "It Gets Better" campaign, it's only right to ask: Why are these kids so fragile and suicidal? Bullying of any group is terrible—and sometimes, no doubt, deadly—but plenty of other kids get bullied in school, and only the tiniest percentage take their lives. Could it be there are other issues troubling suicidal gay and lesbian kids that need to be addressed? Put another way, are they only killing themselves because of the rejection they experience (and the lack of hope for the future)? Are there other factors at work? And is it possible to give them hope without affirming their homosexuality?

A few years back I had some extensive online interaction with a man who had gone through sex-change surgery and now identified as a woman, claiming to be deeply committed to Jesus the whole time. He had been married for thirty-seven years when he had the surgery, and he told me that as a result of him becoming a woman, he had destroyed his marriage and effectively rendered his wife a widow. When I asked him what he did with Ephesians 5:25, "Husbands, love your wives, as Christ loved the church and gave himself up for her," he explained to me that after decades of trying everything he knew to come to grips with his struggles and live as a man, it was either sex-change or suicide.

Of course, I can't relate to the torment he experienced, and I know he claims to be happy and fulfilled living as a woman. At the same time I don't believe for a moment that the only way this dear man could get relief was by destroying his marriage and rendering his wife a virtual widow. And Walt Heyer, a man who had sex-change surgery and lived for years as Laura, also destroying his marriage, only to try to reverse his surgery and become a man again, also believes that there are deeper issues that must be addressed in the lives of those who identify as transgender. As he explained to me during a radio interview on August 28, 2013, the fact that someone *threatens to commit suicide* if they cannot be affirmed as gay or change their gender identity is proof that there are other issues that need to be addressed.[14]

The specific word Walt used in our interview was *comorbidity*, meaning "the presence of one or more disorders (or diseases) co-occurring with a primary disease or disorder; or the effect of such additional disorders or diseases."[15] So rather than just saying, "She's a boy trapped in a girl's body and is suicidal because of it," or, "He's gay and is suicidal because his family won't accept him," we should look for other issues in this person's life that could be contributing to his distress.

Did you know that under the leadership of Dr. Paul McHugh, a nationally respected psychology professor, the medical center of Johns Hopkins University *stopped performing sex-change surgeries* years ago? As I related in *A Queer Thing Happened to America*, in 1975, when McHugh became psychiatrist-in-chief at Johns Hopkins Hospital, he decided "to test the claim that men who had undergone sex-change surgery found resolution for their many general psychological problems," demanding more information before and after surgery. With the help of a fellow psychiatrist, he "found that most of the patients [his colleague] tracked down some years after their surgery were contented with what they had done and that only a few regretted it."[16]

But that was only part of the story. McHugh notes that "in every other respect, they were little changed in their psychological condition."

> They had much the same problems with relationships, work, and emotions as before. The hope that they would emerge now from their emotional difficulties to flourish psychologically had not been fulfilled.
>
> We saw the results as demonstrating that just as these men enjoyed cross-dressing as women before the operation so they enjoyed cross-living after it. But they were no better in their psychological integration or any easier to live with. With these facts in hand I concluded that Hopkins was fundamentally cooperating with a mental illness. We psychiatrists, I thought, would do better to concentrate on trying to fix their minds and not their genitalia.[17]

Those are striking words! For obvious reasons Walt Heyer has read voraciously in this area (he is now in his early seventies and has been happily married to his second wife for more than sixteen years) and has launched a website called SexChangeRegret.com. He regularly hears from people who realize *after* undergoing sex-change surgery that they made a terrible mistake, seeing now that there were underlying issues in their lives that were the real cause of their torment and suicidal pain. A major study from Sweden, which followed the lives of men and women who underwent sex-change surgery, came to similar conclusions: "Persons with transsexualism, after sex reassignment, have considerably higher risks for mortality, suicidal behaviour, and psychiatric morbidity [diseased state] than the general population. Our findings suggest that sex reassignment, although alleviating gender dysphoria, may not suffice as treatment for transsexualism."[18]

To repeat: there are often other factors that lead to LGBT suicide, and it is both unfair and misleading to tell the church, "Unless you affirm people in their sexual orientation and gender identity, you will contribute to their suicide."

Am I denying the story of Bobby Griffith? Not at all. Am I endorsing the way his mother initially handled his situation? Certainly not. In fact, when I'm asked by parents what to do when their child comes out as gay, I tell them this: Sit down with them and say, "You know that we don't believe that God made you gay or that homosexuality is His will, but we want to make it clear to you that we love you unconditionally, that you are our child no matter what, that we will always be here for you, that we are totally committed to you, that we want to be involved in your life, and that what you shared with us doesn't change your relationship with us or diminish our love for you in any way." After that I encourage them not to bring the subject up to their child but rather to pray for him or her and demonstrate that unconditional love.[19]

But this is where so many well-meaning Christians have fallen into a trap: we have believed the lie that a person is primarily defined by their romantic attractions and sexual desires (as in, "I'm gay"), leading to notions such as this, expressed by the gay-affirming New Testament professor Dan Via:

> I would hope for a proclamation of the gospel in relation to human sexuality that can be heard in the same way by homosexuals and heterosexuals: God extends to you forgiveness and restoration and empowers you to realize all the possibilities for good given in your created destiny. Remember that you are required to actualize these possibilities in a morally responsible way. You are liberated *for* the enactment of your sexual identity and—it is hoped—*from* forces in church and society that would compel you to deny who you are.[20]

Do you recognize the fundamental flaw in Professor Via's thinking? Do you see how he is misconstruing the purpose of the gospel, as if Jesus died so that we could fulfill our sexual identity?

Of course, Christians are quick to say to homosexual men and women, "We love you, but we hate your sin," to which they reply, "That means you hate me. This is not what I do. This is who I am."

Well, I want to challenge that. You are more than your romantic attractions or sexual desires. You are more than someone attracted to the opposite sex or the same sex. You are created to be a child of God, a servant of the Lord Jesus, a world-changer and a history-maker in Him—and it is Jesus who tells us that the first step we must take in following Him is *not* to affirm ourselves but rather to *deny ourselves*.

That's where new life starts, not by seeking a liberation "*for* the enactment of [our] sexual identity," as Professor Via alleges, but by the total and complete surrender of our entire lives to God, giving Him the absolute right to do whatever He desires with us and to work whatever He desires into us (or out of us). As one theological dictionary expressed it, "Following Jesus as a disciple means the unconditional sacrifice of his whole life…for the whole of his life.…To be a disciple means (as Matthew in particular emphasizes) to be bound to Jesus and to do God's will (Matt. 12:46–50; cf. Mark 3:31–35)."[21] C. S. Lewis was right on target when he said, "Until you have given up your self to Him you will not have a real self."[22]

And this exposes one of the major roots of the problem we face when dealing with the difficult subject of homosexuality and the church: we start our thinking with the contemporary American value system that begins with, "It's all about me," which means that right and wrong is largely determined by how I feel about it. And then we weave the gospel into this, which is one reason we are in such spiritual error and deception today, not just in the area of "gay Christianity" but in so many other ways as well.[23]

More than fifty years ago, in his classic article "The Old Cross and the New," A. W. Tozer wrote, "The old cross would have no truck with the world. For Adam's proud flesh it meant the end of the journey." In contrast, he noted with profound insight, "the new cross does not slay the sinner, it redirects him."[24] Today we could take this one step further and say, "The new cross does not slay the sinner; it empowers him (or her)."

Yes, the contemporary "gospel" proclaims, "Jesus came to make you into a bigger and better you! Jesus came to help you fulfill your dreams and your destiny!" Put another way, "The gospel is all about you!"

So when it comes to homosexuality, if we start with the premise of, "This is who I am and Jesus died to affirm who I am," then we will end up denying the real gospel message and the consistent and clear testimony of Scripture. Can you see how confused and wrongheaded this whole approach is?

In December 2011 Matt Comer, the editor of *Q-Notes*, the gay newspaper of the Carolinas, wrote an editorial titled "A Prayer for Michael Brown," which ended with these words:

> Brown tells us that it's his goal to see gay and lesbian people's lives transformed and brought to Christ. I think he honestly has faith in the power of Christ to transform. So do I. In this instance, however, I'm afraid it is Brown, not LGBT people, who really needs the transformation. He'll never recognize or admit his words are

hateful or hurtful because he's blind to the truth, the kind of truth that really sets people free and brings them into a radically inclusive communion with each other, the world around them and the Divine. That is a truer, more Christ-like Gospel message I hope Brown one day hears and receives.[25]

In a guest editorial written in response to Matt's piece, I addressed the issue of "the meaning of Christlike inclusion," ending my editorial with these words:

> GLBT leaders often point out (rightly so) that Jesus spent time with those whom society marginalized, specifically the prostitutes and corrupt tax-collectors, commonly viewed as sinners. But what did Jesus do? Did he encourage the prostitutes to serve their clients better? Did he teach the tax-collectors how to extort more money? Of course not. Rather, he reached out to them, got involved in their lives, and changed them. He practiced transformational inclusion, which I wholeheartedly advocate, not affirmational inclusion, which the GLBT community advocates.
>
> I for one am eternally grateful that Jesus didn't affirm me in my lifestyle. Rather, he died for me and transformed me. And so it is my fervent prayer and hope that Matt will experience this same transforming love. Who would want to resist the life-changing love of God?[26]

Today I have friends who are committed Christians and are enjoying His blessings but who still have same-sex attractions. They recognize that those attractions are contrary to God's design, they do not act on them or feed them, they do not embrace a "gay identity," and even though they are currently single, they wouldn't go back to their old way of life for all the money in the world.

I also have friends who assure me that they have been completely delivered from homosexual attractions and are happily married. Their spouses affirm this too! And just as I believe the gut-wrenching stories of those who tell me they tried to change from homosexual to heterosexual and could not—causing them tremendous pain and anguish—I also believe the stories of those who tell me they *have* changed, especially when I see evidence of a changed life over a period of many years.

Don't let anyone tell you such people don't exist. That is an extremely bigoted, intolerant, and even cruel position to take, not to mention a denial of the power of the gospel.[27]

I knew one fine Christian man who had been involved with other men (and not women) before he was saved—in other words, he was homosexual, not bisexual—but when he was born again, he surrendered his whole life to the Lord, which included his sexuality. Over a period of time, to his surprise, he found himself attracted to women, ultimately getting married to a fine Christian woman, and they were happily married until the day of his death.

I heard the story of another man who was exclusively attracted to other men before he became a believer. After he came to the Lord, he desired to marry a woman and have children, which meant becoming heterosexual. But then he thought to himself, "Wait a second. Every heterosexual man I know struggles with lust for women. Who needs that?" So he prayed that God would give him love and attraction only for the woman he would marry, and that's exactly what happened to him—and it has lasted for years.

In April of 2013 I received an e-mail from a man named Randy who regularly listened to my radio show on WMCA in New York City. He wrote this to me via Facebook in response to a question I had asked him:

> For 39 years, I have had to struggle with being gay and loving Jesus. I am jealous of people who claim to have gone heterosexual....It is so far out of my reach, I cannot even fathom such a thing. I have been to more counseling, therapy, Exodus meetings, ex-gay ministries, even electric-shock therapy in a mental hospital....I turned 57 years old on April 18th, and I'm still gay. I did not choose to live a difficult lifestyle where you are belittled and hated—especially when the Baptist church I was brought up in, found out that I was gay. It's just a fact of life for me. I knew I was different when I was still a very little lad. I loved playing with girls...I detested sports (and still do)...I loved hanging out with my mother all the time...sure you have heard this all before...I truly believe I was born this way....I don't want to go to hell...just hope that God knows the struggles I have dealt with and I know He will judge me fairly...[28]

One day later he wrote this:

> Dr. Brown, I fear that I have been given over to a "reprobate mind," and there is now no help for me. I will burn in hell for eternity.
>
> I have already started paying a price for my gay lifestyle—my last lover had HIV and committed suicide. I now have advanced HIV disease and numerous health problems and many of my family had turned away from me. However, these days, that doesn't seem to be so bad—since the gay thing is now pretty much accepted, they have come back to me...a little at a time.
>
> What more can I say, Dr. Brown? Please pray for me—perhaps it is too late.[29]

When I read his e-mails on the air—with his permission—I had to hold myself back from breaking down and weeping. What a painful, painful story. You may say, "Can't you see the problem? All his pain was caused by homophobia, especially in the church. If you Christians had simply affirmed him as a gay Christian, he would not have gone through such living hell. That's the real issue!"

Randy would beg to differ with that, as he explained in another e-mail to me dated September 23, 2013: "No...you cannot be gay and Christian...you can have homosexual feelings which you must fight minute to minute, day to day, month to month, year to year...but you cannot be intimate with a man and be a Christian...I have tried...with utter and dismal emotional failure."[30]

In stark contrast, when I assured him that God had not given him over to a reprobate mind, when I told him that Jesus died to forgive him of *every* sin he had ever committed, and when I encouraged him that he could live without sex or without another man, but he could not live without God, he had a dramatic breakthrough.[31] A few days later, after seeing the responses to an article I had written about his story and hearing the reports about listeners who were praying for him, he posted this on the AskDrBrown Facebook page:

> I am sitting here with tears practically falling on my computer keyboard. I can't believe there are this many people out there who give a [rip] about me! I am "floored"! Why would these people care

about a[n] AIDS-ridden homosexual guy that they have never met before! I am basically speechless at this time. I can't thank all those people enough for their kind words and support. I believe God is going to bring someone into my life who will really, THIS TIME, be able to help me overcome this unhappy lifestyle. Thank you so much, Dr. Brown!…and thank you again to all those wonderful people who care about me…I CAN'T BELIEVE HOW MANY PEOPLE CARE!!![32]

The last time I heard from him, he was doing well, strong in his faith and speaking out clearly against "gay Christianity," saying no to the same-sex desires that had tormented him for so many years.

A CALL TO HOLINESS AND COMPLETE SURRENDER

Everyone's story is different, but the bottom line is that God doesn't call us to heterosexuality as much He calls us to holiness.[33] More than that, He calls us to Himself—to the complete surrender of all that we are and all that we have and all that we desire to Him. And that is how we now define ourselves: as children of God, as sons and daughters of the Most High, as servants of the Lord.

Christopher Yuan is a committed Christian whom I had the pleasure of meeting a few years ago, and today he is teaching at Moody Bible Institute in Chicago and completing his doctor of ministry degree. He had lived a promiscuous, drug-filled, homosexual life before ending up in prison, where, with plenty of time on his hands, he began to read the Bible along with a book that the gay-affirming prison chaplain gave him, telling him that he could be a "gay Christian."

He writes, "I had that book in one hand and the Bible in the other. I had every reason to accept the book's assertions to justify same-sex relationships. But God's indwelling Spirit convicted me that this book was distorting his Word."[34]

And so he explains, "I eventually realized I'd put great emphasis on 'being gay.' Now I needed to place my primary identity in Christ." Yes, "Newfound identity in Christ compelled me to live in obedience to God whether my temptations changed or not. The gospel is about more than just correct beliefs; it leads to correct living as a result of correct beliefs.

Biblical change is not the absence of struggles but the freedom to choose holiness in the midst of our struggles."[35]

In contrast, he finds that Justin Lee's *Torn* sends the wrong message: "*Torn* is an honest memoir of a Christian wrestling through issues of sexuality, but Lee's conclusions for how to live appear to be more anthropocentric than Christocentric."[36] In other words, Lee's conclusions are more "about me" than they are "about Him"—more man-centered than Christ-centered, and that is a central problem with the "gay Christian" approach: it sees the Scriptures through the lens of homosexuality rather than seeing homosexuality through the lens of the Scriptures.[37] As I stated before, this is part of the faulty mentality of the contemporary American "gospel."

As expressed by Princeton University professor Kenda Creasy Dean in her book *Almost Christian: What the Faith of Our Teenagers Is Telling the American Church*, our churches today:

> …seem to have offered teenagers a kind of "diner theology": a bargain religion, cheap but satisfying, whose gods require little in the way of fidelity or sacrifice. Never mind that centuries of Christians have read Jesus' call to lay down one's life for others as the signature feature of Christian love (John 15:13), or that God's self-giving enables us to share the grace of Christ when ours is pitifully insufficient. Diner theology is much easier to digest than all this—and it is far safer, especially for malleable youth. So who can blame churches, really, for earnestly ladling this stew into teenagers, filling them with an agreeable porridge about the importance of being nice, feeling good about yourself, and saving God for emergencies? We have convinced ourselves that this is the gospel, but in fact it is much closer to another mess of pottage, an unacknowledged but widely held religious outlook among American teenagers that is primarily dedicated, not to loving God, but to avoiding interpersonal friction….
>
> In the view of American teenagers, God is more object than subject, an Idea but not a companion. The problem does not seem to be that churches are teaching young people badly, but that we are doing an exceedingly good job of teaching youth what we really believe: namely, that Christianity is not a big deal, that God requires little, and the church is a helpful social institution

filled with nice people focused primarily on "folks like us"—which, of course, begs the question of whether we are really the church at all.[38]

This was from the first part of Professor Dean's book, a section called "Worshipping at the Church of Benign Whatever-ism," with the opening chapters titled, "Becoming Christian-ish" (meaning, not really Christian at all), and "The Triumph of the 'Cult of Nice'" (meaning that Christian teens in America seem to think the end-all of the gospel is simply to be nice). She asks:

> What if the *church* models a way of life that asks, not passionate surrender but ho-hum assent? What if we are preaching moral affirmation, a feel-better faith, and a hands-off God instead of the decisively involved, impossibly loving, radically sending God of Abraham and Mary, who desired us enough to enter creation in Jesus Christ and whose Spirit is active in the church and in the world today? If this is the case—if theological malpractice explains teenagers' half-hearted religious identities—then perhaps most young people practice Moralistic Therapeutic Deism not because they reject Christianity, but because this is the only "Christianity" they know.[39]

It is this mentality that has helped to create the perfect storm for today's "gay Christianity," combining several critical factors all at once. First, more and more young people today have gay friends or siblings or neighbors or parents, which helps to break down a lot of exaggerated, negative stereotypes. There's nothing wrong with that. Second, our society is quick to stand with victims and underdogs, and to the extent LGBT people are perceived as victims, to that extent young people in particular will stand with them and identify with them, which is fully understandable. Third, we have bought into the lie that homosexuality, like skin color, is innate, immutable, and completely neutral (in other words, it is inborn, it cannot be altered, and it is no better or worse than heterosexuality), and so "gay is the new black" in terms of civil rights causes in America.[40]

Fourth, the secular media bombards us with a steady pro-gay, anti-Bible diet, to the point that film critic and radio host Michael Medved once observed, "A Martian gathering evidence about American society, simply by monitoring our television, would certainly assume that there were more gay people in America than there are evangelical Christians."[41] Or, as Elizabeth Taylor once said, "If it weren't for gays, honey, there wouldn't be a Hollywood."[42]

We cannot underestimate the power of the media's influence on our culture today, and it did not happen by accident. As two Harvard-trained gay activists explained in 1989, their goal was the "conversion of the average American's emotions, mind, and will, through a planned psychological attack, in the form of propaganda fed to the nation via the media."[43] As explained by Professor David Eisenbach, himself a gay historian:

> Gay activists in the 1960s and 1970s understood that only after the public saw that homosexuals were not threats to society could gay rights make any political and legal progress. By manipulating the media and forcing more sympathetic characterizations of homosexuals on television shows, the gay rights movement offered powerful challenges to common stereotypes.[44]

Fifth, gay activists have succeeded in portraying all those who do not affirm homosexuality as "haters," as if a compassionate pastor who simply believes that God intended men to be with women is a hate-filled, intolerant bigot. Again, it is not an accident that someone like Rev. Fred Phelps, leader of the notorious "God Hates Fags" Westboro Baptist Church, has become the media's poster boy for conservative Christianity, despite the fact that 99.99 percent of all true believers utterly repudiate his words and sentiments.

This too was a stated strategy of gay activists more than twenty-five years ago, as they spoke of "jamming" people's emotions by associating "homohatred" with Nazi horror, bringing to mind images such as "Klansmen demanding that gays be slaughtered," "hysterical backwoods preachers," "menacing punks," and "a tour of Nazi concentration camps where homosexuals were tortured and gassed."[45]

As observed by Jeff Jacoby, a conservative columnist with the *Boston Globe,* "Dare to suggest that homosexuality may not be something to celebrate…and you instantly are a Nazi….Offer to share your teachings of

Christianity or Judaism with students 'struggling with homosexuality' and you become as vile as a Ku Kluxer."[46]

Do a little test for yourself and take issue with "gay Christianity" or with same-sex "marriage," and do it with care, love, and sensitivity. Watch how long it takes before you are called a hater and an intolerant bigot (or worse).

Sixth, there is a tremendous amount of biblical illiteracy in today's church, and so the false gospel of "affirmational inclusion" fits in perfectly— the "diner theology" that Professor Dean spoke of.

Seventh, in response to aggressive, powerful, and well-funded gay activism, many Christian leaders and ministries have responded by taking strong public stands against same-sex "marriage" and other gay causes, because of which they have been dubbed homophobic and judgmental.

"But that's where you're missing things," you might say. "The church *has* become homophobic and judgmental, and yet Jesus plainly taught us not to judge. That's why so many young people are turned off by church today, and that's why most gays and lesbians wouldn't dare step foot into any church that wasn't gay affirming. Don't you get it?"

Speaking for many other college-aged kids, Dannika Nash wrote an article on her blog titled "An Open Letter to the Church From My Generation." She explained how the pro-gay song of Mackelmore and Ryan, "Same Love," was a theme song for her generation, and she noted that:

> Things are changing—the world is becoming a safer place for my gay friends. They're going to get equal rights. I'm writing this because I'm worried about the safety of the Church. The Church keeps scratching its head, wondering why 70% of 23-30 year-olds who were brought up in church leave. I'm going to offer a pretty candid answer, and it's going to make some people upset, but I care about the Church too much to be quiet. We're scared of change. We always have been. When scientists proposed that the Earth could be moving through space, church bishops condemned the teaching, citing Psalm 104:5 to say that God "set the earth on its foundations; it can never be moved." But the scientific theory continued, and the Church still exists. I'm saying this: we cannot keep pitting the church against humanity, or progress. DON'T hear me saying that we can't fight culture on anything. Lots of things in culture are absolutely contradictory to love and equality,

and we should be battling those things. The way culture treats women, or pornography? Get AT that, church. I'll be right there with you. But my generation, the generation that can smell [expletive], especially holy [expletive], from a mile away, will not stick around to see the church fight gay marriage against our better judgment. It's my generation who is overwhelmingly supporting marriage equality, and Church, as a young person and as a theologian, it is not in your best interest to give them that ultimatum.[47]

But there's more:

My whole life, I've been told again and again that Christianity is not conducive with homosexuality. It just doesn't work out. I was forced to choose between the love I had for my gay friends and so-called biblical authority. I chose gay people, and I'm willing to wager I'm not the only one. I said, "If the Bible really says this about gay people, I'm not too keen on trusting what it says about God." And I left my church. It has only been lately that I have seen evidence that the Bible could be saying something completely different about love and equality.[48]

And this really highlights the problem once again: "If I have to choose between the Bible and my gay friends, I will choose my gay friends—unless, of course, the Bible says something different than what my church has taught me."

Am I saying that the whole problem is that young people aren't spiritual enough and don't know the Bible well enough? Actually, even if that is true in some cases, that's not my point here at all. And, in my opinion, to the extent that it is true, a large part of the blame must be placed at the feet of the preachers and pastors and parents who failed to lead the younger generation into a real encounter with the Lord. And so, in a real sense, I see today's young people as victims of a compromised, defective church.

Am I denying that the evangelical church has put its trust in politics, to the point that white evangelical Christians have almost equated working for social change with voting Republican? Not at all. In fact, I have been an outspoken critic of our dependence on the political system, also criticizing black evangelicals for their wholehearted allegiance with the Democratic

Party and noting that there is often a big difference between the kingdom of God and patriotism.

Am I claiming that the church has not been guilty of loudly proclaiming its opposition to gay activism while quietly proclaiming its love for LGBT people? Certainly not. So here too I'm sympathetic to what Dannika and other young people are saying. But would you allow me to present another side to the story?

To be sure, I do understand how weighty these issues are, and the findings of Kinnaman and Lyons are as undeniable as they are shocking:

> In our research, the perception that Christians are "against" gays and lesbians—not only objecting to their lifestyles but also harboring irrational fear and unmerited scorn toward them—has reached critical mass. The gay issue has become the "big one," the negative image most likely to be intertwined with Christianity's reputation. It is also the dimension that most clearly demonstrates the unChristian faith to young people today, surfacing a spate of negative perceptions: judgmental, bigoted, sheltered, right-wingers, hypocritical, insincere, and uncaring. Outsiders say our hostility toward gays—not just opposition to homosexual politics and behaviors but disdain for gay individuals—has become virtually synonymous with the Christian faith....
>
> Out of twenty attributes that we assessed, both positive and negative, as they related to Christianity, the perception of being antihomosexual was at the top of the list. More than nine out of ten Mosaic and Buster outsiders (91 percent) said "antihomosexual" accurately describes present-day Christianity. And two-thirds of outsiders have very strong opinions about Christians in this regard, easily generating the largest group of vocal critics. When you introduce yourself as a Christian to a friend, neighbor, or business associate who is an outsider, you might as well have it tattooed on your arm: antihomosexual, gay-hater, homophobic. I doubt you think of yourself in these terms, but that's what outsiders think of you.[49]

So, again, I'm fully aware of this, but as I asked a moment ago, may I share another perspective with you? Perhaps there is another side to the story that many young people in particular are not seeing. Here are some questions to consider.

First, is it possible that some of the anti-Christian hostility has been fueled by the media? Think back to Michael Medved's words, namely, "A Martian gathering evidence about American society, simply by monitoring our television, would certainly assume that there were more gay people in America than there are evangelical Christians." We could easily take this one step further and say: "The Martian would also conclude that gay people were, with rare or no exception, incredibly nice, family-oriented, creative, and considerate, while evangelical Christians were all mean-spirited, judgmental, dull, greedy, and hypocritical."

And get this: whereas survey after survey tells us that gays and lesbians make up about 3 percent of our population,[50] a 2011 Gallup poll indicated that, on average, Americans believe that gays and lesbians make up *25 percent* of the population! Even more shocking is the fact the younger generation (those aged eighteen to twenty-nine) believed that *almost 30 percent* of the population was gay—meaning, *roughly one out of every three people rather than one out of every thirty-three*.[51] What a difference that makes—and surely the media played a big role in this grossly false perception.

As for evangelical Christians being gay bashers, the fact is that the vast majority of evangelical churches in America rarely address the issue of homosexuality in any way—I've done surveys about this and examined lists of sermons and book and article titles—yet the popular perception is that we are obsessed with this subject and that on any given Sunday you are likely to hear an antigay, homophobic sermon. Nothing could be further from the truth.

Second, is it possible that where Christians have gotten involved with these issues—and it is primarily major, family-oriented ministries that have led the way—they have done so because they were responding to real life issues that needed to be addressed from a scriptural standpoint? According to Justin Lee, it is not only true that American society, especially among the younger generation, is uncomfortable with the increasingly nasty culture between gays and Christianity, but it is who have allegedly *"fired the first shot."*[52]

Once again, that is simply not true. It was only with the rise of an in-your-face gay activism that the church was forced to address these issues.

And can you really fault these Christian leaders for having somewhat exaggerated pictures of the "average" gay or lesbian when the most prominent images they were presented with were quite vulgar and extreme—like gay pride parades featuring public male nudity, phallus-shaped floats, topless lesbians, and signs declaring, "God is gay" and "We want your boys"?

To be perfectly clear, I do not believe this speaks for the great majority of gays and lesbians, but you need to understand that to the extent "gay pride" was associated with bold, perverted, sexual promiscuity, it was all too easy for Christians to think the worst about all homosexual men and women. Added to this is the fact that, on average, gays *are* more promiscuous than straights, not to mention the massively higher rates of STDs in the gay (male) community, and you can understand why Christian leaders sounded the alarm about homosexual practice.[53] We were hardly firing "the first shot."

Third, is it possible that the "gay rights" movement is more connected to the sexual revolution of the 1960s than it is to the civil rights movement of that same era? I know that many homosexuals say "Love is love" and "I have the right to marry the one I love," and they compare the ban on same-sex "marriage" to the ban on interracial marriage. But there's another way to look at this, namely, understanding the attempt to radically redefine marriage as another sign of the deterioration of marriage, a deterioration accelerated by no-fault heterosexual divorce, rampant pornography, and promiscuity.

In fact, once you place same-sex "marriage" in the context of the sexual revolution, it all becomes clear: marriage and family are under assault. In 1960 23 percent of all births to black Americans were out of wedlock; by 1970 it was up to 37.6 percent. By the 1990s it averaged *more than 68 percent*, and it is no better today.[54] In white America in 1960 out-of-wedlock births made up only 2.3 percent of all births, rising only to 5.7 percent in 1970 and 7.3 percent in 1975. But by 1997 it had reached 25.8 *percent*—amounting to an increase of more than ten to one from 1960.[55] And if you want a snapshot of where our culture stands today, in 2013 48 percent of all first-time births (meaning, babies born to first-time mothers) were out of wedlock.[56] That is an absolutely staggering statistic.

As noted by Robert Rector, Senior Research Fellow of the DeVos Center for Religion and Civil Society Domestic Policy Studies:

> In 1964, 93 percent of children born in the United States were born to married parents. Since that time, births within marriage have declined sharply. In 2010, only 59 percent of all births in the nation occurred to married couples.
>
> …When the War on Poverty began in the mid-1960s, only 6 percent of children were born out of wedlock. Over the next four and a half decades, the number rose rapidly. In 2010, 40.8 percent of all children born in the U.S. were born outside of marriage.[57]

It is against this backdrop that the push for same-sex "marriage" must be seen. It is not a step forward but another step backward.

We can see the same downward cycle in the media, and it's no surprise that just a few years ago major cable TV networks featured groundbreaking programs celebrating homosexuality and lesbianism (such as *Queer as Folk* and *The L Word*), while today they are featuring groundbreaking programs celebrating polygamy (*Sister Wives* and *Big Love*), teenage pregnancy (*Teen Moms*—where the moms become TV celebrities, even if teen pregnancy is not celebrated), and polyamory (*Polyamory: Married and Dating*). Do you see how all of these subjects are tied together?

On August 16, 2010, *Newsweek* asked the question, "Are We Facing a Genderless Future?" One year earlier *Newsweek* featured a major article on "relationships with multiple, mutually consenting partners." The article, titled "Polyamory: The Next Sexual Revolution," stated, "It's enough to make any monogamist's head spin. But traditionalists had better get used to it."[58] Just two years before that (in 2007), *Time* magazine raised the question, "Should Incest Be Legal?"

And in December 2010, when Columbia University professor David Epstein was arrested for a three-year consensual affair with his adult daughter, his attorney noted, "It's OK for homosexuals to do whatever they want in their own home. How is this so different? We have to figure out why some behavior is tolerated and some is not."[59] Not surprisingly, quite a few Columbia students got online and asked why any sexual acts committed by consenting adults (in this case, a father and daughter!) should be considered a crime.

In light of all this (and I could write a whole book on these subjects—in fact, I did, and it was 700 pages long, with 1,500 endnotes of documentation[60]), is it such a mystery why many Christians are so concerned about the direction our society is going? Is it so shocking that it would be important to us to stand for marriage and family and sexuality as God intended it, even if it means offending our gay friends whom we love and care for?

Fourth, could it be that there really *is* a gay agenda—meaning, common goals shared by gay activist organizations and their allies—and that agenda really *is* a threat to our freedoms of speech, conscience, and religion, not to mention a threat to marriage, family, and gender distinctions as well? If you're tempted to write me off as a religious fanatic, I challenge you to look at the evidence. Will you at least keep reading to see what I have to say?

I assume you've heard of Rosa Parks, the African American woman who helped ignite the modern civil rights movement. But have you heard of another African American woman named Crystal Dixon? No? How about another woman named Julea Ward? No? How about one more woman, Angela McCaskill? Still not ringing a bell?

Well, Crystal Dixon served as the administrator for human resources at the University of Toledo when she wrote an op-ed piece for her local newspaper (on her own time and as an individual citizen) in which she respectively took issue with the idea that being black was like being gay (in particular, in terms of social status and the history of the civil rights movement). As a result of writing that editorial, she was fired by the university. Fired![61]

Julea Ward was a grad student in the counseling program of Eastern Michigan University when she was asked to counsel a gay client and instructed to affirm that client's gay relationship. When she said she couldn't do this in good conscience as a Christian, her professor told her to refer the client to another counselor, after which she was reported to the administration and then subjected to a degrading, anti-Christian inquisition before being expelled from the program. Expelled![62]

Dr. Angela McCaskill was the first deaf African America woman to earn a PhD from Gallaudet University in Washington DC, hailed as the nation's top school for the deaf, and after working at the school for years, she was appointed as the university's first chief diversity officer in January 2011. (For the record, her job description did *not* focus on LGBT "diversity.") In July 2012, as a private citizen and resident of Maryland, she signed a petition supporting marriage as the union of a man and woman. And she signed this petition with her husband on the way out of a church service where her pastor had preached against redefining marriage.

Almost three months later a lesbian faculty member became aware of this and issued a complaint to the university, and McCaskill was immediately relieved of her responsibilities. Out you go! She was put on paid administrative leave and became so distraught she required doctor's care. Thankfully the public outcry on her behalf was so strong that she was eventually reinstated, but only after being terribly traumatized and mistreated—and this, my friends, is not even the tip of the iceberg.[63]

Similar instances are taking place across the country—a worker is fired because he explains to his lesbian supervisor, who keeps telling him about her upcoming gay wedding, that he disagrees with homosexual practice according to the Bible; an eleven-year old girl receives death threats after testifying before her state senate that marriage is the union of a man and woman; a schoolteacher is fired for posting comments against gay activism on her private Facebook page; a Catholic professor is terminated because he taught his students what the Catholic Church believes about homosexuality in a class in the religion department on Catholicism. And almost every month (if not every week) Christians are being taken to court in different states because they cannot in good conscience provide services (such as photography or floral arrangements or cakes) for same-sex "wedding" ceremonies or the like.[64]

Yes, those who came out of the closet forty-plus years ago want to put us in the closet, and those who claim to be tolerant have become increasingly intolerant. Is it so odd that Christian leaders have been concerned about the erosion of our freedoms? It was Dietrich Bonhoeffer who said, "The ultimate test of a moral society is the kind of world it leaves to its children."[65] What kind of world are we leaving to *our* children?

People can call us homophobic all they like, but are we really overreacting when we raise concerns about three new bills that recently passed in California? The first, SB 777, *requires* all school districts and all grades, K–12, to *celebrate* gay, lesbian, bisexual, and transgender history in America.[66] The second, SB 1172, makes it illegal for a minor with unwanted same-sex attractions to go for professional counseling[67] (meaning, a seventeen-year-old boy who does not want to be attracted to other boys is *not* allowed to get counseling; a similar bill has been passed in New Jersey, with more states planning to follow suit). Yet it is perfectly legal in California for parents to put their ten-year-old child on hormone blockers to stop the onset of puberty if the child feels he or she is trapped in the wrong body! The third bill, AB 1266, now allows a boy who believes he is a girl (or vice versa) to use the girl's bathroom in school (from K–12) as well as to play on the girls' sports teams and use the girls' locker room—and no test of any kind is required.[68] The child simply has to say, "This is who I perceive myself to be."

Are Christians to sit idly by and do nothing to help when our own kids and grandkids are being affected by all this? Are we not to stand *for* righteousness—and therefore *against* unrighteousness?

There are preschools in America where the teachers are not allowed to call the children "boys and girls" since that would be making a gender distinction. And in several countries Toys "R" Us has announced that it will move to *gender-neutral toy stores*.[69] In fact, some of their catalogs already feature boys playing with princess dolls and girls playing with guns, all because some people were offended with gender stereotypes. And on the university level there are professors calling for war on the "gendered world."[70]

So, I ask you, is it wrong for us to be concerned when headlines celebrate the news that a sixteen-year-old boy, who now identifies as a girl, has been elected homecoming *queen* of his school?[71] (My heart goes out to this kid, but he is a boy—biologically and chromosomally—and real compassion would try to help him from the inside out.) Should we be happy when a student in another high school (who had voted for a *girl* to be prom *king*) explained, "It's not like the stereotype where the [prom] king has to be a jock and he's there with the cheerleaders anymore....We live in a generation now where dudes are chicks and chicks are dudes."[72] This is supposed to be a good thing?

And is it praiseworthy that a *six-year-old* boy in Argentina has been allowed to change his birth certificate from male to female? Kids that age hardly understand the difference between fantasy and reality, yet a gay news outlet reports that, "A six-year-old girl *who was assigned male at birth* won her legal battle to change her national ID card and birth certificate to reflect her accurate gender."[73] This is nothing less than social insanity.

And is it supposed to be good when LGBT college students, responding to a survey, identified themselves with descriptions like: "21-year-old genderqueer lesbian, senior"; "22-year-old queer F-M dyke, senior" (F-M stands for female to male); "21-year-old bisexual queer female, junior"; and, "20-year-old bi-curious questioning female, senior."[74] This is something to celebrate?

This is how far off course we get when we depart from the male-female, man-woman order God has established. And this is why we're starting off on the wrong foot when we simply tell people, "You are defined by your sexual identity, whatever that identity—or identities—might be." It leads to bizarre policies like this one from the Los Angeles Unified School District Reference Guide: "'Gender identity' refers to one's understanding, interests, outlook, and feelings about whether one is female or male, or both, or neither, regardless of one's biological sex."[75] What?

And once we find the male-female dichotomy to be restrictive and oppressive, and we consider homosexuality and bisexuality to be perfectly good options to heterosexuality, we end up with a list of terms like this, all of which have been used in contemporary LGBT circles:

Androgeny, Androgenous, Bigendered, Bi-Dyke, Boi, Boidyke (or, Boydyke), Bro-sis, Butch, ButchDyke, Camp, Cross Dresser (CD), Cross-Living, Drag (In Drag), Drag King, Drag Queen, Dyke, FTM or F->M or F2M (Female to Male), Femme, Femme Dyke, Female Bodied, Female Impersonator (FI), Fetishistic Transvestite, Gender Illusionist, Gender Neutral, Gender-Bender, Gender-Blender, Genderqueer, Genetic Boy, Genetic Male/Man (GM), Genetic Female/Woman (GF/GW), Genetic Girl (GG), Grrl, Half-dyke, Heteroflexible, Hir, Intersex, MTF or M->F or M2F (Male to Female), Male Impersonator, Metamorph, Monogendered, Multigendered, Neuter, No-gendered, Non-op, Omnisexual, Pansexual, Pre-operative Transsexual (Pre-op TS), Polygendered, Post-operative Transsexual, Queer, Queerboi, Shape Shifter, Stem (a feminine-identified lesbian), Stud (a masculine-identified lesbian), Trannyboi, Trannydyke, Trannyfag, Transboi, Transgendered, Transgenderist, Transitioning, Transmale, Transsexual (TS), Transvestite, Transidentified, Trisexual, Two-Spirit, Ze.[76]

How far this is from Genesis 1:27: "So God created man in his own image, in the image of God he created him; male and female he created them." But it is inevitable once we begin to affirm gay identity, which means we must recognize bi and trans and genderqueer and pansexual…and on and on it goes.

REACH OUT AND RESIST

Of course, we must shout from the rooftops that Jesus shed His blood for each of these individuals as much as He shed His blood for the straightest person in the world. But we can preach the gospel without affirming everyone's sexual desires, romantic attractions, and gender identities.

That's why I said we have to navigate through a difficult minefield, showing compassion and love for LGBT individuals—in every way, being Jesus to them—while standing for marriage and family and morality in society: being the salt of the earth and the light of the world that Jesus called us to be. In short, we are to *reach out and resist*, meaning, reaching out to LGBT people with compassion and resisting gay activism with courage.

We tend to put all our emphasis on one side or the other, leading to a dangerous imbalance. And while the local church should certainly focus its energies on compassionate outreach to all, it cannot ignore the social issues that are impacting the families of our nation. Do you see now that the issue is not as cut-and-dried as you might have thought?

Perhaps some of you who only cared about social issues now realize that you have wrongly judged most gays and lesbians, as if they were all activists trying to take away your rights. That is certainly not the case. Perhaps others of you have only cared about being a friend to your gay and lesbian neighbor, and you have wrongly judged socially minded Christians as if they were gay-haters because of their strong moral stands. That too is certainly not the case.

But what about Jesus's words that we are not to judge? Isn't that really the bottom line here? And doesn't it simply come down to the fact that it is not our job as Christians to judge *anyone*?

Well, do you really believe that? We'll look at Jesus's words in a moment, but are you telling me that if you saw a football player in your high school punching a gay kid in the face and calling him a sissy that you wouldn't judge the football player and say what he was doing was wrong?

If you lived in the days of slavery, are you telling me that you wouldn't have judged the slave traders for their actions and told them what they were doing was wrong? After all, Jesus said, "Don't judge!" And how do you feel about the college professor I just mentioned who was having sex with his grown daughter? Aren't you judging them if you say what they're doing is wrong?

According to Hollywood director Nick Cassavetes, it *is* wrong to judge family members for committing incest. Promoting his 2012 movie *Yellow*, which features an adult incestuous relationship, he said, "We had heard a few stories where brothers and sisters were completely, absolutely in love with one another. You know what? This whole movie is about judgment, and lack of it, and doing what you want."[77] Exactly. Who are you to judge?

So, do you honestly believe that as Christians it is not our job to judge anyone? Perhaps what you mean is that we shouldn't be judgmental. In that case, I agree! Being judgmental is one thing. Making good moral judgments is another thing entirely.

Here's what Jesus said:

> Judge not, that you be not judged. For with the judgment you pronounce you will be judged, and with the measure you use it will be measured to you. Why do you see the speck that is in your brother's eye, but do not notice the log that is in your own eye? Or how can you say to your brother, "Let me take the speck out of your eye," when there is the log in your own eye? You hypocrite, first take the log out of your own eye, and then you will see clearly to take the speck out of your brother's eye.
>
> —Matthew 7:1–5

What exactly did Jesus mean? In his commentary on Matthew, New Testament scholar D. A. Carson explained that Jesus's words in Matthew 7:1 clearly do not:

> ...forbid all judging of any kind, for the moral distinctions drawn in the Sermon on the Mount require that decisive judgments be made. Jesus himself goes on to speak of some people as dogs and pigs (v. 6) and to warn against false prophets (vv. 15–20). Elsewhere he demands that people "make a right judgment" (Jn 7:24; cf. 1 Co

5:5; Gal 1:8–9; Php 3:2; 1 Jn 4:1). All this presupposes that some kinds of judging are not only legitimate but mandated.

Jesus' demand here is for his disciplines not to be judgmental and censorious. The verb *krinō* has the same force in Romans 14:10–13 (cf. Jas 4:11–12). The rigor of the disciples' commitment to God's kingdom and the righteousness demanded of them do not authorize them to adopt a judgmental attitude.[78]

I wonder why people are so quick to quote Jesus's words here in Matthew 7:1, "Judge not"—which clearly means do not judge hypocritically; do not judge unfairly; do not judge superficially; do not condemn—but they never seem to quote Jesus's words in John 7:24, "Do not judge according to external appearance, but judge with proper judgment" (NET). Jesus calls us to "judge with proper judgment"! And, as Professor Carson noted, Jesus's teaching in the Sermon on the Mount *requires* us to make proper judgments: recognizing the kind of people who will just mock our message ("casting pearls before swine"), recognizing false prophets (whom we will know by their bad fruit), and recognizing the speck that is in our brother's eye so we can remove it once we have removed the beam from our own eye.

To be clear, according to the Scriptures, I am not your judge and you are not my judge. The Word warns us strongly about this: "There is only one lawgiver and judge, he who is able to save and to destroy. But who are you to judge your neighbor?" (Jacob [James] 4:12) "Why do you pass judgment on your brother? Or you, why do you despise your brother? For we will all stand before the judgment seat of God" (Rom. 14:10).

At the same time, we *are* required to judge moral behavior, as Paul explained in 1 Corinthians 5:11–13:

> But now I am writing to you not to associate with anyone who bears the name of brother if he is guilty of sexual immorality or greed, or is an idolater, reviler, drunkard, or swindler—not even to eat with such a one. For what have I to do with judging outsiders? Is it not those inside the church whom you are to judge? God judges those outside. "Purge the evil person from among you."

So, if someone claims to be a follower of Jesus and is living in open, unrepentant sin, we are to "judge" him and break off all fellowship with him (with the goal of leading him back in repentance). As for unrepentant sinners outside the church, Paul writes that God will judge them. (Notice that he doesn't say God will *bless* them but that He will *judge* them.)

The ironic thing with all this is that some who constantly say, "You have no right to judge me! You are so judgmental! Jesus said, 'Don't judge,'" are often very judgmental themselves. As a colleague of mine once asked a woman who accused him of judging her, "But aren't you judging me for judging you?" Even more ironic still is that many of those who claim to preach a message of grace, love, and acceptance become fiercely judgmental and hostile when their message is challenged.[79] Somehow I don't feel their love.

So where does that leave us when it comes to the subject of the Bible and homosexuality? It leaves us in a place of humility before God, not condemning others, not judging with a harsh and censorious spirit, and searching our own hearts for sin and hypocrisy. It also leaves us jealous for God's best, recognizing that His ways alone are the path of life. And it leaves us clinging tightly to the Lord and His Word, not wanting to impose our values, standards, and opinions on God's Word but rather asking our heavenly Father to help us form our values, standards, and opinions based on the Scriptures. Otherwise, as Augustine once warned, "If you believe what you like in the gospels, and reject what you don't like, it is not the gospel you believe, but yourself."[80]

Why not stop for a moment and pray this prayer with me before turning the page?

> *Father, in Jesus's name, I ask You to help me to open my heart and my mind to Your truth, whatever the cost or consequence. Help me to humble myself and to be teachable and correctable, and in keeping with Your promises, lead me in the way of truth and life and freedom. Where I have been deceived, undeceive me, and where I have hardened my heart through sin, pride, fear, tradition, control, or man-made religion, forgive me and cleanse me. Lord, I want to please You, not myself, and more than anything in this world I just want to love You, know You, and live for You. By Your grace I will. Amen!*

Now, go ahead and turn the page. Are you ready?

Chapter 3

ARE WE USING the BIBLE to SANCTION ANTIHOMOSEXUAL PREJUDICE?

The "gay Christian" argument: Just as the church misused the Bible to justify and even sanction slavery, segregation, and the oppression of women, it continues to misuse the Bible to justify and sanction antihomosexual prejudice.

The biblical response: The Bible has been misused to justify and even sanction slavery, segregation, and the oppression of women. In stark contrast, the church is rightly using the Bible to reject homosexual practice and to proclaim to LGBT people that God has a better way. It's also important to remember that it was Christians, rightly using the Bible, who helped put an end to slavery, segregation, and the oppression of women.

IN JANUARY 2013 I spent ten days in Hong Kong teaching the Book of Jeremiah to Chinese pastors from the mainland as part of a special seminary program. Two other professors from the States were also teaching classes that week, and one afternoon we spent a few hours together getting a tour of the island.

One of these professors was a well-known New Testament Greek scholar, a graduate of Fuller Theological Seminary, and as we traveled around Hong Kong, the subject of "gay Christianity" came up. This scholar then told me that when he was at Fuller, if he wanted to hear the Word of God preached in depth and with clarity, he would go listen to Dr. Mel White, a professor at Fuller, a pastor, and a ghostwriter for men like Jerry Falwell, Pat Robertson, and Billy Graham.

But what Dr. White's students and parishioners didn't know was that this respected Christian leader, apparently a happily married man, not to mention a father and grandfather, was secretly struggling with same-sex attractions, and all of his efforts to change had failed, including prayer, counseling, and even exorcism. After his homosexuality was discovered by others in the publishing industry, he came out publicly, left his wife, and moved in with his male lover, sending shock waves through parts of the evangelical Christian world.

Mel White? Gay?

After coming out and becoming a leading "gay Christian" activist, Dr. White wrote this open letter to Rev. Jerry Falwell, containing a heartfelt appeal:

> I've been reading your autobiography again. It still moves me. And I'm not just saying that because I wrote it. *Strength for the Journey* inspires and informs readers because you talk about your failures and not just your success.
>
> I'm especially moved by those twenty short pages in Chapter Eleven that describe your transformation from 1964, when you were a staunch segregationist, to 1968, when you baptized the first black member of Thomas Road Baptist Church.
>
> When I asked you what happened in four short years to change your mind about segregation, you told me stories about the African-Americans you had known and loved from childhood.
>
> "It wasn't the Congress, the courts, or the demonstrators," you assured me. "It was Lewis, the shoeshine man, and Lump Jones, the mechanic, and David Brown, the sensitive, loving black man without a wife or family who lived for most of his adult life in the backroom of our large family home in Lynchburg."
>
> It was obvious that you really cared about those black men, especially David Brown. "He was a good man," you told me. "He helped my mother with the cooking and cleaning. He cared for me and my brother Gene when we were children. He bathed and fed us both. He was like a member of our family."
>
> Then, one day, you and Gene found David Brown lying

unconscious and unattended in the lobby of Lynchburg's General Hospital. One portion of his head and face had been crushed from a severe blow with a dull pipe or the barrel of a pistol. He suffered cuts and bruises over his entire body; yet because he was black, he lay dying in that waiting room for forty-eight hours without medical help. You and your brother intervened but your friend was permanently damaged by the racist thugs who left him for dead and by the racist hospital policies that denied him treatment in time.

Do you remember how your eyes filled with tears when you told me, "I am sorry that I did not take a stand on behalf of the civil rights of David Brown and my other black friends and acquaintances during those early years."[1]

As Dr. Falwell himself stated in an open reply to Dr. White, "I was born and raised in a segregationist culture. As a young believer, this was one of the first things that the Holy Spirit began purging from my life."[2]

Could it be, then, that just as Dr. Falwell inherited wrong views about blacks, views that "the Holy Spirit began purging" from his life as a young believer, he also inherited wrong views about homosexuals, and it was now high time for the Holy Spirit to purge him from those views as well?

Dr. White pressed this point home:

I knew from the sound of your voice, Jerry, that you are still sorry that you did not take a stand for equality in those early years of ministry. Nevertheless, after condemning President Johnson's Civil Rights legislation as an act of "Civil wrong" and after preaching fervently against integration, you had the courage to acknowledge your sinfulness and to end your racist ways.

"In all those years," you told me, "it didn't cross my mind that segregation and its consequences for the human family were evil. I was blind to that reality. I didn't realize it then, but if the church had done its job from the beginning of this nation's history, there would have been no need for the civil rights movement."

Well said, friend. But now I have to ask you one more time. Has it ever crossed your mind that you might be just as wrong about homosexuality as you were about segregation? Could it be that you are blind to a tragic new reality, that the consequences of your anti-homosexual rhetoric are as evil for the human family as were your sermons against integration? Have you even thought about the possibility that you are ruining lives, destroying families, and causing endless suffering with your false claims that we are "sick and sinful," that we "abuse and recruit children," that we "undermine family values."

In the 1950s and 60s, you misused the Bible to support segregation. In the 1990s you are misusing it again, this time to caricature and condemn God's gay and lesbian children. Once you denied black Christians the rights (and the rites) of church membership. Now it's gay, lesbian, bisexual, and transgendered Christians you reject.[3]

And Dr. White ended his letter with these piercing words:

Please, Jerry, hear your own words about segregation and apply them to my homosexual sisters and brothers. "I can see from the earliest days of my new faith in Christ," you told me, "that God had tried to get me to understand and to acknowledge my own racial sinfulness. In Bible College, the Scriptures had been perfectly clear about the equality of all men and women, about loving all people equally, about fighting injustice, and about obeying God and standing against the immoral and dehumanizing traditions of man."

The Scriptures are still clear about the equality of all men and women. The Scriptures are still clear about loving all people equally. The Scriptures are still clear about fighting injustice and standing against the immoral and dehumanizing traditions of man. Why can't you apply THOSE Scriptures to us instead of the six verses you misuse over and over again to clobber and condemn GLBT people?

For years you supported the "immoral and dehumanizing traditions" used to persecute people of color. Then, finally, the Spirit of Truth set you free. Now, you are a supporter of "immoral and dehumanizing traditions" used to persecute homosexuals. Please, Jerry, let the Spirit of Truth set you free again.[4]

Is this what the spirit of truth is saying to the church today? Is God challenging our bigotries, misconceptions, and biases afresh? Are we, in fact, using the Bible to sanction antihomosexual prejudice?

Retired South African Archbishop Desmond Tutu answers with a resounding yes. In a September 2013 interview he was asked, "What is the most pressing issue in which Christians need to relate their faith to power and injustice?" He replied:

> Anywhere where the humanity of people is undermined, anywhere where people are left in the dust, there we will find our cause. Sometimes you wish you could keep quiet. It's the kind of thing you heard the prophet Jeremiah complain of where he says, "You know God, I didn't want to be a prophet and you made me speak words of condemnation against a people I love deeply. Your word is like a fire burning in my breast."
>
> It isn't that it's questionable when you speak up for the right of people with different sexual orientation. People took some part of us and used it to discriminate against us. In our case, it was our ethnicity; it's precisely the same thing for sexual orientation. People are killed because they're gay. I don't think, "What do I want to do today? I want to speak up on gay rights." No. It's God catching me by my neck.... The God who was there and showed that we should become free is the God described in the Scriptures as the same yesterday, today and forever.[5]

Pastor Brian McClaren, a well-known "Emergent Church" leader, would also say yes, the church needs to make major changes in its dealing with gays, lesbians, and transgenders, noting that:

> ...although the debate has been agonizing, liberals have blazed the trail in seeking to treat homosexual and transgender persons with compassion. Conservatives may follow in their footsteps in this issue just as they have in others, several decades down the road, once the pioneers have cleared the way (and once their old guard has passed away).[6]

To be sure, many conservative Christians would immediately protest this exaggerated statement, as if the only way to treat homosexual and transgender-identified people with compassion was to affirm their sexual desires, romantic attractions, or gender confusion. But is there truth to Pastor McClaren's larger point that liberal Christians—often called "progressive" Christians today—are the ones who break down walls of prejudice and bigotry, only to be followed decades later by the new generation of conservative Christians?

The late Rev. Dr. Peter Gomes, longtime minister of Harvard University's Memorial Church, Plummer Professor of Christian Morals, and one of the most celebrated leaders in the African American church, would certainly echo McClaren's sentiments. (In 1991 Gomes famously stated, "I am a Christian who happens as well to be gay."[7]) In his 1996 best seller, *The Good Book: Reading the Bible With Heart and Mind*, Gomes devotes a whole chapter to "The Bible and Homosexuality," referring to the moral rejection of homosexual practice as a "biblically sanctioned prejudice."

Dr. Gomes writes:

> The legitimization of violence against homosexuals and Jews and women and blacks...comes from the view that the Bible stigmatizes these people, thereby making them fair game. If the Bible expresses such a prejudice, then it certainly cannot be wrong to act on that prejudice. This, of course, is the argument every anti-Semite and racist has used with demonstrably devastating consequences, as our social history all too vividly shows.[8]

According to Dr. Gomes, it is fear that is "at the heart of homophobia, as it was at the heart of racism, and as with racism, religion—particularly the Protestant evangelical kind that had nourished me—[is] the moral fig leaf that covered prejudice."[9]

Bruce Bawer, another articulate "gay Christian" voice, adds this further confirming testimony:

> When I was a boy in the early 1970s, spending summers in my mother's South Carolina hometown, I met some white kids who had recently withdrawn from public school and began attending a new private academy. They explained the switch: Their public schools had been integrated by Supreme Court order, and their parents were sending them to this new institution in order to

protect them from attending school with "[expletive]." Thus did I witness the birth of the Religious Right.[10]

Could it be, then, that "the Religious Right"—or, more broadly, conservative evangelical Christianity—that opposes homosexual practice today is simply continuing in its bigoted, prejudiced ways of the recent past? Is this charge true?

I'm sure there *are* some professing Christians who are continuing in their bigoted ways, and their negative evaluation of homosexuality is not based on the Scriptures but on their own feelings, similar to negative feelings they had about blacks or others in the past. They might even think that all gay men are pedophiles or that all homosexuals are atheists or God-haters.

But the existence of bigoted people in the church, be their numbers large or small, proves nothing at all about what the Scriptures actually say. And if we'll look at the Word honestly, we'll have to admit that there is no comparison between the promotion of slavery, segregation, the oppression of women, and the rejection of homosexual practice.

Are you willing to follow the truth of God's Word wherever it leads? Then let's carefully examine the testimony of Scripture and history.

A self-described "transsexual woman" on the Ex-Gay Watch blog posted these comments to me on January 27, 2008: "Mr Brown, since you claim to adhere so much to the Holy book for your politicalization, in the face of only 6 verses in the Bible that is interpreted by the religious right to condemn homosexuality, do you sanction the return of slavery then?"[11]

She then listed scores of verses from the Bible, all of which seemed to sanction slavery, asking, "Surely this is a far more serious matter than whether homosexuals should be given rights?"[12]

Coming at this from the viewpoint of a gay atheist philosophy professor, John Corvino states, "I think the most plausible reading of Leviticus 18:22 is 'No male-male sex, period,' and unlike loophole-seeking teenagers, I think oral sex is sex."[13] But, given that many biblical laws no longer apply today (especially the ones sanctioning slavery), Corvino concludes:

> Yet when one reads [the Bible] in its entirety, it's hard to avoid the sense that this book contains not, in fact, the unerring word of an all-good, all-knowing, all-powerful God, but instead the

occasionally reasonable but often flawed rules of fallible human beings, rules that are intricately bound to the author's cultural circumstances.[14]

More pointedly, he notes that whether or not the gay reinterpretation "works for the homosexuality passages (or for that matter, the divorce passages), it's untenable for the slavery passages." In other words:

> It seems pretty clear that the Bible endorses slavery, and the Bible is just wrong about that. But once we admit that the Bible reflects the mistaken cultural prejudices about slavery, we must concede that it may also reflect mistaken cultural prejudices about other things, homosexuality included. Either it's infallible, or it isn't.[15]

So, Professor Corvino is able to dismiss what Scripture says about homosexual practice—recognizing that it does prohibit it—by writing off the Bible as a whole because of the Bible's apparent sanction of slavery.

How should we respond to forthright and fair challenges like this? I would suggest that all of us ask ourselves some honest questions:

+ Am I using the Bible to confirm my own beliefs and prejudices and biases, or am I willing to challenge who I am and what I believe based on God's Word?

+ What if I were to use the Scriptures alone to inform my views about other races, about slavery, about women, about homosexuality? What conclusions would I draw?

+ Is there more to scriptural interpretation than just quoting a few verses? Are there larger issues and greater moral principles that must also be addressed in evaluating the testimony of Scripture?

Mennonite professor Willard Swartley raises some further questions for reflection, noting that:

> ...on the one hand, the biblical call to holiness and noncomformity to the world's way, especially its sexual sins, is strong and clear. On the other hand, Scripture as a whole...is equally strong in its call

for justice-mercy and acceptance of the marginalized, which might thus lead us to accept gay and lesbians together with homosexual practice in light of their being stigmatized by religion and society. Resolving these tensions is the hermeneutical-interpretive task, as we live with Scripture in our world today.[16]

He continues:

How do we manage these mixed ethical signals in the biblical text? How do we balance biblical justice with its concern also for boundaries and discipline? How does biblical holiness fit with compassion and inclusion? Does the strong gospel principle of inclusion override the texts that call for boundaries and ethical discipline (Matt. 18:15–18; 1 Cor. 5)? Are inclusiveness and discipline incompatible?[17]

These are important questions! And let's be totally candid: these are not merely questions of how we interpret Scripture. We are dealing with people's lives, and we dare not trivialize the difficulty and sensitivity of these subjects.

So, for me, it is with care and concern before the Lord that I take any of the stands that I take, and I never do so without much introspection and, often, genuine pain, not wanting to hurt the LGBT community more than it has been hurt, not wanting to reflect my heart rather than God's heart, not wanting to be a poor witness of Jesus, not wanting to reject those whom He is affirming, and always wanting to be sensitive to the voice of the Spirit, the voice of conscience, and the voice of the disenfranchised. And while awaiting the ultimate day of accounting before God's throne, I bring myself before Him (often daily), asking Him to examine my heart, my life, my motives, my responses, my words, my actions, praying for both mercy and forgiveness where I fall short and for courage to stand where His truth requires it, regardless of the cost or consequences.

My personal upbringing is also important in this regard, since I grew up in a very open, liberally minded home, to the point that the first organ teacher my sister and I had was an openly gay man named Russ. (I was barely six years old when we started taking music lessons; my sister was about nine.) Sometimes Russ and his partner Ed would commute together from Manhattan to our home on Long Island, often staying for dinner with us afterward. (Ed was a hair dresser, and one time, as a family, we visited Russ and Ed in their apartment in Manhattan.)

My sister and I knew that they were different—that much was obvious— but we didn't understand sexual issues at such young ages, and, in any case, my parents didn't have the least concern with Russ being our organ teacher. This was obviously not a "homophobic" household!

It was not a racially biased home either, and so our next organ teacher was a black man who was married to a white woman (this was in the mid- 1960s), and they had been ostracized by family members and friends because of their interracial marriage. I remember my father explaining to us what happened and how wrong this treatment was. Again, this is a picture of the environment in which I was raised.

When I came to faith in Jesus in 1971 as a heroin-shooting, LSD-using, sixteen-year-old, hippie-rebel, rock drummer, I began to read the Bible voraciously and certainly believed that homosexual practice was sinful. But to be perfectly honest, I don't remember hearing much (or even any) preaching about the subject, nor was it something that concerned me at the time. For me the big issue was giving up drugs and drinking (which, by God's grace, I did almost overnight once the Lord's love became real to me), then living in sexual purity, staying close to the Lord, and reaching out to others with the good news of Jesus.

This pattern continued in my life over the next decades, and so, out of the first nineteen books I wrote (from 1985–2010), if you took out all the material dealing with homosexuality and put it together, it would barely fill one page, even though a close relative of mine married a man who came out of homosexuality. Still, this was simply not a major focus of mine, nor was I uptight about the subject of homosexuality, nor could anyone who listened to me preach over the decades think that I had it in for LGBT people. Once God began to burden me about this subject (starting in 2004), I went out of my way to listen to the stories of LGBT individuals, to read their books and articles, to see the world (and the Word) through their eyes—as much as a straight Christian could do so—and to prayerfully consider all sides of the relevant issues.

So you will have a hard time of accusing me of bringing a small-minded, homophobic mind-set to the biblical text. I am simply committed to following the Lord and His truth, wherever it leads. I hope you are too.

Before getting into the specific subjects of slavery, the oppression of women, and homosexuality, it is clear to me the vast majority of those who have changed their views on what the Bible says about homosexuality and now find the two compatible have done so based on: (1) their own same-sex desires and attractions, (2) their interaction with "gay Christians" (or with any gay or lesbian person who challenges their assumptions), or (3) contemporary understandings of homosexuality. In other words, they have not changed their thinking based on study of the Scriptures alone, since, the truth be told, *no new textual, archeological, sociological, anthropological, or philological discoveries have been made in the last fifty years that would cause us to read any of these biblical texts differently.* Put another way, it is not that we have gained some new insights into what the biblical text means based on the study of the Hebrew and Greek texts. Instead, people's interaction with the LGBT community has caused them to understand the biblical text differently.

Consider this case in point. Luke Timothy Johnson is a highly respected New Testament scholar and professor who had a change of heart regarding the Bible and homosexual practice, but he states that the scriptural testimony is clear: "The task demands intellectual honesty," he writes. "I have little patience with efforts to make Scripture say something other than what it says, through appeals to linguistic or cultural subtleties. The exegetical situation is straightforward: we know what the text says."[18]

What a candid admission! We know what the biblical text says about homosexual practice, and it is clearly prohibited in the Scriptures.

For Professor Johnson, however, there's more to the story, and he asks the question, "But what are we to do with what the text says?"[19] He explains:

> We must state our grounds for standing in tension with the clear commands of Scripture, and include in those grounds some basis in Scripture itself. To avoid this task is to put ourselves in the very position that others insist we already occupy—that of liberal despisers of the tradition and of the church's sacred writings, people who have no care for the shared symbols that define us as Christian. If we see ourselves as liberal, then we must be liberal in

the name of the gospel, and not, as so often has been the case, liberal despite the gospel.[20]

But what if this means rejecting what the Bible clearly teaches "in the name of the gospel"? Professor Johnson writes: "I think it important to state clearly that *we do, in fact, reject the straightforward commands of Scripture,* and appeal instead to another authority when we declare that same-sex unions can be holy and good" (my emphasis).[21]

What possible kind of "authority" would allow a Christian to "reject the straightforward commands of Scripture"?

> We appeal explicitly to the weight of our own experience and the experience thousands of others have witnessed to, which tells us that to claim our own sexual orientation is in fact to accept the way in which God has created us. By so doing, we explicitly reject as well the premises of the scriptural statements condemning homosexuality—namely, that it is a vice freely chosen, a symptom of human corruption, and disobedience to God's created order.[22]

That is quite a statement! We reject what the Bible explicitly teaches based on "the weight of our own experience" coupled with the experience of thousands of other "gay Christians" who are convinced that God made them gay. Really? This is what a leading New Testament scholar is saying? (And note also his claim that "we explicitly reject...the premises of the scriptural statements condemning homosexuality," as if there's no way to harmonize what these verses say with contemporary views of homosexuality." We'll return to that subject in chapters 6–8.)

On what basis, then, can a Scripture scholar put personal experience on a higher plane of authority than God's Word? He explains:

> Implicit in an appeal to experience is also an appeal to the living God whose creative work never ceases, who continues to shape humans in his image every day, in ways that can surprise and even shock us. Equally important, such an appeal goes to the deepest truth revealed by Scripture itself—namely, that God does create the world anew at every moment, does call into being that which is not, and does raise the dead to new and greater forms of life.[23]

This too is an astounding proposition, one that could theoretically lead to the complete abandonment of everything written in the Bible based on the idea that the "creative work" of our living God "never ceases," and so we might learn something today that would cause us to throw out what was written in the Bible two thousand to three thousand years ago. How could a biblical scholar like Johnson make such a serious mistake?

It is true that his daughter came out as a lesbian, which clearly impacted his viewpoint. But that is not the "experience" that Professor Johnson wants to discuss here (although it obviously carried a lot of weight in his own life). Instead, his argument about the power of experience can be summed up in one word: slavery.

He writes, "Our situation vis-à-vis the authority of Scripture is not unlike that of abolitionists in nineteenth-century America. During the 1850s, arguments raged over the morality of slave-holding, and the exegesis of Scripture played a key role in those debates."[24]

According to Johnson:

> The exegetical battles were one-sided: all abolitionists could point to was Galatians 3:28 and the Letter of Philemon, while slave owners had the rest of the Old and New Testaments, which gave every indication that slaveholding was a legitimate, indeed God-ordained social arrangement, one to which neither Moses nor Jesus nor Paul raised a fundamental objection.[25]

In light of this assessment—one that we'll challenge shortly—Johnson asks, "So how is it that now, in the early twenty-first century, the authority of the scriptural texts on slavery and the arguments made on their basis appear to all of us, without exception, as completely beside the point and deeply wrong?"[26]

> The answer is that over time the human experience of slavery and its horror came home to the popular conscience—through personal testimony and direct personal contact, through fiction like *Uncle Tom's Cabin*, and, of course, through a great Civil War in which ghastly numbers of people gave their lives so that slaves could be seen not as property but as persons. As persons, they could be treated by the same law of love that governed relations

among all Christians, and could therefore eventually also realize full civil rights within society. And once that experience of their full humanity and the evil of their bondage reached a stage of critical consciousness, this nation could neither turn back to the practice of slavery nor ever read the Bible in the same way again.[27]

Professor Johnson then makes the obvious application, claiming that, "Many of us who stand for the full recognition of gay and lesbian persons within the Christian communion find ourselves in a position similar to that of the early abolitionists—and of the early advocates for women's full and equal roles in church and society."[28]

Nonetheless, his argument still rings hollow as he sums things up by saying:

> We are fully aware of the weight of scriptural evidence pointing away from our position, yet place our trust in the power of the living God to reveal as powerfully through personal experience and testimony as through written texts. To justify this trust, we invoke the basic Pauline principle that the Spirit gives life but the letter kills (2 Corinthians 3:6). And if the letter of Scripture cannot find room for the activity of the living God in the transformation of human lives, then trust and obedience must be paid to the living God rather than to the words of Scripture.[29]

How revealing it is that Johnson's knowledge of the Bible compels him to repeat, "We are fully aware of the weight of scriptural evidence pointing away from our position," meaning that, even with the alleged weight of experience favoring "gay Christianity," he still must admit that God's Word endorses no such thing. Equally damning to his position is that to compare slavery and the oppression of women to homosexual practice is to compare apples to oranges—really, it's more extreme than that, like comparing apples to baseballs—while the argument from "experience" works against him as much as for him.

Let me unpack these items one at a time, as succinctly and clearly as possible. For those wanting an extremely detailed hermeneutical discussion, I would recommend William Webb's book *Slaves, Women and Homosexuals: Exploring the Hermeneutics of Cultural Analysis*, which I'll be citing below.

Also highly recommended (and less technical) is Willard Swartley's *Homosexuality: Biblical Interpretation and Moral Discernment.* I'll be citing from this book as well.

So what does the Bible say about slavery, women's rights, and homosexual practice? How do these subjects compare? Obviously we'll be spending most of the rest of this book looking at the major biblical texts that address homosexual practice, so our focus here is on a simple question: Did the church use the Bible rightly when it endorsed slavery (and segregation) and oppressed women? Is it using the Bible rightly when it speaks against homosexual practice?

SLAVERY IN THE BIBLE

Without a doubt, certain forms of slavery *were* instituted by God in the Torah, and the slave did not have the same rights as his or her master. It is also true that during certain times of warfare the Israelites enslaved their captives. (See Deuteronomy 21:10–14.) In one passage that most contemporary readers find very distressing, the Israelites were allowed to buy slaves from the neighboring peoples or from foreigners living among them, even passing these slaves on to their children as an inheritance:

> As for your male and female slaves whom you may have: you may buy male and female slaves from among the nations that are around you. You may also buy from among the strangers who sojourn with you and their clans that are with you, who have been born in your land, and they may be your property. You may bequeath them to your sons after you to inherit as a possession forever. You may make slaves of them, but over your brothers the people of Israel you shall not rule, one over another ruthlessly.[30]
> —LEVITICUS 25:44–46

Clearly none of us today would endorse this as a godly or acceptable practice, and yet nowhere in the Hebrew Scriptures is slavery itself denounced as inhuman or immoral. It would seem that Christians *were* simply following the Scriptures when they practiced slavery in the past, right?

In New Testament times, slavery was a way of life in the Greco-Roman world in which Jesus and the apostles lived, yet at no time did any of them call for a direct revolt against the system. To the contrary, Peter and Paul actually commanded slaves to obey their masters, while Paul even counseled the masters to treat their slaves kindly rather than ordering them to free their slaves.[31]

Could it be true, then, that a fair and honest reading of the Scriptures would support slavery today, including the barbaric African slave trade of America's past (not to mention many other barbaric slave trade industries that exist today in other parts of the world)? Not a chance.

First, we need to see that within the Bible itself the seeds of liberation from slavery were already being planted, and where Old Testament law did institute slavery, it called for a completely different standard for the treatment of slaves when compared to slavery as it was practiced in America and beyond.

Summing up the Old Testament evidence, we see:

+ The deliverance from Egypt was in response to Israel crying out to God from the midst of oppressive slavery (Exod. 2:23–24), and this theme is commemorated throughout the Old Testament. (See, for example, Deuteronomy 15:15.)

+ One reason the Sabbath command was given was to help the people of Israel remember that very liberation from Egyptian slavery and that it was to be a day of rest for slave and free alike. So one of the Ten Commandments states, "Six days you shall labor and do all your work, but the seventh day is a Sabbath to the LORD your God. On it you shall not do any work, you or your son or your daughter or your male servant or your female servant, or your ox or your donkey or any of your livestock, or the sojourner who is within your gates, that your male servant and your female servant may rest as well as you. You shall remember that you were a slave in the land of Egypt, and the LORD your God brought you out from there with a mighty hand and an outstretched arm. Therefore the LORD your God commanded you to keep the Sabbath day" (Deut. 5:13–15).

+ Hebrew servitude was primarily based on economic need as opposed to forcibly imposed slavery (see, for example, Deuteronomy 15:7–18), and an Israelite would serve for only six years as a slave, going free in the seventh year unless he decided he wanted to stay in that household for life (or until the year of jubilee, whichever came first; see Exodus 21:5–6 with Leviticus 25).[32] So, Israelite slavery was much closer to indentured servitude than to the slavery most of us think of when we hear the word *slavery*, meaning a slavery that involved kidnapping, massive fatalities in transport (in the passage from Africa to America), and all kinds of brutal oppression.

+ An Israelite was not allowed to enslave a fellow Israelite, in particular a family member. And under no circumstances could an Israelite be sold as a slave. This is reflected in laws such as these: "If your brother becomes poor beside you and sells himself to you, you shall not make him serve as a slave: he shall be with you as a hired worker and as a sojourner. He shall serve with you until the year of the jubilee. Then he shall go out from you, he and his children with him, and go back to his own clan and return to the possession of his fathers. For they are my servants, whom I brought out of the land of Egypt; they shall not be sold as slaves. You shall not rule over him ruthlessly but shall fear your God" (Lev. 25:39–43).

+ The Torah system of laws was extremely humanitarian in terms of slaves and masters. (See, e.g., Exodus 21:1–11.) So not only did the slaves rest on the Sabbath along with the rest of the Israelites, but if the master seriously mistreated the slave, the slave would go free: "When a man strikes the eye of his slave, male or female, and destroys it, he shall let the slave go free because of his eye. If he knocks out the tooth of his slave, male or female, he shall let the slave go free because of his tooth" (vv. 26–27).

+ In Jeremiah 34 the Judeans were rebuked for failing to release their slaves in the seventh year, as required by the Torah. Then, after releasing the slaves and subsequently changing their minds, enslaving them again, Jeremiah

declared that God would severely judge them for their
sinful actions.

+ The Book of Deuteronomy contains this remarkable legislation: "You shall not give up to his master a slave who has
escaped from his master to you. He shall dwell with you, in
your midst, in the place that he shall choose within one of
your towns, wherever it suits him. You shall not wrong him"
(Deut. 23:15–16). While it is possible that this refers to
slaves of foreigners rather than Israelites, it is still unprecedented in the ancient Near East and, again, carries within
it the seeds of liberty and mercy.[33]

So while I do not minimize the fact that Torah Law did allow the
Israelites to purchase slaves from the neighboring countries as well as from
foreigners dwelling in their midst (as we noted above in Leviticus 25), those
slaves would rest every week on the Sabbath and would still be guaran-
teed humane treatment. Otherwise they too would be released, just as an
Israelite slave would.

Also, while we will see in the following chapters that the New Testament
clearly expresses God's disapproval of homosexual practice, thereby rein-
forcing what is taught in the Old Testament, the New Testament teaches
that in Jesus, any caste or class distinctions that previously existed between
Jew and Gentile are now dissolved. This means that Old Testament laws
that treated Gentiles on a lower plane than Jews would be null and void in
the new covenant Jesus established. So a law like Leviticus 25:44–46, in
which foreign slaves could be kept as the "possession" of Israelites, would
no longer apply. But, to repeat, there are no similar comparisons that exist
with regard to homosexual practice, despite the best arguments of gay theologians. This will be demonstrated clearly throughout the rest of this book.

It is also noteworthy that the people of Israel never entered "into the
capture and sale of human life as did the Phoenician and Philistine traders
and later the European nations."[34] As summarized in the *Hard Sayings of
the Bible*:

The laws concerning slavery in the Old Testament appear to function to moderate a practice that worked as a means of loaning

money for Jewish people to one another or for handling the problem of the prisoners of war. Nowhere was the institution of slavery as such condemned; but then, neither did it have anything like the connotations it grew to have during the days of those who traded human life as if it were a mere commodity for sale. This type of slavery was voluntary for the Hebrew...; only the war prisoner was shackled involuntarily. But in all cases the institution was closely watched and divine judgment was declared by the prophets and others for all abuses they spotted.[35]

In addition to this, every fiftieth year in Israel would be a year of jubilee (or release; see Leviticus 25:10–55), a time in which Israelites who had decided to serve their masters for life (rather than be released in the seventh year) would go free, a time to "proclaim liberty" (v. 10). Debts would also be canceled, and family land that had been sold out of financial need would return to the original owners. And it is this very theme, "proclaiming liberty" to the captives, that is found in Isaiah 61:1 as the prophet speaks of God's end-time release of the captives. Significantly, when Jesus began His public ministry, He took these words from Isaiah 61 and made them His own, proclaiming liberty to the poor and the oppressed. (See Luke 4:18.) Jesus Himself gave future abolitionists a great text to use in their preaching.

And so, while it is true that there was not an attempt by the church in its infancy to overthrow the system of slavery in the ancient Greco-Roman world—that would be similar to a small, new religious movement trying to outlaw the military in America today—the seeds of liberation and equality were clearly planted in the New Testament. For example:

- Paul taught that "there is no slave or free" in Christ (Gal. 3:28; Col. 3:11), a truly radical concept at that time (or any time).[36]

- Paul taught that both masters and slaves serve the same Master and that the slave is the Lord's freeman (Eph. 6:5–9), another radical concept.

- Paul encouraged slaves to obtain their freedom if possible (1 Cor. 7:21–23), which is hardly an endorsement of the system.

✦ In the letter to Philemon, Paul writes to his friend Philemon on behalf of a man named Onesimus who had previously been Philemon's slave but had escaped, after which Paul led Onesimus to Jesus. Paul then appeals to Philemon to receive Onesimus back, not as a slave but rather as a Christian brother! This too was a radical, new way of thinking and quite revolutionary in its implications.

As noted in the *Hard Sayings of the Bible*, when dealing with social relationships that called on the subordinates to submit to their superiors:

> Paul adds a new twist in that in one form or another he reframes the traditional duty in terms of a relationship to Christ. In other words, he takes it out of the earthly context and puts it in the context of something that the Lord will reward. In doing this he qualifies the absoluteness of the duty, for obviously one cannot do something "as unto the Lord" or "like slaves of Christ" if it is something that the Lord has made it perfectly clear that he hates.... Paul has raised the status of the subordinate to that of a full human being before God, yet he has done this without calling for rebellion.
>
> ...Paul also addresses the social superior and points out that he...has responsibilities toward his subordinate.... The master is to treat slaves appropriately in the light of knowing that in reality both he and they are slaves of the same heavenly Master (Eph. 6:9). After all, even Paul calls himself a slave of Jesus Christ. This part of Paul's teaching is revolutionary. It was unheard of to call a social superior to respect and respond to a call to duty toward social inferiors. In fact, one could say that Paul brings the masters down to the level of their slaves and makes them treat their slave as a brother or sister.[37]

But why not just try to overthrow the system in one fell swoop? Again, it's important to remember the social realities of the hour:

> In the social world of Paul's day slavery was an accepted institution. There was also a genuine fear of slaves. In Rome slaves were prohibited from wearing distinctive clothing for fear that they would

discover how numerous they were and start a revolt. Slaves all over the Roman world were under the total control of their masters. If a master wished, he could have a slave executed (or kill the slave himself)....A slave in the first century was property.

Given this context, what would it look like if Christianity were believed to be calling slaves to disobedience? Christianity was already viewed as a subversive form of thought. It rejected the traditional gods (which made it seem treasonous to city and country, for worship of the traditional gods was a major expression of patriotism) and did not allow any compromises in this matter. It rejected many of the "normal" forms of recreation (drinking bouts, use of prostitutes and the like). It formed its members into "secret societies" (at least in the eyes of pagan observers), and in those societies it was rumored master and slave ate the same food at the same table and that wives were present along with their husbands. In other words, first-century social decorum was not observed in the church. Notice that in the New Testament there is no separation of religious duty according to social status. Every member is spiritually gifted, whatever their social status. Any person can become an elder, not just freeborn males. Every member of the church is called to the same obedience to Christ, slave or free, male or female.[38]

So, New Testament Christianity was already quite revolutionary, and there would be no way to advance this new faith—let alone avoid massive bloodshed—by calling on slaves to rebel against their masters or ordering all masters to give up their slaves the moment the masters were converted. But the effects of the new message, in which slaves and free were equal in Jesus, did have a revolutionary effect:

...it raised the slave to a new status of an equal human being before Christ. After all, in the eyes of the church slavery was just a job, and what job or social status one had on earth did not matter (Jesus did not have a great social status at any time in his life either, and he died a most shameful death, an executed slave's death). If the job was done "as a slave of Christ" the reward was equal, whether one was a human slave or a human master. Paul's strategy was thus that of producing an expression of the kingdom of God in the church, not that of trying to change society.

What was the result of this strategy? The church never adopted a rule that converts had to give up their slaves. Christians were not under law but under grace. *Yet we read in the literature of the second century and later of many masters who upon their conversion freed their slaves. The reality stands that it is difficult to call a person a slave during the week and treat them like a brother or sister in the church.* Sooner or later the implications of the kingdom they experienced in church seeped into the behavior of the masters during the week. Paul did in the end create a revolution, not one from without, but one from within, in which a changed heart produced changed behavior and through that in the end brought about social change. This change happened wherever the kingdom of God was expressed through the church, so the world could see that faith in Christ really was a transformation of the whole person.[39]

It makes perfect sense, then, that the antislavery movement in British and American history was driven by Bible-believing Christians, including:

+ William Wilberforce, the courageous British Parliamentarian who fought tirelessly to abolish slavery and the slave trade in the British Empire. And he succeeded!

+ John Newton, the former slave trader who encouraged Wilberforce and is best known for writing the hymn "Amazing Grace."

+ Charles Grandison Finney, considered to be one of the greatest American evangelists in history. Although he put evangelism and revival first, he was also a strong abolitionist to the point that under his presidency, Oberlin College became part of the Underground Railroad, the escape route for slaves.

+ William Lloyd Garrison, publisher of the radical antislavery newspaper called *The Liberator*.

+ Theodore Dwight Weld, speaker, editor, organizer, and coauthor of the book *American Slavery as It Is: Testimony of a Thousand Witnesses*.

+ Harriet Beecher Stowe, author of the massively influential book *Uncle Tom's Cabin*. According to the common account (although not verifiable), when President Lincoln met her after the Civil War, he said to her, "So you are the little woman who wrote the book that started this great war!"

And let's not forget that the modern civil rights movement in America started largely in the church, led by men such as Rev. Martin Luther King Jr. who made frequent appeals to Scripture in their writing and preaching.[40]

Of course, there were plenty of white ministers who, sad to say, supported segregation. But there were also white ministers such as Rev. Billy Graham who were among the first to endorse the call for unity and equality.

> During the 1960s Graham opposed segregation and refused to speak to segregated auditoriums. Once he dramatically tore down the ropes that organizers had put up to separate the audience. Graham said, "There is no scriptural basis for segregation....The ground at the foot of the cross is level, and it touches my heart when I see whites standing shoulder to shoulder with blacks at the cross." Graham paid bail money to secure the release of Martin Luther King, Jr. from jail during the 1960s civil rights struggle. He invited Dr. King to join him in the pulpit at his 16-week revival in New York City in 1957.[41]

This important concept that "the ground at the foot of the cross is level," coupled with the command to "love your neighbor as yourself," speaks directly against the practices of slavery and segregation. In contrast, as we shall see, to say that "the ground at the foot of the cross is level" and to advocate love of our neighbors does *not* provide endorsement for same-sex practices—although it absolutely *does* call for compassionate, caring outreach to those who are marginalized and outcast, including those who identify as LGBT.

We also need to remember that nowhere in the Bible are other races, as such, universally condemned or criticized. In other words, there is no wholesale condemnation or criticism of people of one particular color, contrary to some terribly misguided interpretations of certain verses that actually say no such thing.[42] That means there is not a stitch of biblical support for the view that Christians should oppress another people group because of their ethnicity or the color of their skin, whereas there is consistent biblical support in both the Old Testament and New Testament for the view that homosexual practice is sinful in God's sight.

To summarize, then, although slavery was legislated in the Old Testament and permitted in the New Testament, the Torah laws stood out for their humanitarian aspects, while the seeds of liberation from slavery were already planted in the Old Testament. With the coming of Jesus into the world, these seeds of liberation were planted even more deeply and widely, which is why the New Testament paved the way for the freeing of slaves individually and, over time, on a society-wide basis. And so it is only by a misuse of the Bible that a Christian could advocate for the modern slave trade (or support segregation).

THE STATUS OF WOMEN IN THE BIBLE

Clearly, women do not stand on equal footing with men in many ways in the biblical world, especially in the Old Testament. For example, the biblical world was totally patriarchal; the Torah gave men the right to divorce but not women (see, for example, Deuteronomy 24:1–4); polygamy was practiced, along with other forms of marriage that could be considered degrading to women; and women could not serve in the priesthood.

In the New Testament women had to be veiled or have their heads covered in church gatherings, according to 1 Corinthians 11, while in 1 Corinthians 14 Paul wrote, "As in all the churches of the saints, the women should keep silent in the churches. For they are not permitted to speak, but should be in submission, as the Law also says" (vv. 33–34). Similarly, in 1 Timothy 2:11–15 he wrote:

> Let a woman learn quietly with all submissiveness. I do not permit a woman to teach or to exercise authority over a man; rather, she is to remain quiet. For Adam was formed first, then Eve; and Adam was not deceived, but the woman was deceived and became

a transgressor. Yet she will be saved through childbearing—if they continue in faith and love and holiness, with self-control.

On the other hand, there is no doubt but that the Bible is a book of liberation for women. Consider the following:

- Eve, the first woman, plays an essential and irreplaceable role both as the suitable companion for Adam and "the mother of all living." And from the start it is the man who is called to leave father and mother and cleave to his wife. (See Genesis 2:18–24; 3:20.)

- The Torah also called for the humanitarian treatment of women and wives. (See Exodus 21:7–11, which actually deals with required fair treatment of a female slave.)

- The Old Testament celebrates powerful women such as Deborah, who led the nation and was a hero of the faith, and Esther, the courageous queen who saved the Jewish people from destruction. (See Judges 4–5; the Book of Esther.)

- In biblical wisdom literature (especially the Song of Solomon) female sexuality is celebrated.

- The long poem in praise of godly wives in Proverbs 31:10–31 extols the woman who makes business decisions, provides for her family, and runs the affairs of the household with such shrewdness that her husband is free to talk theology and ethics with the other men at the city gate. The poem, which is twenty-two verses long, ends with these words: "Charm is deceptive, and beauty is fleeting; but a woman who fears the LORD is to be praised. Give her the reward she has earned, and let her works bring her praise at the city gate" (vv. 30–31, NIV).

In stark contrast there is not one syllable in the Scriptures praising homosexuality or homosexual practice, nor is a single homosexual leader or individual recognized or commended as such.[43]

When we move into the New Testament, we note that women played a prominent role in the ministry of Jesus:

- His mother Miriam (Mary) is highly regarded in the Gospels and continues in ministry with the apostles after Jesus's death and resurrection.

- Luke records that a number of women accompanied Jesus and His twelve disciples (this was certainly out of the norm), and some of them helped underwrite their expenses (Luke 8:1–3).

- Some of these women are prominently involved in the events surrounding Jesus's death, and the sacrificial and compassionate acts of one of them—another woman named Miriam (Mary)—are commemorated in the Gospels as a lasting witness. (See Matthew 26:6–13.)

- These women also play a prominent role in the events surrounding Jesus's resurrection, and they are the first to see Him after He rose, the first to believe that it was really Him, and the ones to report to the male disciples that He had risen. This is major, since the resurrection of Jesus is one of the most pivotal events in the history of the world, and it was women who were the first to witness it. Not surprisingly the men were skeptical when they first heard the report from these women, even though Jesus had assured His followers that He would rise.

Women also played a major role in the ministry (and letters) of Paul, as evidenced from this one section from Romans 16:1–7 (NIV):

I commend to you our sister Phoebe, a servant of the church in Cenchrea. I ask you to receive her in the Lord in a way worthy of the saints and to give her any help she may need from you, for she has been a great help to many people, including me. Greet Priscilla and Aquila, my fellow workers in Christ Jesus.[44] They risked their lives for me. Not only I but all the churches of the Gentiles are grateful to them....Greet Mary, who worked very hard for you.

> Greet Andronicus and Junias, my relatives who have been in prison with me. They are outstanding among the apostles, and they were in Christ before I was.[45]

And let's not forget that the same Paul who taught there was no Jew or Gentile in Jesus and no slave or free in Him also taught that there was no male or female in Christ—an absolutely radical concept.[46] Did Paul mean that these categories no longer existed in real life? Hardly. Instead he was saying that in Jesus there is no caste system and no class system, that all of us are equal in Jesus—as Billy Graham said, the ground is level at the foot of the cross.

Interestingly, to this day, when a traditional Jewish man wakes up in the morning, he thanks God that he is not a woman, not a Gentile, and not a slave. Why? Because it is only a free Jewish male who is obligated to keep all the commandments of the Torah, and that is considered a sacred privilege.[47]

Paul says something quite the opposite: even though each group clearly exists, and even though men are called to do some things that women are not, and vice versa (the same with Jew and Gentile and slave and free), we share absolute equality as brothers and sisters in Jesus. To repeat: there is no caste system or class system in Jesus, and this concept alone had revolutionary effects on the growing church.

WOMEN IN THE EARLY CHURCH

How then did these teachings and principles play out in the life of the early church? What was the status of women? The positive pattern continued, and some of the most celebrated and courageous martyrs were women, such as Perpetua and Felicity, and their stories were told and retold for centuries. More significantly, as the new faith spread in the ancient world, it had a liberating effect on women, just as it has a liberating effect when it impacts Islamic-dominated societies today.

As noted by the respected anthropologist Rodney Stark, "Amidst contemporary denunciations of Christianity as patriarchal and sexist, it is easily forgotten that the church was so especially attractive to women that in 370 the emperor Valentinian issued a written order to Pope Damasus I requiring that Christian missionaries cease calling at the homes of pagan women."[48]

Stark also explained that, "Christian women did indeed enjoy considerably greater status and power than did pagan women."[49] He explains, "First of all, a major aspect of women's improved status in the Christian subculture is that Christians did not condone female infanticide," which was another revolutionary breakthrough brought about by the new faith.[50]

Professor Stark pointed out that males clearly outnumbered females in the ancient Greco-Roman world, meaning that human life was being tampered with: "Exposure of unwanted female infants and deformed male infants was legal, morally accepted, and widely practiced by all social classes in the Greco-Roman world."[51] And Stark cites this famous letter from the year 1 BC written by a man named Hilarion to his pregnant wife Alis:

> Know that I am still in Alexandria. And do not worry if they all come back and I remain in Alexandria. I ask and beg you to take good care of our baby son, and as soon as I receive payment I shall send it up to you. If you are delivered for a child [before I come home], if it is a boy keep it, if a girl discard it. You have sent me word, "Don't forget me." How can I forget you. I beg you not to worry.[52]

How extraordinary! The Jesus movement changed that mind-set dramatically, and infanticide was largely obliterated by the Christian faith as it spread, which was of special benefit to females.

And there's more. Stark notes that, "The more favorable Christian view of women is also demonstrated in their condemnation of divorce, incest, marital infidelity, and polygamy.... Like pagans, early Christians prized female chastity, but unlike pagans they rejected the double standard that gave pagan men so much sexual license."[53] So, the double standard that required sexual purity for women but not for men was also obliterated by the cross.

Stark also adds that, "Should they be widowed, Christian women also enjoyed very substantial advantages," noting that, "Close examination of Roman persecutions also suggests that women held positions of power and status within the Christian churches."[54]

As for the passages in the New Testament that seem to subordinate women—calling on them to respect their husbands and submit to them—those same passages also call on the husbands to love their wives the way Christ loved the church, laying down His life for her. And yes, it is true that husbands are called to be the heads of their homes, but the biblical model is one of responsibility and care, not oppression or abuse.

There are also verses that must be understood in the context of the culture of the day, such as women wearing head coverings when they gathered with men for meetings. You see, it was the norm for married women to wear head coverings in public, so the question here was, "When we gather in our homes for Scripture study and prayer, do the ladies need to be veiled?" It was hardly some oppressive, chauvinistic culture that Paul was advocating, and, as Professor Robert Gagnon noted, "Paul did not make head coverings an issue vital for inclusion in God's kingdom, but he did put same-sex intercourse on that level."[55]

There is even a simple explanation for Paul's rather harsh-sounding admonition that "the women should keep silent in the churches. For they are not permitted to speak, but should be in submission, as the Law also says. If there is anything they desire to learn, let them ask their husbands at home. For it is shameful for a woman to speak in church" (1 Cor. 14:34–35).

As Bible background expert Craig Keener explains, "The issue here is…their weakness in Scripture, not their gender."[56] In fact, just a few chapters earlier, Paul had given clear guidelines in which women could pray and prophesy in a public meeting (1 Cor. 11:1–5), so his call for them to "remain silent" was in a specific context and for a specific purpose. As Keener explains:

> Informed listeners customarily asked questions during lectures, but it was considered rude for the ignorant to do so. Although by modern standards literacy was generally low in antiquity (less so in the cities), women were far less trained in the Scriptures and public reasoning than men were. Paul does not expect these uneducated women to refrain from learning (indeed, that most of their culture had kept them from learning was the problem). Instead he provides the most progressive model of his day: their husbands are to respect their intellectual capabilities and give them private instruction. He wants them to stop interrupting the teaching

period of the church service, however, because until they know more, they are distracting everyone and disrupting church order.[57]

It is also possible (if not likely) that the men sat on one side of the room (or building) and the women on the other, as is still common in certain cultures and religions to this day, therefore the women calling out and asking their husbands questions during the meeting would be all the more disruptive. So what seems extreme to us today would hardly have been extreme back then.[58]

Summing up the evidence, then, while it is clear that there was not total social equality between men and women in biblical days, including during the time of the New Testament, it is equally clear that women could be raised up by God as leaders, that women were to be highly respected and regarded by their husbands, that women played a prominent role in the ministry of Jesus and the early church, and that the gospel message itself is liberating for women. So it is only by a misuse of the Scriptures that the church could oppress women and treat them like second-class citizens.[59]

This is in stark contrast to the Bible's depiction of homosexual practice, which, as we will learn, is always seen as contrary to God's established order, while it is heterosexual practice and male-female unions that are the only option. And while liberation from slavery is pointed to as a positive ideal in the Scriptures, and while the Word has much to say that is positive about women, there is not a single positive statement about homosexuality in the Bible. In fact, every time it is mentioned, it is condemned in the clearest of terms.

A WORD TO MY GAY AND LESBIAN READERS

At this point, though, I realize that some of you reading this identify as gay and are about to throw the book down, feeling that I have ripped open old wounds that you have carried for years, as if *you* are an abomination or as if God hates you and has predetermined to damn you. Nothing could be further from the truth. In fact, I personally believe that the Father has a special tenderness in His heart for those who have struggled with same-sex attractions (or gender identity issues), understanding the internal (and even external) torment that many of you have lived through. And the Scriptures assure us that Jesus, our great High Priest, does understand![60]

I simply encourage you to realize that you are more than your romantic attractions and sexual desires, that there is quite a difference between having a desire and acting on it,[61] and if you will give yourself completely to the Lord, holding nothing back from Him, He will hold back nothing from you. There is a place of freedom and fulfillment in Jesus—whether or not you experience a change in your attractions and desires. Do you believe the Lord is big enough and good enough to be your all in all?

Professor Luke Johnson had stated that:

> We appeal explicitly to the weight of our own experience and the experience thousands of others have witnessed to, which tells us that to claim our own sexual orientation is in fact to accept the way in which God has created us. By so doing, we explicitly reject as well the premises of the scriptural statements condemning homosexuality—namely, that it is a vice freely chosen, a symptom of human corruption, and disobedience to God's created order.[62]

But the Scriptures warn us repeatedly about the deceitful nature of our own hearts—our experience confirms this too—and it is extremely dangerous to reject what the Word plainly says about homosexual practice because we have a sweet child or close friend or caring minister who identifies as gay or lesbian. None of that changes what the Word of God clearly says, and none of that changes the deceitfulness of sin, which is why the Word often warns not to be deceived or to deceive ourselves.[63] As someone once said, the problem with deception is that it's so deceiving!

Contrast the penetrating, truth-revealing power of God's Word with the deceitful nature of our own hearts:

> For the word of God is living and active, sharper than any two-edged sword, piercing to the division of soul and of spirit, of joints and of marrow, and discerning the thoughts and intentions of the heart. And no creature is hidden from his sight, but all are naked and exposed to the eyes of him to whom we must give account.
> —Hebrews 4:12–13

> The heart is deceitful above all things, and desperately sick; who can understand it?
> —Jeremiah 17:9

Which will you follow? Your heart or the Word of God?

The reality is that all of us are created in the image of God, and all of us, by nature, are fallen and broken, in need of redemption and forgiveness. Homosexuality is just one of many manifestations of our fallen nature, whatever its causes and origins.[64] And so, rather than seeing yourself as uniquely cursed or condemned because you are same-sex attracted, why not simply see yourself as a fellow sinner in need of mercy and transformation? Why not see yourself as a candidate for God's grace?

To be sure, there are biblical scholars and theologians, both gay and straight, who claim that we really can't be sure how Moses, Jesus, and Paul would feel about committed, monogamous gay relationships, while others claim we can be fairly sure that they would approve and accept. But on the day you stand before God to give account, you will do it alone, without those scholars, pastors, theologians, and friends.

How much of your life are you willing to leave to speculation? And given the importance of this issue, would a loving God leave so many of you hanging on a thread of uncertainty, conjecture, and guesswork? Would He inspire His servants (or, at the least, allow them) to make so many categorical statements against homosexual practice in the Bible, recognizing that no one would rightly understand the allegedly gay-friendly intent of these verses until the late twentieth century (or that no one would understand "sexual orientation" until this time)?

This, as we have seen, is in complete contrast to the biblical texts regarding slavery and women, especially in light of the New Testament. Yet it is the New Testament that makes God's disapproval of homosexual practice even clearer.

And if experience is to be our guide, what do we tell people with sexual orientations other than heterosexuality or homosexuality? What do we tell them when they explain that to the core of their beings they have attractions and desires that the Word of God clearly prohibits? What do we tell them when they insist they were born this way and cannot change?[65] Do we rewrite the Bible for them as well? And do we deny the stories of those who say that the Lord has actually changed their orientation from gay to straight? Do we deny their experiences and call them liars?[66]

Professor Richard Hays has some words of wisdom for us:

In view of the considerable uncertainty surrounding the scientific and experiential evidence, in view of our culture's present swirling confusion about gender roles, in view of our propensity for self-deception, I think it prudent and necessary to let the univocal testimony of Scripture and the Christian tradition order the life of the church on this painfully controversial matter.

We must affirm that the New Testament tells us the truth about ourselves as sinners and as God's sexual creatures: Marriage between man and woman is the normative form for human sexual fulfillment, and homosexuality is one among many tragic signs that we are a broken people, alienated from God's loving purpose.[67]

And so we come back to the theme of this chapter: Are we using the Bible to sanction antihomosexual prejudice? The conclusions of Professor William Webb are relevant. He writes that we are "asking the questions of what aspects of the [biblical] text we should continue to practice and what aspects we should discontinue or modify due to differences between cultures."[68]

He recognizes the importance of contemporary culture:

Of course, I must thank our modern culture for raising the issues addressed in this book. But our culture only raises the issues for me; it does not resolve the issues. When it comes to cultural assessment, it matters little where our culture is on any of the issues discussed in this book! Scripture, rather than contemporary culture, always needs to set the course of our critical reflection.[69]

And so, after detailed, sensitive, and lengthy analysis, he states:

If our modern culture were at some point in the future to accept slavery, it would not influence my conclusions to the slightest degree. I would still be an abolitionist. If our modern culture were to embrace an extremely strong form of patriarchy down the road, it would not change my thinking at all. I would still affirm either ultra-soft patriarchy or complementary egalitarianism (my own preference being for the latter).

If our culture eventually accepts homosexual lifestyles with their complete and unreserved blessing, such a position would not alter my conclusions. I would still advocate a heterosexuality-only position as a Christian sexual ethic. I do not wish to encourage a callous attitude toward our culture. My point is simply that our modern culture must not determine the outcome of any cultural/transcultural analysis of Scripture.[70]

He sums up his position on slavery in the Bible as follows:

Our analysis of the slavery texts has led to a fairly firm conclusion that the sociological structure of slavery along with much of the legislation related to slaves be viewed as culturally relative.... While Scripture has a positive influence in its time, we should take that redemptive spirit and move to an even better, more fully realized ethic today.... The abolition of slavery and its many related injustices should be a passionate value of modern Christians.[71]

Regarding the Bible and women, Webb writes:

It is reasonable to say that much of the portrait of patriarchy within Scripture contains culturally bound components and is not uniformly transcultural in nature.... Like the slavery issue, we need to reapply the spirit of the [biblical] text and attempt to make things fairer and more equitable for women.... Our ethic needs to embrace the renewing spirit of the original text (in its social setting) and move to an even more equitable and just treatment of women today.[72]

Regarding homosexuality and the Bible, he writes:

The same canons of cultural analysis, which show a liberalizing or less restrictive tendency in the slavery and women texts relative to the original culture, demonstrate a more restrictive tendency in homosexuality texts relative to the original culture. Furthermore, the biblical texts not only hold an aversion to associative features (e.g., rape, pederasty), they appear to voice a concern about the more basic or core issue of same-gender sexual acts themselves (i.e., male with male; female with female).

Once this factor is paired with finding a more restrictive

movement within Scripture compared to the surrounding cultures, the covenant homosexual argument fails to be persuasive. Virtually all of the criteria applicable to the issue suggest to varying degrees that the biblical prohibitions regarding homosexuality, even within a covenant form, should be maintained today. There is no significant dissonance within the biblical data.

A comparison of homosexuality with other sexual-intercourse prohibitions in Scripture reveals that the lack of covenant or the lack of equal-partner status is simply not a substantive issue....

Although it is not a popular stance today, only by retaining heterosexuality as normative and homosexuality as aberrant do we perpetuate the redemptive spirit of that text, as it was invoked in the original setting.[73]

And so he concludes, "The comparative outcome is this: the homosexual texts are in a different category than the women and slavery texts. The former are almost entirely transcultural in nature, while the latter are heavily bound by culture."[74]

The observations of Professor Willard M. Swartley are similar. He had written a fascinating book titled *Slavery, Sabbath, War, and Women: Case Issues in Biblical Interpretation*, addressing the fact that, "The Bible appears to give mixed and even conflicting signals on [these] four case issues."[75] He then wrote the volume *Homosexuality: Biblical Interpretation and Moral Discernment*, and he explained the contrast in the subject matter:

On three issues—slavery, war, and role of women—the accusation of the status quo proponents is that those who deem themselves progressive want to "set for [themselves] a higher law than the Bible." The new way, argued by abolitionists, pacifists, and feminists, emerges from God's redemptive action, grace, and kingdom justice. It contrasts to practices in that culture in which slavery, war, and hierarchical gender structures prevailed.

God's way is different, liberating and loving, replacing dominion and self-defensiveness with mutuality and trust. In contrast, homosexual practice is not related to grace-energized behavior in even a single-text. Nor is the practice regulated by permeation of or juxtaposition with a qualifying gospel ethic. For example, the husband-wife hierarchy is virtually transformed by the Christian

ethic of mutual submission and the christologically rooted husband's self-giving love in Ephesians 5:21–33.[76]

To explain this further, he notes that:

> …homosexual practice on the surface of the biblical texts…always
> appears in prohibitive language. It is a deviation from the model of
> life fitting to God's community. Freeing slaves, refusing war, and
> celebrating male-female unity and interdependence are possibili-
> ties of grace, through nonconforming values to the world's cultural
> practices of that time.
>
> Scripture thus moves in a redemptive trajectory on those issues
> when compared to the cultures of the Hebrew and early Christian
> environment. But on homosexuality, Scripture takes as strong or
> even stronger a negative view, and consistently so, than does the
> culture of its environment.[77]

Let's stand with God and His Word and confront the culture with His
redemptive love rather than trying to conform God and His Word to the
culture. This is always the path of wisdom and life.

Chapter 4

THE BIBLE IS a HETEROSEXUAL BOOK

The "gay Christian" argument: Although many Christians put a great emphasis on the sinfulness of homosexuality, there are only a handful of passages in the Bible that touch on the subject at all, which means it was hardly that important to the biblical authors.

The biblical response: Actually, it is because the Bible explicitly states that heterosexuality is God's intended norm for the human race and the only form of union acceptable to God in marriage that the biblical authors didn't say more about homo-sexual practice. The little they said was more than enough given the fact that the Bible, from beginning to end, is a heterosexual book.

AY CHRISTIANS" OFTEN make reference to the so-called "clobber passages" in the Scriptures, by which they mean the main verses the church has used to clobber them over the head with the Bible.[1] They raise two main arguments against the use of these verses. First, they claim that the verses have been mistranslated, misinterpreted, or misused, and so, in reality, these scriptures do not prohibit monogamous, committed, homosexual relationships. In the appropriate chapters in this book we'll look at these key passages in depth.

Second, and perhaps more importantly, they point out that out of more than thirty-one thousand total verses in the Bible, there are between six and eight "clobber passages" consisting of a total of less than twenty-five verses. In other words, out of tens of thousands of verses in the Scriptures, less than one in a thousand deal with the issue of homosexuality. How important can it actually be? And why in the world does the church make such a big deal about something that God's Word hardly addresses? Isn't this evidence of homophobic attitudes in the church rather than a careful representation of God's heart as expressed in His Word?

To consider this second argument in more detail, even if we agree that the references to homosexuality in the Bible are negative, proponents of "gay Christianity" would point out that there is but one reference to homosexual practice in Genesis, none in Exodus, two in Leviticus, none in Numbers, and one in Deuteronomy—meaning, just a handful of negative references in the entire Pentateuch, also known as the Torah. Yet the impression most Christians have is that the Law of Moses condemns homosexual practice over and over again. That seems not to be the case.

In the historical books, meaning from Joshua to Esther, a total of twelve books, references to homosexual practice are found in only three books (Judg. 19:16–24; 1 Kings 14:24; 15:12; 2 Kings 23:7), while in the prophetic books, meaning from Isaiah to Malachi, a total of seventeen books, there is not a single reference to homosexual practice, nor are any to be found in all the poetry and wisdom books, a total of five books, including Psalms, Proverbs, and Job.

Moving to the New Testament, it is often pointed out Jesus never mentioned homosexuality explicitly (nor did the authors of the Gospels), and that Paul only mentioned it three times in his letters, and two of those times the primary word he used to describe homosexual practice is disputed in meaning. Otherwise, the argument goes, homosexuality is never mentioned clearly and directly throughout the rest of the New Testament. (Again, we'll review all these arguments later in the book.)

Can it be honestly said, then, that homosexual practice was a major issue to the human authors of the Bible? More importantly, can it be fairly said that homosexual practice was a major issue to the divine Author who inspired them? Why then do so many right-wing preachers make such a big deal about homosexuality when God apparently didn't make such a big deal about this?

Those are definitely fair questions, but the reality is that the evidence goes in the exact opposite direction. In other words, without any doubt, the Bible is a heterosexual book. From Genesis to Revelation the Bible explicitly presents and presupposes heterosexuality as the divinely intended norm. In fact, rather than accusing the church of making LGBT people feel uncomfortable, it would be more accurate to accuse the Bible as a whole of making them feel uncomfortable.

Now, before I'm misunderstood (and misquoted!), I want to state clearly that an honest reading of the Scriptures makes plain that all of us have sinned and fallen short of God's standards, that all of us are in need of a Savior, that all of us are broken in one way or another, and that without God's mercy all of us are lost. God's Word also makes plain that Jesus died for all human beings alike and that He consistently reached out to the marginalized and disenfranchised, which today would especially include those who identify as LGBT.

That being said, the Bible clearly presents heterosexuality as the divinely intended pattern for the human race, sanctioning sexual acts only within the context of heterosexual marriage. But before I expand on this, let me share a helpful illustration used by my friend Larry Tomczak.[2]

Let's say you buy a new cookbook featuring healthy dessert recipes, none of which use sugar. In the introduction to the book the author explains her reasons for avoiding sugar products, telling you that you will find sumptuous, sweet dessert recipes—but all without sugar. And so, throughout the rest of the book, the word *sugar* is not found a single time—not once! Would it be right to conclude that avoiding sugar was not important to the author? To the contrary, it was so important that every single recipe in the book makes no mention of sugar.

It is exactly the same when it comes to the Bible and homosexuality. There are a few very strong, very clear references to homosexual practice— every one of them decidedly negative—and then not a single reference to homosexual practice throughout the rest of the Bible. Was it because avoiding homosexual practice was not important to the authors of the Scriptures? To the contrary, the only relationships that were acceptable in God's sight or considered normal for society were heterosexual relationships, so homosexual practice was either irrelevant (because it had nothing to do with the God-ordained relationships of marriage and family and society) or, if mentioned, explicitly condemned.

A CONSISTENT MESSAGE

Let's do a brief survey of the contents of Scripture from the beginning to end and see what the Word has to say.

In Genesis 1 God creates humankind (*'adam* in Hebrew) in His own image, creating them male and female, and He blesses them with these words: "Be fruitful and multiply and fill the earth…" (v. 28). This is quite significant, since, while it is true that there are impotent men and barren women, only a man and a woman can conceive. And so, from the very beginning, when human beings were created in God's image and blessed by Him, we were created heterosexual, blessed with a divine purpose that only heterosexuals can fulfill.

Of course, I'm fully aware of the gay argument that heterosexuals have done a good job of procreating and filling the earth and that: (1) homosexual couples are not needed to procreate, and (2) homosexual couples will not stop heterosexual couples from procreating. I'm simply saying that when God created us in His image, He created us male and female, and the blessing that He spoke over us from the start was a heterosexual blessing. So, from the first chapter of the first book of the Bible, a gay couple reading Genesis 1 could easily feel excluded, since God's unique creation of our race presupposes heterosexuality—or, more specifically, makes clear that God created us heterosexual from the beginning.

Moving into Genesis 2, God forms Adam first and then states, "It is not good that the man should be alone; I will make him a helper fit for him" (v. 18), after which God brings the different animals to Adam, and he gives names to each of them. "But for Adam there was not found a helper fit for him" (v. 20)—not a lion, tiger, bear, zebra, gorilla, chimpanzee, or dog. None of them—obviously!—could possibly be the suitable helper that Adam needed.

> So the LORD God caused a deep sleep to fall upon the man, and while he slept took one of his ribs and closed up its place with flesh. And the rib that the LORD God had taken from the man he made into a woman and brought her to the man.
>
> —GENESIS 2:21–22

So it is out of Adam that God forms Eve, the two of them uniquely complementing each other to the point that when Adam sees his helper and counterpart, he exclaims, "This at last is bone of my bones and flesh of my flesh; she shall be called Woman [Hebrew *'ishah*], because she was taken out of Man [*'ish*]" (v. 23). As Old Testament scholar Gordon Wenham notes, "In ecstasy man bursts into poetry on meeting his perfect helpmeet."[3]

85

And this is what we cannot miss: it is because the woman was taken out of the man that the very next verse says this: "*Therefore* a man shall leave his father and his mother and hold fast to his wife, and they shall become one flesh" (v. 24). The author of Genesis is explaining to us that *because* the woman was taken out of the man, the two are now joined back together as one in marital union, each one uniquely complementing the other. And notice: there's not a word here about reproduction or procreation, simply about union (even if procreation is the presupposed outcome).

As A. B. Simpson explains:

> Man was created male and female. This does not mean, as it would seem at first from the language, that he created the male and the female at the same time, but He created male and female in one person. The woman was included in the man physically and psychically, and afterwards was taken out of the man and constituted in her own individuality.[4]

Only a man and a woman can be joined (rejoined!) together in this way. A man plus a man or a woman plus a woman cannot possibly share the same union as a man and a woman, since they do not share the essential of fundamental sameness and difference. To rephrase the famous saying of John Gray, namely, that men are from Mars and women are from Venus, Mars + Mars or Venus + Venus cannot ever equal Mars + Venus.

The fact is that no matter how much two gay men or two lesbian women may feel they love each other, they cannot form a complementary couple the way God intended, nor they can form the biological couple that God intended. Yes, God's design of the male and female body tells you something as well in terms of His ultimate intent and plan.[5]

Now, you might think I'm making too much of Genesis 1–2, but there are two points worth noting here: First, God created the first human beings as heterosexuals, and everything about the way He formed them biologically and emotionally was to complement one another. A male-female couple is the only couple countenanced here, and so it is impossible for a "gay Christian" to read these foundational chapters and relate to them the way a heterosexual Christian would, and no one but the author (and ultimately Author) of Genesis can be blamed for that. (In other words, this has nothing to do with an alleged "homophobic" interpretation.) Second, heterosexual unions (maritally and therefore sexually) are the only unions throughout the entire Bible blessed by God, sanctioned by God, or referenced in any explicit or positive way by any author in the entire Bible. That is really saying something.[6]

In fact, gay activists have often argued against the view that God established marriage as only the union of one man and one woman by pointing to polygamous marriages in the Bible as well as several other unusual variations. There's even a viral YouTube video with a famous illustration underscoring this point:

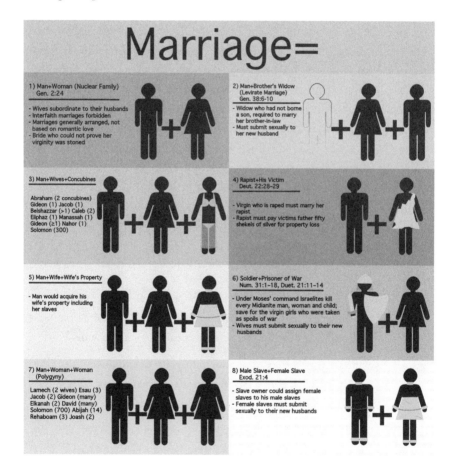

Of course, many of these relationships were far from God's ideal,[7] but the irony of this illustration is simple: all these relationships are heterosexual! Homosexual "marriages" are nowhere to be found on this list, because they did not exist in the Bible, and they were certainly never sanctioned by God in any shape, size, or form. So, in a strange way, this popular chart is one of the best illustrations that the Bible is a heterosexual book.

As we continue to read the Book of Genesis (and the rest of the Bible), we see men and women marrying and having children, and we see promises of blessing and reproduction over couples who couldn't have children, but every single relationship is heterosexual. And when we come to the legal sections of the Pentateuch, in Exodus, Leviticus, Numbers, and Deuteronomy, there are many laws and regulations concerning marital relationships and sexual purity, and once again, every single law and every single regulation presupposes heterosexuality. Even the Ten Commandments presuppose heterosexuality with the famous words, "Honor your father and your mother."

You might say, "But what does that prove? Everything was heterosexual, and homosexual relationships were not sanctioned."

Exactly. The Bible is a heterosexual book, and that's why it doesn't need to constantly speak against homosexual practice. It is heterosexual from beginning to end, and my heart truly goes out to "gay Christians" trying to read the Bible as "their book." For them it cannot be read as is; it must be adjusted, adapted, and changed to fit homosexual couples and families. In short, "gay Christians" must read God-approved homosexuality into the biblical text since it simply isn't there.

And this is the pattern throughout the entire Bible in book after book.

+ Every single reference to marriage in the entire Bible speaks of heterosexual unions, without exception, to the point that a Hebrew idiom for marriage is for a man to "take a wife."[8]

+ Every warning to men about sexual purity presupposes heterosexuality, with the married man often warned not to lust after another woman.[9]

+ Every discussion about family order and structure speaks explicitly in heterosexual terms, referring to husbands and wives, fathers and mothers.[10]

+ Every law or instruction given to children presupposes heterosexuality, as children are urged to heed or obey or follow the counsel or example of their father and mother.[11]

- Every parable, illustration, or metaphor having to do with marriage is presented in exclusively heterosexual terms.[12]

- In the Old Testament God depicts His relationship with Israel as that of a groom and a bride; in the New Testament the image shifts to the marital union of husband and wife as a picture of Christ and the church.[13]

- Since there was no such thing as in vitro fertilization and the like in biblical times, the only parents were heterosexual (it still takes a man and woman to produce a child), and there is not a hint of homosexual couples adopting children.

The Bible is a heterosexual book, and that is a simple, pervasive, undeniable fact that cannot be avoided, and, to repeat, this observation has nothing to do with a disputed passage, verse, or word. It is a universal, all pervasive, completely transparent fact. And so, when a gay couple reads the Word—two men or two women—and they come to Paul's words in Ephesians 5:22, 25, "Wives, submit to your own husbands, as to the Lord....Husbands, love your wives, as Christ loved the church and gave himself up for her," they cannot possibly relate to those words the way a heterosexual couple relates to them.

Which one is the husband and which one the wife? Or are they both husbands or both wives? And which one follows the example of Jesus? Which one relates to the image of the church?

I'm sure a "gay Christian" couple would say, "Actually, we both take on both roles and give ourselves to each other and submit to each other," but that just proves the point I am making. They cannot simply apply these words to their lives as God intended because He never intended a man to "marry" a man or a woman to "marry" a woman.

In the same way a "gay Christian" couple cannot tell their child, "Remember that God commanded you to honor your father and your mother," since the child is not connected to both his (or her) father and mother, and so the verse must either be quoted generically ("Honor your parents")[14] or fundamentally changed to, "Honor your mothers (or fathers)."

Again, I'm not saying that gay couples don't love each other or that they don't love the children they raise. I'm simply saying that whenever they read the Scriptures regarding marriage and family and parenting as God intended, they cannot possibly relate to the stories, instructions, parables, and illustrations the way a heterosexual couple can because the Bible is a heterosexual book. As summarized by New Testament scholar Robert Gagnon, "Indeed, every narrative, law, proverb, exhortation, poetry, and metaphor in the pages of Scripture that has anything to do with sexual relations presupposes a male-female prerequisite for sexual relations and marriage."[15]

As I noted in a July 2013 article titled, "It's an Avalanche, Not a Slippery Slope":

> "As England moves toward redefining marriage," the *Daily Telegraph* reports, "the word 'husband' will in future be applied to women and the word 'wife' will refer to men, the Government has decided." According to John Bingham, "Civil servants have overruled the Oxford English Dictionary and hundreds years of common usage, effectively abolishing the traditional meaning of the words for spouses."
>
> In the government's proposed guidelines, "'Husband' here will include a man or a woman in a **same-sex marriage**, as well as a man married to a woman. In a similar way, 'wife' will include a woman married to another woman or a man married to a man."
>
> So, a man could be a wife if married to another man (or not), while a woman could be a husband if married to another woman (or not), all of which begs the question: Why use words at all if they have utterly lost their meaning? It's like saying that up is down (or up) and down is up (or down), while north is south (or north) and south is north (or south).
>
> But this is what happens when marriage is redefined.[16]

MISREADING THE SCRIPTURES

The heterosexual nature of the Bible is underscored when gay scholars "cruise" the Scriptures looking for alleged examples of same-sex activity (in particular, supposedly with divine sanction), leading to horrific misreadings of the text. Consider these interpretations by gay pastor and Old Testament scholar Timothy Koch.

Since the Bible describes the prophet Elijah as a hairy man who wore a leather belt (2 Kings 1:8), according to Dr. Koch that means that he is "the Hairy Leather-Man,"[17] also deducing through a bizarre reading of the Hebrew that Elijah may not only be thought of as a hairy man but also as "Lord of the Goats." Dr. Koch writes:

> At this point in my cruising, I felt suddenly as if bells and whistles were going off all over the place. Elijah as a goat god, wrapped in goat skins?! Judy Grahn, in *Another Mother Tongue: Gay Words, Gay Worlds*, devotes an *entire section* to detailing holy homosexuals who, through history, dressed up in goat skins, channeling goat gods (gods who were often thunder gods as well).[18]

So Elijah the prophet, one of the most extraordinary figures in both Jewish and Christian tradition, now becomes a gay leather man, perhaps even clad in goat skins and channeling goat gods!

Koch makes other remarkable "discoveries," such as: Jehu, the zealous king of Israel who slaughtered the idol worshippers, was an "ancient Lawrence of Arabia" (famous, of course, for his homosexuality). Koch bases this on 2 Kings 10:12–17 (you'll be amazed at his deductions when you read the verses), where Jehu took the hand of a man named Jehonadab and helped him into his chariot after questioning his loyalty and devotion. Through Koch's interpretive method, Jehu's question to Jehonadab becomes, "'Are you thinking what I'm thinking?!' The answer is YES! and suddenly these men are holding hands and riding together in the chariot."[19]

More bizarre is his reading of Judges 3:12–26, where Ehud, a left-handed Israelite, hid an eighteen-inch sword on his right thigh then gained a private audience with the Moabite king, Eglon, before plunging the knife all the way into the obese king's stomach. For Koch, it is significant that Ehud was left-handed (since many gay men are left-handed), while the eighteen-inch knife "would certainly be an impressive measurement for *anything* found snaking down (okay, okay 'fastened' to) a young man's right thigh!"[20] (Did I say already that the author of these words is a pastor?) And, having gained a private audience with the king, Koch comments, "What, may I ask, do you actually think that the king believes Ehud to be removing at this point from the folds of his garment, that cubit along his thigh?!"[21]

He concludes, "There are dozen [sic] of these gems scattered and buried in the pages of the Bible."[22] Gems? What kind of biblical interpretation is this? A long knife on a man's thigh—used to kill his enemy—becomes an eighteen-inch phallus, and this is an interpretive gem?[23] (For the record, Dr. Koch was an ordained pastor with the Metropolitan Community Churches, the world's largest gay denomination.)

I'm sure that many readers who identify as "gay Christians" are as offended as I am when they read these "interpretations," and this does not represent the way they see the Scriptures. But it *is* the way many gay theologians see the Scriptures (see chapter 9; note also chapter 6), and it *does* illustrate just how much the biblical text must be radically rewritten in order to "find" alleged positive examples of homosexual unions or homosexual activity in the Scriptures.

Some gay interpreters point to Ruth and Naomi, claiming they had a lesbian relationship despite the fact that the text presents them explicitly as heterosexuals—they were both married and then Ruth remarried after her husband died. And how many thousands of times has a daughter-in-law become very close to her mother-in-law, remaining as a close part of the family after her husband's death (which is what happened with Ruth and Naomi)? Why must lesbianism be read into an explicitly heterosexual family bond?

The best argument gay theologians can give is that, when Naomi is returning to her home country and she urges Ruth, who was a foreigner, to stay with her people in her homeland, Ruth says to her mother-in-law: "Intreat me not to leave thee, or to return from following after thee: for whither thou goest, I will go; and where thou lodgest, I will lodge: thy people shall be my people, and thy God my God: Where thou diest, will I die, and there will I be buried: the Lord do so to me, and more also, if ought but death part thee and me" (Ruth 1:16–17, KJV).

You might ask, "But what does that have to do with a lesbian relationship?" Obviously nothing, but it is argued that because these words are often used by Christian couples when they get married, that means that the words must have had a similar meaning back then. I kid you not!

So, because a heterosexual daughter-in-law whose husband has died feels closely joined to her mother-in-law whose husband also died (she also feels close to her mother-in-law's faith; Naomi was an Israelite; Ruth had come from a pagan background), and because three thousand years later some Christians use her words in a marriage ceremony, then Ruth and her mother-in-law must have been lesbians! (And to repeat: after Ruth accompanies Naomi back to Israel, she marries a man named Boaz, and they have kids together.)

To make them into lesbians is not simply a matter of special pleading. It is a matter of complete fabrication, creating something out of nothing, thereby providing another indication of just how much the Bible is a heterosexual book, to the point that alleged lesbian relationships like this have to be created out of whole cloth since the Bible never once says a single word about a lesbian relationship other than to condemn lesbian sexual acts as a violation of God's intended order. (For more on this, see chapter 6.)

And so, Professor Daniel A. Helminiak, who holds two PhDs, states that, "Unfortunately, we have very little evidence about Ruth and Naomi, so it is impossible to say whether or not they shared a sexual relationship. Nonetheless, given what we know about the women's world in antiquity, the possibility of such a relationship is good."[24] Nonsense![25]

Even worse, Helminiak cites Daniel 1:9, "And God disposed the chief officer [or, chief of the eunuchs] to be kind and compassionate toward Daniel" (NJV), stating, "This text could also be translated to read that Daniel received 'devoted love,'"[26] which is also complete nonsense. The Hebrew says no such thing. Yet, building on this bogus foundation, Helminiak suggests that the chief officer was not actually a eunuch (meaning, a castrated man) but rather a man with same-sex attractions, and so, "some people suggest that Daniel's role in Nebuchadnezzar's court included a homosexual liaison with the palace master."[27] I kid you not. He even makes the claim that, "The romantic connection would explain in part why Daniel's career at court advanced so favorably."[28]

Honestly, I am not making this up in order to make Professor Helminiak look bad, but the truth be told, he is creating things out of whole cloth, making the Hebrew say what it doesn't say, ignoring what the Hebrew text does say, and finding homosexual relationships where they don't exist. Yet his book *What the Bible Really Says About Homosexuality* is widely cited among "gay Christians," tragically so. What he writes is pure (or, more accurately, impure) fiction, and it reminds me of the joke about an imprisoned sex offender who was being interviewed by the prison psychiatrist.

The psychiatrist showed him a picture of a circle and asked him what he saw, and the sex offender gave him a profane, sexual answer. The same thing happened when he showed him a picture of a square, a triangle, and a straight line.

The psychiatrist then said to him, "Sir, I must tell you that you have a filthy mind!"

The prisoner replied, "But you're the one showing me all the dirty pictures!"

While I am *not* comparing Helminiak with an imprisoned sex offender (that is *not* my point!), I *am* saying that this gay reading of the Scriptures is a perfect example of projecting one's own thoughts and desires into the text, just as the sex offender in this joke saw things that were not there, projecting what was in his own heart.

For an even more glaring example of this tendency, some have argued that when Jesus healed the servant of a Roman soldier, He was actually sanctioning their alleged same-sex relationship, since it was common for Roman soldiers to have boy-toy slaves, and this was surely one of them. As unthinkable as this "interpretation" is, it is becoming increasingly common in "gay Christian" circles, and we will actually devote the next chapter to analyzing and refuting this rewriting of the text.

Others point to Mary, Martha, and Lazarus, two sisters and their brother, assuring us that they must have been gay since they were all unmarried adults living in the same house, whereas one would have expected them to have been married based on Jewish practice of the day. (This is not to imply that they were sexually involved with one another but rather that they were not married, raising questions as to why.)

Not only is this theory creating gays and lesbians out of thin air (very thin air at that), but it also begs the question of why these allegedly homosexual siblings weren't living with their same-sex lovers. Why were they all living in the same familial home instead? And how common is it that all three siblings in a family are gay?

More to the point: (1) There is no evidence from the first-century Jewish world that all young men and women would automatically be married, just as Jesus never married (and Paul might never have been married), and no special attention is given to this. (2) It is possible that one or more of the siblings was already widowed or divorced. (3) The biblical text does not say explicitly that Lazarus was not married. (4) There might have been a family situation that called for them to delay marriage or to live together after one or more was widowed or divorced. All in all, no big deal and nothing in the least bit exceptional.

In fact, the whole "they must have been gay" argument is so forced and preposterous that lifelong New Testament scholars are astounded when they hear it for the first time. It never dawned on them for a split second, and one reason is that ancient Jewish literature freely describes the sins of the Jewish people—including prostitution, fornication, and adultery—but almost never speaks of homosexual acts, either because they were so taboo that they were not practiced or because they were completely outside the pale of Jewish culture, considered to be a Gentile vice. So aside from there being a sum total of zero evidence that Mary, Martha, and Lazarus were gay siblings, it is completely ludicrous to think that the Gospel authors, writing in this first-century Jewish context, just casually painted a picture of this lovely gay trio. Again, the thought of it is utterly absurd, and there's not a stitch of evidence to support it.

What about Jonathan and David? Does the Bible present them as gay lovers—and in a positive, deeply moving way?

Rev. James D. Cunningham devotes a chapter of his book *Gay Christian Survivors* to their story, titling it "A Biblical Gay Marriage: Did the Church Just Miss This One—or Did They Intentionally Ignore It?"[29] And it is very common for gay theologians to point to the Jonathan and David narrative as clear evidence of a biblically sanctioned same-sex relationship. In reality, as we shall see, the evidence is decidedly against this interpretation.

For a moment, though, let's go along with the gay reading of the text and ask, "What then can we conclude from this?" (Again, I don't accept for a moment that the Scriptures teach that Jonathan and David were gay. I'm just going along with this to make a simple point.) At the very most, it would indicate that they were bisexual men who had a sexual and romantic relationship, one that was considered reproachful by Jonathan's father, and one that was never connected with David once he became king. In other words, even if the gay interpretation was right, it would point to David, who was clearly heterosexual, having a bisexual fling with Jonathan when he was a young man, and nothing more.

It would say nothing about them being "gay" in any exclusive sense, and it would say even less about a "biblical gay marriage." At most, it would have pointed to a bisexual relationship between two young men, and even that would go way beyond what the Bible says.

Before presenting the pro-gay arguments, let's recount what we do know about these two men.

1. We know that Jonathan later married and had children. (See 2 Samuel 9, which references Jonathan's son.)

2. We know that David was very much into women, the Bible recording the names of *eight women* that he married (Michal, Ahinoam, Abigail, Maacah, Haggith, Abital, Eglah, Bathsheba), also noting, "David took more concubines and wives from Jerusalem, after he came from Hebron, and more sons and daughters were born to David" (2 Sam. 5:13), which could point to additional wives. He obviously had quite a strong heterosexual appetite.

3. David's heterosexual lust got him in trouble later in life when he saw a beautiful married woman named Bathsheba bathing. He wanted her so badly that he had sex with her, and then, when he found she was pregnant, he had her husband killed (2 Sam. 11).

David hardly fits the description of being gay! Is it possible, though, that at least one time in his life he had a homosexual relationship with Jonathan? Here's the evidence as presented by J. D. Cunningham, who makes his case as if he is presenting it in a court of law:

1. According to 1 Samuel 18:1, "The soul of Jonathan was knit to the soul of David, and Jonathan loved him as his own soul," and, "Only lovers have their souls 'knit together in love.' To suddenly redefine these words would be to overthrow our entire language."[30]

2. According to 1 Samuel 18:2, Saul, Jonathan's father, "took [David] that day and would not let him return to his father's house," which proves that "David was brought into the royal home because the king's son had entered into a marriage covenant with him."[31]

3. Based on the explicit language of 1 Samuel 18:3–4, which speaks of Jonathan, who was the royal heir, loving David as his own soul and then stripping off his robe and giving it to David, along with his sword and bow, it is clear that "they entered into a marriage covenant with the bestowing upon David even the very Royal Vesture & Sword, as well as everything else that was upon his Royal Person."[32]

4. According to 1 Samuel 20:30, King Saul "knew about David and Jonathan's romantic and sexual relationship."[33]

5. When David had to flee for his life from Saul, David and Jonathan "kissed one another and wept with one another, David weeping the most" (1 Sam. 20:41; for some reason, Cunningham doesn't cite this text when presenting his argument before the judge).

6. David adopted Jonathan's orphaned son after Jonathan was killed in battle.

7. After Jonathan's death David composed a poem for him, saying, "I am distressed for you, my brother Jonathan; very pleasant have you been to me; your love to me was extraordinary, surpassing the love of women" (2 Sam. 1:26).

Now, some of you reading these arguments are shaking your heads saying, "Surely, that author can't be serious. No one reading the Bible on their own would ever think that Jonathan and David were gay lovers!" Others, however, are saying, "Yes, that is so clear! How could anyone argue against this?"

Well, let's step back and look at the relevant verses again, noting that:

1. There is actually not a single reference to them committing a sexual act together; had the biblical author wanted to portray their relationship as sexual, there were plenty of words to use, but none of them were included.

2. You would have to turn the text upside down to claim that Saul encouraged them to be lovers, and you would have to actually completely rewrite it to claim that Saul helped

them enter into a homosexual marriage. You could honestly make a better case for all of them being Martian invaders.

3. Rev. Cunningham acknowledges that, "No one's arguing" that David and Jonathan were not "best friends and 'godly brothers in the Lord,'" and that is all that is actually required to make sense of this beautiful section of Scripture that speaks of the deep friendship and covenantal love between two male (heterosexual!) friends.[34]

We need to remember first that David was already an important person in Saul's life, playing the harp for him when Saul came under the influence of a demonic spirit (1 Sam. 16:14–23) and then defeating Goliath in battle, and that's why he was in Saul's house in the first place. It was in that context that he met Jonathan:

> As soon as he had finished speaking to Saul, the soul of Jonathan was knit to the soul of David, and Jonathan loved him as his own soul. And Saul took him that day and would not let him return to his father's house. Then Jonathan made a covenant with David, because he loved him as his own soul. And Jonathan stripped himself of the robe that was on him and gave it to David, and his armor, and even his sword and his bow and his belt.
>
> —1 Samuel 18:1–4

Is there anything sexual here? Only if read through a hyper-sexualized lens since first, contrary to Cunningham, the Hebrew words "the soul of X was knit to the soul of Y" are *never* once used in the Old Testament for a sexual or romantic relationship.[35] Second, the covenant Jonathan made with David was not sexual—obviously—and the garments he gave him may well have implied his recognition that David, not him, was to be the next king, something that would absolutely infuriate his father Saul. As a team of Old Testament scholars noted:

> The word for the robe that Jonathan gave to David often denotes a royal robe. Ugaritic texts refer to a special robe worn by the crown prince. [Ugarit was an ancient city located in what today is Syria.] If Israel had the same custom, Jonathan would be renouncing his

claim to the throne by giving David that robe. He also gave to him his daily warrior's garment and bow....Jonathan's gifts to David may very well represent his willingness to give up and transfer his particular position as heir apparent to the throne of Israel. He thus was expressing loyalty and possibly submission to David.[36]

This is further confirmed by 1 Samuel 20:16: "And Jonathan made a covenant *with the house of David*"—as if David already had a dynasty, saying, "May the LORD take vengeance on David's enemies" (meaning, in the future.)

Third, the theme of "love" for David occurs throughout this portion of Scripture: "Saul loved him greatly, and he became his armor-bearer" (1 Sam. 16:21); Jonathan loved David (again, 1 Sam. 18:1, 3); "all Israel and Judah loved David" (1 Sam. 18:16); "Saul's daughter Michal loved David" (1 Sam. 18:20; see also v. 28); Saul instructs his messengers to tell David, "All his [i.e., Saul's] servants love you" (1 Sam. 18:22). So, in this context, Jonathan is just one of a number of players who "love" David—including his father, King Saul; Saul's daughter Michal; all the people; and, allegedly, all the king's servants. To read something sexual and romantic into the "love" expressed here is ridiculous, except in the case of Michal, who actually becomes David's wife.

Was Jonathan specially attached to David (1 Sam. 20:17)? Yes, they were soul mates, and they fought the Lord's battles together and risked their lives for their people, and, frankly, to have this kind of especially close-knit relationships is hardly unusual among heterosexuals. Talk to people who have played professional sports together for a period of years on the same team; talk to people who fought in the trenches and lived together during war; talk to lifelong best friends who share many memories in common. Unfortunately, these gay scholars have a hard time recognizing that such close, loving, devoted heterosexual relationships can and do exist, but they surely do, and Jonathan and David are a great example of this. (Can any gay readers relate to super close, loving, nonsexual and non-romantic relationships with people of the opposite sex? I believe so.)

THE TRUTH ABOUT DAVID AND JONATHAN

Saul, on his part, was becoming increasingly neurotic and insecure, especially when he heard the people singing, "Saul has struck down his thousands, and David his ten thousands." As a result of this, the biblical text tells us that, "Saul was very angry, and this saying displeased him. He said, 'They have ascribed to David ten thousands, and to me they have ascribed thousands, and what more can he have but the kingdom?' And Saul eyed David from that day on" (1 Sam. 18:7–9).

It is in this context that you can see why Saul was so upset by Jonathan's close relationship to David. Not only was his son siding with his enemy—again, Saul perceived David to be his enemy because of David's great popularity, being loved by all the people—but also his son seemed willing to give up the throne to David, relinquishing his right to be the next king because he recognized that David was chosen by God for that role. And that's why Saul—an unstable man even before this—tried to kill David. (See 1 Samuel 18:11; 19:1 for the first attempts.)

Look carefully at these words speaking of the last time David and Jonathan saw each other, when Jonathan came to meet with him when he was fleeing for his life from Saul:

> David saw that Saul had come out to seek his life. David was in the wilderness of Ziph at Horesh. And Jonathan, Saul's son, rose and went to David at Horesh, and strengthened his hand in God. And he said to him, "Do not fear, for the hand of Saul my father shall not find you. You shall be king over Israel, and I shall be next to you. Saul my father also knows this." And the two of them made a covenant before the LORD.
>
> —1 SAMUEL 23:15–18

Again, the issue was David being chosen by God to take Saul's throne—which should have gone to Jonathan—and the covenant they made was in recognition of that, pledging their loyalty one to another. (Please don't tell me you think that their covenant meant that Jonathan was pledging to sit next to David as his queen!)

Ultimately, when Saul planned to kill David and he realized that Jonathan was in league with David and warning him, things reached a boiling point:

> Then Saul's anger was kindled against Jonathan, and he said to him, "You son of a perverse, rebellious woman, do I not know that you have chosen the son of Jesse to your own shame, and to the

shame of your mother's nakedness? For as long as the son of Jesse lives on the earth, neither you nor your kingdom shall be established. Therefore send and bring him to me, for he shall surely die."

—1 Samuel 20:30–31

Gay theologians commonly point to this passage as making explicitly clear that Saul knew that Jonathan and David were sexually involved, based on some of the specific Hebrew expressions used. Of course, if that was the case, it would only indicate that such conduct was considered absolutely shameful and wrong. But in reality, that's not what the text is saying at all. As explained by Old Testament scholar Ralph W. Klein:

> The king called his wife (Ahinoam?) a rebellious woman, and his oldest son was just like his mother (cf. Jdt 16:12)![37] Jonathan was accused of forsaking his father to whom, as son and subject, he owed allegiance. While Jonathan had repeatedly referred to Saul as "my father," Saul referred to him neither as "my son" nor by his name. Saul accused Jonathan of being a comrade or ally of David, a friendship that should be embarrassing to him as it was embarrassing to the nakedness, or genitals, of his mother. Saul treated Jonathan as if he had been a mistake from the start! By Jonathan's friendship with David he was foolishly destroying his chance to continue the dynasty....Saul's fear of David's power anticipates what Jonathan reports in 23:17: "My father Saul knows you are going to be king."[38]

Regarding the expression "to the shame of your mother's nakedness," Samuel commentator R. D. Bergen explains that "Saul noted that Jonathan's actions were also bringing shame on 'the mother who bore you' (lit., 'the shame of the nakedness of your mother'), that is, Ahinoam (cf. 14:50), whom he himself had just shamed by calling her 'perverse and rebellious.'"[39] Thus a Bible translator's handbook to Samuel notes that the Revised English Bible translates this expression with "to bring dishonour on your mother," while the Contemporary English Version renders it with "your own mother should be ashamed that you were ever born."[40] Why? Because Jonathan's friendship with David was perceived to be a direct betrayal of his family line, thereby shaming his own mother.

But note carefully: there is nothing in the idiom that connects anything sexual with Jonathan. That is not what the words mean at all. In short, "Saul now accused his dynastic heir of being in league with the very one whom Saul believed would destroy the family dynasty."[41] As another Samuel commentary explains:

> Saul observes that Jonathan is on the side of David, whom he wishes to destroy as an aspirant after the throne and therefore a rebel. And so he looks on Jonathan also as a rebel....David is making a rebellious attempt on the royal throne, and Jonathan, bound to him in intimate friendship, is therefore a rebel. He calls this rebellion "perversity," because "as long as the son of Jesse lives on the earth, he (Jonathan) and his kingdom will not be established." It is therefore Saul's determined and permanent purpose to slay David as a rebel.[42]

And in an extensive translation note in the New English Translation, the force of this idiom in question is explained:

> *Heb* "son of a perverse woman of rebelliousness." But such an overly literal and domesticated translation of the Hebrew expression fails to capture the force of Saul's unrestrained reaction. Saul, now incensed and enraged over Jonathan's liaison with David, is actually hurling very coarse and emotionally charged words at his son. The translation of this phrase suggested by Koehler and Baumgartner [a standard biblical Hebrew lexicon] is "bastard of a wayward woman"...but this is not an expression commonly used in English. A better English approximation of the sentiments expressed here by the Hebrew phrase would be "You stupid [expletive]!" However, sensitivity to the various public formats in which the Bible is read aloud has led to a less startling English rendering which focuses on the semantic value of Saul's utterance (i.e., the behavior of his own son Jonathan, which he viewed as both a personal and a political betrayal [= "traitor"]). But this concession should not obscure the fact that Saul is full of bitterness and frustration. That he would address his son Jonathan with such language, not to mention his apparent readiness even to kill his own

son over this friendship with David (v. 33), indicates something of the extreme depth of Saul's jealousy and hatred of David.[43]

Yes, Saul was so enraged that he now tried to kill Jonathan, who then made his way to David, who was in hiding and awaiting Jonathan's report. And when he saw Jonathan, "David rose from beside the stone heap and fell on his face to the ground and bowed three times. And they kissed one another and wept with one another, David weeping the most" (1 Sam. 20:41).

Should we make anything of the fact that they kissed? Certainly not! In the biblical world the act of kissing (as distinguished from "making out") was a common way of saying hello or good-bye, as it is in many cultures to this day. In fact, this is so common in the Scriptures that if all the kisses the Bible recorded were interpreted in sexual terms, then Isaac would have been erotically involved with his own son (Gen. 27:26, "Then his father Isaac said to him, 'Come near and kiss me, my son.'"), Laban would have been erotically involved with his nephew Jacob (Gen. 29:13, "He ran to meet him and embraced him and kissed him and brought him to his house"), Laban would have been erotically involved with his grandchildren and daughters (Gen. 31:55, "Early in the morning Laban arose and kissed his grandchildren and his daughters and blessed them"), Esau would have been erotically involved with his brother Jacob (Gen. 33:4, "But Esau ran to meet him and embraced him and fell on his neck and kissed him, and they wept"), Joseph would have been erotically involved with all his brothers (Gen. 45:15, "And he kissed all his brothers and wept upon them"), Jacob would have been erotically involved with his grandsons (Gen. 48:10, "So Joseph brought them [his sons] near him [Jacob], and he kissed them and embraced them"), and Joseph would have been erotically involved with his just-deceased father Jacob (Gen. 50:1, "Then Joseph fell on his father's face and wept over him and kissed him")—and these are just examples from the first book of the Bible, Genesis! Obviously all this public kissing was not in the least bit sexual!

In the next book of the Bible, Exodus, we see Moses kissing his brother, Aaron, and his father-in-law, Jethro (Exod. 4:27; 18:7). For some examples of nonrelatives kissing, we see the prophet Samuel kissing Saul (1 Sam. 10:1), David kissing Jonathan (1 Sam. 20:41), the prince Absalom kissing all who would approach him asking him to adjudicate on their behalf (2 Sam.

15:5), the king David kissing the old man Barzillai (2 Sam. 19:39), and Joab kissing Amasa (2 Sam. 20:9).

Kissing as a form of greeting was so customary in New Testament times that Paul and Peter taught the believers to "greet one another with a holy kiss" (Rom. 16:16; see also 1 Cor. 16:20; 2 Cor. 13:12; 1 Thess. 5:26; 1 Pet. 5:13), the ancient equivalent of a handshake, and presumably men with men and women with women. Note also that when the Bible wanted to speak of a sensual kiss, it certainly knew how, as in the bride's words in Song of Solomon 1:2, "Let him kiss me with the kisses of his mouth! For your love is better than wine," or as seen in the context of Proverbs 7:13 (read the whole chapter!). And since there is not a single erotic term used with regard to David and Jonathan's relationship, since the terms "love" and "kiss" are used all over the Bible in nonsexual ways, since both of them were eventually married to women and David got in trouble because of his heterosexual lust, and since everything we know about the ancient Hebrew culture indicates that a homosexual relationship would not have been tolerated let alone celebrated—remember David *loved* the very Torah that calls male-male sex an abomination[44]—it is completely unconscionable to make David and Jonathan into gay lovers.

And so, if we read David's lament for Jonathan after he was killed in battle in heterosexual terms, it makes perfect sense and is consistent with the rest of the Bible: "How the mighty have fallen in the midst of the battle! Jonathan lies slain on your high places. I am distressed for you, my brother Jonathan; very pleasant have you been to me; your love to me was extraordinary, surpassing the love of women" (2 Sam. 1:25–26)—meaning, "I have been involved with a number of women, sexually and romantically, but the love we had between us, the covenantal bond that existed between us, the depth of loyalty and friendship, was more extraordinary that anything I've enjoyed with a woman."

Rev. Cunningham asks the question, "So were they lovers, or just 'close buddies'? Be sure you make that decision based on biblical facts, not on personal feelings."[45] There is only one possible answer: they were godly friends—no doubt about it.

And that leads us full circle to where we started this chapter. The issue is not the interpretation of the so-called "clobber passages," which, as a sacred part of God's sacred Word, are actually liberation verses, since embracing

God's truth sets us free. The issue is the testimony of the entire Bible, from beginning to end, and without a doubt, it is a heterosexual book—as one psychologist commented, "Our bodies tell us who we are—that humanity was designed and created for heterosexuality"[46]—which is why marriage and family models in the Word are exclusively heterosexual.

So when the gay-edited Queen James Bible made some completely unjustified changes to a few verses in the Bible, it failed on two accounts: first, it butchered the verses that it did change;[47] and second, to succeed, it would have had to change the whole Bible!

The good news is that God's arms are open wide to every human being on the planet, no matter how you or I identify ourselves, and there is new life through Jesus available for all. And since we don't have the power to change ourselves from sinner to saint—and, to repeat a common theme of Scripture, all of us have sinned and fallen short of God's glory (Rom. 3:23), there's only one way any of us can come to the Lord, and that is the way we are, asking Him for mercy, grace, forgiveness, and new life.

All of us start as outsiders, regardless of our ethnicity, skin color, social stature, or even the nature of our sin. We all come as lost people needing a Savior. And Jesus is the Savior we all need. Don't let your sexual desires, romantic attractions, or gender identity issues stop you from coming to Him today.

And as a former lesbian once said in a meeting I attended, "God never said, 'Be thou heterosexual because I the Lord thy God am heterosexual.' He said, 'Be thou holy because I the Lord thy God am holy.'"

So while it is true that God designed us for heterosexuality, He called us first and foremost to holiness, and that must be our first priority and goal.

Chapter 5

LEVITICAL LAWS and the MEANING of TO'EVAH (ABOMINATION)

The "gay Christian" argument: The prohibition against homosexual practice in ancient Israel was part of the ceremonial, Levitical law, which also prohibited things such as eating shellfish and pork or wearing a garment made of two kinds of fabrics. Obviously, those laws no longer apply to us today. Plus, the word **abomination** in the Hebrew simply speaks of ritual defilement, not moral sin.

The biblical response: There were some laws that God gave to Israel to keep them separated from the nations, such as the dietary laws, while other laws were based on universal moral prohibitions that applied to all people, such as laws against murder, adultery, and homosexual practice. These universal moral prohibitions obviously apply to all believers today, while the dietary laws do not. As for the word **abomination**, it often speaks of that which is morally detestable before God.

F YOU'VE EVER been to a large gay pride event, you've probably seen some Christians holding big signs featuring one particular verse, normally cited in the King James Version: "Thou shalt not lie with mankind, as with womankind: it is abomination" (Lev. 18:22). You might also see signs with another verse from Leviticus: "If a man also lie with mankind, as he lieth with a woman, both of them have committed an abomination: they shall surely be put to death; their blood shall be upon them" (Lev. 20:13, KJV).

So there you have it in black and white. Homosexual practice is an "abomination" in God's sight, and those who practice it should be put to death under the Law of Moses. Simple, right?

Not so fast. According to Leviticus it's also forbidden to eat shrimp and lobster (Lev. 11:9–12), to plant two different types of seeds in one's field (Lev. 19:19), to wear a garment with mixed fabrics (v. 19 again), or for a man to trim the corners of his beard (v. 27). It's also forbidden for a man to have sex with his wife during her menstrual period (Lev. 18:19; 20:18). As for the death penalty, it's not only practicing homosexuals who should be killed; it's also kids who curse their parents: "For every one that curseth his father or his mother shall be surely put to death: he hath cursed his father or his mother; his blood shall be upon him" (v. 9, KJV).

Why, then, should we make such a big deal about homosexual practice while ignoring or downplaying these other Levitical prohibitions? Isn't that the height of hypocrisy?

Back in 2000 an anonymous author (later identified as J. Kent Ashcraft)[1] penned a very clever letter to conservative radio show host Dr. Laura Schlessinger, asking for her help in sorting out some issues of biblical interpretation:

> Dear Dr. Laura,
>
> Thank you for doing so much to educate people regarding God's law. I have learned a great deal from you, and I try to share that knowledge with as many people as I can. When someone tries to defend homosexuality, for example, I will simply remind him or her that Leviticus 18:22 clearly states it to be an abomination. End of debate.
>
> I do need some advice from you, however, regarding some of the other laws in Leviticus and Exodus and how to best follow them.
>
> 1. When I burn a bull on the altar as a sacrifice, I know it creates a pleasing odor for the Lord (Leviticus 1:9). The problem is my neighbors. They claim the odor is not pleasing to them. How should I deal with this?
>
> 2. I would like to sell my daughter into slavery, as stated in Exodus 21:7. In this day and age, what do you think would be a fair price for her?
>
> 3. I know that I am allowed no contact with a woman while she

is in her period of menstrual uncleanliness (Leviticus 15:19–24). The problem is, how can I tell? I have tried asking, but most women take offense.

4. Leviticus 25:44 states that I may buy slaves from the nations that are around us. A friend of mine claims that this applies to Mexicans, but not Canadians. Can you clarify?

5. I have a neighbor who insists on working on the Sabbath. Exodus 35:2 clearly states he should be put to death. Am I morally obligated to kill him myself?

6. A friend of mine says that even though eating shellfish is an abomination (Leviticus 10:10), it is a lesser abomination than homosexuality. I don't agree. Can you settle this?

7. Leviticus 20:20 states that I may not approach the altar of God if I have a defect in my sight. I have to admit that I wear reading glasses. Does my vision have to be 20/20, or is there some wiggle room here?

I know you have studied these things extensively, so I am confident you can help. Thank you again for reminding us that God's Word is eternal and unchanging.[2]

To be candid, most conservative Christians would be stumped by this letter, probably responding with something like, "Well, you may be clever, but you'll never convince me that homosexuality is right in God's sight. After all, the Bible says it's an abomination!" Can we do no better than that?

Things get even worse for the conservative Christian side when it is argued that the word *abomination* (*to'evah* in Hebrew) doesn't mean something "morally detestable" but rather something "ritually unfit" or "contrary to custom." And so, it is argued, even if we took Leviticus 18:22 at face value, it simply means that a man having sex with another man was a matter of ritual impurity under Old Testament Law and nothing more. Others would argue that, according to the immediate context of Leviticus 18:22, the prohibition is against homosexual acts carried out in conjunction with idolatry (in other words, as part of an act of cult prostitution), not against two men engaged in a consensual, loving (and monogamous) act.

Gay anthropologist Patrick Chapman sums up the most common pro-homosexuality arguments:

William Countryman believes that the purpose of the prohibition of male-male sex is not an ethical or moral one, but as part of the Hebrew purity regulations, it is designed to help keep Jewish identity strong. Daniel Helminiak compares the religious prohibition to one found in the Catholic church:

> There used to be a church law that forbade Roman Catholics to eat meat on Fridays....That church law was considered so serious that violation was a mortal sin, supposedly punishable by hell. Yet no one believes that eating meat was something wrong in itself. The offense was against a religious responsibility: one was to act like a Catholic.

This is evident in that the same Hebrew word used to describe the behavior in the Leviticus passages as an "abomination" or "detestable act," *to'evah*, is used to describe various foods as ritually unclean, such as eating camels, rabbits, and pigs. This word is rarely used in the context of sexual behavior that is inherently immoral, although it is used to condemn male temple prostitution. *Zimmah* is typically used to discuss sexual immorality [with reference to Leviticus 18:17; Job 31:11; Ezekiel 16:27; 22:9, 11]. Furthermore, while other sexual behaviors that are considered inherently immoral are mentioned elsewhere in the Old Testament, male homosexuality is not. Given that the focus is solely on ritual and social impurity, Helminiak argues that the prohibition on male homosexuality is no longer important. Christian tradition has viewed the purity concerns and regulations in Leviticus as irrelevant.[3]

But there's more:

> John Boswell criticizes those who use the Leviticus passages to condemn homosexuals, given that Leviticus also condemns many things are not considered wrong by evangelicals, including tattoos, wearing garments made of two types of cloth, and eating pork. As Boswell notes,

Their extreme selectivity in approaching the huge corpus of Levitical law is clear evidence that it was not their respect for the law which created their hostility to homosexuality but their hostility to homosexuality which led them to retain a few passages from a law code largely discarded.[4]

Dr. Chapman concludes with this: "While the passages in Leviticus may have condemned aspects of male homosexual behavior, there is no indication that they condemn all homosexuality, or that the condemnation had any moral implications. The Levitical condemnation was rather a response to issues of ancient Israelite culture and identity."[5]

According to Dr. Jay Michaelson (and others) the prohibition in Leviticus 18:22 refers to "anal sex—and only that."[6] He continues his argument with one of the more nuanced discussions of the word *abomination* found in the pro-homosex writings:

The last key word of the verse is, in my opinion, the most important: *toevah*. As I've lectured and taught across the country, I've been amazed at how everyone thinks they know the meaning of this obscure Hebrew word: Abomination, right? Isn't that what it says in the Bible? No. Whatever *toevah* means, it definitely does not mean "abomination." Colloquially, abominations are things that should not exist on the face of the Earth: three-eyed fish, oceans choked with oil, and maybe Cheez Whiz. The word "abomination" is found in the King James translation of Leviticus 18:22....Yet this is a misleading rendition of the word *toevah*, which actually means something permitted to one group and forbidden to another. Though there is (probably) no etymological relationship, *toevah* means taboo.[7]

Michaelson further argues that:

The term *toevah* (and its plural, *toevot*) occurs 103 times in the Hebrew Bible, and almost always has the connotation of a non-Israelite cultic practice....*Toevah* is also culturally relative. For example, there are things that are *toevah* for Egyptians but perfectly acceptable for Israelites [with reference to Genesis 43:32,

34; Exodus 8:22]....So, if (1) *toevah* is a culturally relative taboo related to boundary between Israelite and foreign, and (2) male anal sex is specifically called a *toevah*, unlike other prohibitions (e.g., incest), then: (3) male anal sex is a culturally relative taboo related to boundary between Israelite and foreign. This isn't about abomination or nature, or even morality—this is about a ritual purity law that distinguishes Israelites from foreigners.[8]

Are these authors right? Actually, it's very easy to see that: (1) the word *abomination* often has moral overtones in the Hebrew Scriptures and consistently refers to things that God's people should abhor; and (2) while there were many laws that God gave to the people of Israel to keep them separate from the nations, the laws against homosexual practice were universal in scope and intent—in other words, not just for Israel but for all nations.[9]

Let's break things down one point at a time, first demonstrating that the prohibition against homosexual practice was universal, for all people, and not given exclusively to Israel, next demonstrating that *to'evah* simply means "something detestable," then demonstrating that the prohibition against homosexual practice was not specifically tied in to idolatry.

Before getting into the meat of our discussion, let me just say that as someone who has earned a doctorate in Near Eastern languages and literatures from New York University, I have spent decades delving into the original Hebrew text of the Bible and seeking to read it in its ancient Near Eastern context.[10] And so, sometimes, I don't know whether to laugh or cry when I hear the latest "gay Christian" argument claiming the Bible does not speak against homosexual practice.

But it's even worse when these authors back up false arguments with completely shoddy Internet scholarship, by which I mean citing a book excerpt they read online—an excerpt that misrepresents the author's view—and then repeating the misrepresented material as if they read the original work and knew where the author stood. And then other "gay Christian" authors quote the same misrepresented material over and over again.

Not surprisingly, this very thing happened with the subject we're discussing now, namely, the interpretation of Leviticus 18:22. It first came to my attention when reading Justin Lee's book *Torn*, in which he cites Professor Robert Gagnon, arguably the world's foremost authority on the

Bible and homosexuality. Lee describes Gagnon as a professor "who has spent much of his career studying and writing in condemnation of homo-sexuality,"[11] yet he cites Gagnon in support of his own pro-gay reading of the text. (It's the only time he cites Gagnon in his entire book.)

When I read this, I thought to myself, "That's not just odd. It's actually dishonest, since anyone reading Gagnon's whole discussion about this point would know that Lee misrepresented him here."

Not long after, Professor Gagnon, who had become aware of this, wrote an open letter to Justin Lee on the Patheos website, stating, "In your book *Torn*, you make a grand total of one reference to my work on the Bible and homosexual practice (unfortunately ignoring all the other arguments and evidence that I bring forward). In that one reference I believe that you are misleading."[12] Gagnon then demonstrated his case in devastating detail, pointing out that anyone reading the "the very next set of sentences (same paragraph, no less)" that Lee did not mention to his readers, along with the sentences that preceded the section cited by Lee, which, again, Lee failed to mention to his readers, along with several other strong arguments Gagnon made, which Lee also overlooked, would see at once that Gagnon had been misrepresented.

Why would Justin Lee do this? While I disagree strongly with some of the conclusions of his book, I didn't think he would intentionally deceive. Why then did he so poorly misrepresent Gagnon?

Lee wrote a blog post in response to Gagnon's open letter (a rather weak response, to be candid),[13] and then Gagnon wrote a further, devastating reply,[14] and sometime later, while doing research for this book, I found the identical, misleading citation from the same page of Gagnon's book cited by another "gay Christian" author, and that's when the light went on.

I sent this e-mail to Professor Gagnon:

> I happened upon a discussion on one of my web pages with a poor homosexual "Christian" struggling with the issues and believing all the wrong arguments, and he too misquoted you, just as Justin Lee did (p. 130) of your book.
>
> When I did a quick search, I realized what happened (you prob-ably figured this out already as well). Justin never got this from your book; he got it from "gay Christian" sites/articles that cite you accord-ingly, as here: http://www.gaychristian101.com/what-does-you

-shall-not-lie-with-a-man-as-with-a-woman-mean.html, cited again here http://homosexualescristianos.wordpress.com/, and here http://wakeupgeneration.wordpress.com/2012/10/17/142/ and on and on it goes.

In other words, despite the fact that Justin Lee wrestled with the issues of what the Bible said about homosexuality for years, and despite the fact that he mentions how he read everything he could get his hands on pertaining to these issues—issues, which, quite understandably, consumed his whole life as he sought to please the Lord and come to grips with his sexuality at the same time—he apparently overlooked the most comprehensive, scholarly book ever written on the Bible and homosexual practice, relying on a misleading Internet citation. Unfortunately, this kind of thing happens all the time—not just in "gay Christian" circles either—and almost overnight, Internet myths and misrepresentations become reality to millions of people around the world.

So let's dig a little deeper here and look at the biblical texts themselves, in the original languages, and let's separate fact from fiction. After all, if we love God and have given our lives to Him, then we never have to fear the truth, right? And with such important questions before us, we dare not rely on shoddy "research."

THE PROHIBITION AGAINST HOMOSEXUALITY WAS UNIVERSAL PROHIBITION

Even a first-time reader of the Bible will recognize that God made a special covenant with the people of Israel in ancient times, giving them special laws to keep and customs to observe. Included in this category would be dietary laws, ritual purity laws, and laws concerning observing special holidays. In keeping with this, in Leviticus 11, when God tells the Israelites which animals they are not allowed to eat, He says to them, "You shall not eat of their flesh or touch their carcasses; *they are unclean for you*" (Lev. 11:8, NJV; see also Lev. 11:26–27; Deut. 14:7). In contrast, the laws concerning murder are universal, for all people, and not just for Israel.

How do we know this? It's simple. The Bible tells us—just to give one example—that God judged Israel for eating unclean animals, but the Bible never tells us that God judged the nations of the world for eating unclean animals. Why? Because it was not intrinsically sinful to eat a pig rather than a cow (although in the ancient world, in particular, it might have been a lot more unhealthy to eat a pig), but it was intrinsically sinful to commit other sins, such as murdering another human being.

That's why laws against murder were established by God for all humanity after Noah's flood, according to Genesis 9:6, whereas God permitted the human race to eat all animals for food (v. 3), as long as the blood was drained. In the same way, the Lord rebuked foreign nations for their sins against one another—acts of murder and violence—because these were wrong for all people, but, as stated, He did not rebuke them for eating animals that were considered unclean for the Israelites. This also carries over to the New Testament, where the authors reiterate God's universal moral code—laws against murder and adultery, for example—while making clear that food in and of itself doesn't defile us or make us holy.[15]

So, to repeat and summarize: there were laws God gave to Israel alone, and there were laws God gave to all people, including Israel, and for the most part, using the entire Bible as our guide, it is easy to see which are which.

Where exactly does the prohibition against homosexuality fit? Was it a law given to Israel alone, or was it a law for all people? Leviticus 18 makes clear that it was a law for all people, meaning that for a man to have sex with another man is detestable in His sight.

We'll let the Scriptures speak for themselves.

> And the LORD spoke to Moses, saying, "Speak to the people of Israel and say to them, I am the LORD your God. You shall not do as they do in the land of Egypt, where you lived, and you shall not do as they do in the land of Canaan, to which I am bringing you. You shall not walk in their statutes. You shall follow my rules and keep my statutes and walk in them. I am the LORD your God. You shall therefore keep my statutes and my rules; if a person does them, he shall live by them: I am the LORD.
>
> —LEVITICUS 18:1–5

We see here that the laws that will follow prohibit the Israelites from doing what the neighboring pagan nations did, but that doesn't necessarily mean it was wrong for those pagan nations. Perhaps the laws that follow were meant for Israel alone, just like dietary laws? Perhaps the sarcastic letter to Dr. Laura was right? Let's keep reading.

Verses 6–18 of Leviticus 18 deal with various forms of incest; verse 19 prohibits a man having sex with a woman during her menstrual period; verse 20 prohibits adultery; verse 21 prohibits offering children as a sacrifice to the god Molech; verse 22, as we already noted, prohibits a man having sex with another man;[16] and finally verse 23 prohibits bestiality. And some of the offenses are further described using different words: *depravity* (v. 17, speaking of a man having sex with a woman and her daughter or grand-daughter);[17] *abomination* (v. 22, speaking of two men having sex);[18] and *perversion* (v. 23, speaking of bestiality).[19]

And note carefully what follows next:

> Do not make yourselves unclean by any of these things, *for by all these the nations I am driving out before you have become unclean, and the land became unclean, so that I punished its iniquity, and the land vomited out its inhabitants.* But you shall keep my statutes and my rules and do none of these abominations, either the native or the stranger who sojourns among you *(for the people of the land, who were before you, did all of these abominations, so that the land became unclean),* lest the land vomit you out when you make it unclean, as it vomited out the nation that was before you. For everyone who does any of these abominations [*to'evot*], the persons who do them shall be cut off from among their people. So keep my charge never to practice any of these abominable customs [*to'evot*] that were practiced before you, and never to make yourselves unclean by them: I am the LORD your God.
>
> —LEVITICUS 18:24–30

Did you see that? God said plainly that He judged the Egyptians and the Canaanites—idol-worshipping pagans, according to the Bible—for committing these very sins, even stating that by them committing these sins, the land became unclean and vomited them out. This is strong language! And that's why God tells the people of Israel not to commit these sins, otherwise they too will defile the land and the land will vomit them out.[20] In contrast, God never said that He judged the nations of the world for eating unclean animals or sowing their fields with two different kinds of seeds or wearing garments with mixed fabrics.[21] Nor did He say that the land vomited them out for doing these things. But He did say that about the sins listed in Leviticus 18, including homosexual practice.[22]

And there's more still: all these sins together are described as *to'evot*, abominations, detestable things, making clear that God included incest, bestiality, homosexual practice, adultery, and sacrificing children to Molech in this category. (For the question of where sex with a menstruating wife fits, keep reading.) They are all "detestable" in His sight, and together they have dreadful consequences for the nations that practice them. But only male homosexual practice is singled out in Leviticus 18 as a *to'evah*, abomination, detestable thing, meaning that it is a *to'evah* among *to'evot*, an abomination among abominations.

In fact, in the entire Book of Leviticus, homosexual practice is the only specific sin singled out as an "abomination," which is certainly saying something. In addition, it is one of the few sins listed in Leviticus that requires the death penalty, along with sacrificing one's children to Molech, cursing one's father or mother, and committing adultery, bestiality, or incest (Lev. 20:1–16)—hardly a list of mere ceremonial infractions!

To be perfectly clear, I am *not* advocating the death penalty for homosexual practice any more than I'm advocating it for adultery or cursing one's parents.[23] I'm simply underscoring how strongly God expressed Himself in His Word regarding this—and, to repeat, this was not just a sin in His eyes for ancient Israel. It was a sin for the pagan nations too. *And if it was a sin for idol-worshipping Egyptians and Canaanites back then, you'd better believe it is a sin for God's holy and chosen people today.*[24]

So we see that God gave Israel certain laws to keep them separate from the nations—in particular, the food laws, since if you can't eat with other people, it's a lot harder to intermingle with them and share life together. But He gave them certain other laws because they applied to all people. If something was sinful for the nations of the world, it was certainly sinful for Israel, a nation that was divinely chosen to live at a particularly high level (often failing, of course, in the process).

The prohibition against homosexual practice, then, was given to Israel because homosexual practice was wrong for all people in all generations, meaning it is intrinsically sinful. Why? One main reason is that God designed men for women and women for men, and to join a man with a man or a woman with a woman is to sin in a fundamental way against His design and purpose. Is it any wonder, then, that as gay activism rises in the society, it brings about so many other radical changes with it, including the redefining of marriage, the undoing of gender, the reeducation of children, and more?[25] And is it any wonder that a reading of the Scriptures that affirms homosexual practice leads to many other abusive readings of the sacred text? (See chapters 7 and 9 for more on this.)

TO'EVAH MEANS "ABHORRENT," NOT SIMPLY "TABOO"

What is commonly overlooked in "gay Christian" treatments of the word *to'evah* is that there is a verb *ta'av*, derived from the same Hebrew root and closely related in meaning, just as the words "drive" and "driver" or "rule" and "ruler" are closely related in meaning in English. What then does *ta'av* mean? Does it mean "to be ritually unclean"? Does it have anything to do with something being "taboo"? Not in the least. Rather, as expected, the verb means "to detest, abhor; to act abhorrently," and it is used twenty-two times in the Old Testament in verses like these (I have italicized the word where it occurs):

> You shall not *abhor* an Edomite, for he is your brother. You shall not *abhor* an Egyptian, because you were a sojourner in his land.
> —DEUTERONOMY 23:7

> All my intimate friends *abhor* me, and those whom I loved have turned against me.
> —JOB 19:19

> They *abhor* me; they keep aloof from me; they do not hesitate to spit at the sight of me.
> —JOB 30:10

> You destroy those who speak lies; the LORD *abhors* the blood-thirsty and deceitful man.
> —PSALM 5:6

> The fool says in his heart, "There is no God." They are corrupt, *they do abominable deeds*, there is none who does good.
> —PSALM 14:1

I hate and *abhor* falsehood, but I love your law.

—PSALM 119:163

Hear this, you heads of the house of Jacob and rulers of the house of Israel, who *detest* justice and make crooked all that is straight.

—MICAH 3:9

What makes this usage all the more interesting is that many Semitic scholars believe that the noun *to'evah* came first and the verb developed out of the noun, just as the noun "paint" came first, and from that noun, the verb "to paint" is derived. So, the verb *ta'av*, "to detest, abhor; to act abhorrently," comes from the noun *to'evah*, "something detestable; abhorrent," giving further support to the fact that *to'evah* does not mean something ritually unclean but rather something abhorrent.

And that's *why* it could be used to describe something ritually unclean or taboo, because in certain cultures and among certain peoples, something considered taboo or ritually unclean *is* abhorrent to them, like pork for a religious Jew or a Muslim. (For a good example of this, see Genesis 46:34, which states that "all shepherds are *detestable* to the Egyptians" [NIV].) But that does not change the meaning of *to'evah*, as if the word itself only meant "something ritually unclean or taboo." That would be like saying, "Well, I was reading in a dieting book that it is detestable to be obese, so I now understand that the word *detestable* refers to being overweight, so when I read in the Bible that homosexual practice is 'detestable,' it must mean that gay men are overweight." Do you see how convoluted such "logic" is?

Let's focus in, then, on the usage of the noun *to'evah* in the Old Testament. According to the authoritative Koehler-Baumgartner *Hebrew and Aramaic Lexicon of the Old Testament*, in Leviticus 18 the phrase "the abhorrent customs" (חֻקּוֹת הַתּוֹעֵבֹת) refers to "the abhorrent customs of the Canaanites (Lv 18:30), by which is meant in particular *sexual perversity*."[26] That certainly speaks of moral violations and not just ritual taboos.

In Deuteronomy 12:31 *to'evah* refers to child sacrifice; in Deuteronomy 7:26 to idolatry; and in Deuteronomy 25:15–16 to dishonest weights and measures. So, just in these three verses, we see serious moral infractions, from the idolatrous practice of child sacrifice to worshipping foreign gods in general to unethical business practices. They all fit under the category of *to'evah*, something abhorrent, detestable (and note in Deuteronomy 25:16

that anyone who is guilty of unethical business practices is *to'evah*, someone abhorrent, detestable).

In Ezekiel 16:50 the prophet declares that the people living in Sodom committed *to'evah*, which either refers back to the previous words in verses 49–50 ("This was the guilt of your sister Sodom: she and her daughters had pride, excess of food, and prosperous ease, but did not aid the poor and needy. They were haughty and did an abomination before me."), in which case *to'evah* refers clearly to these ethical violations. Or else *to'evah* is referring to the wanton homosexual promiscuity reflected in Genesis 19, when the men of the town tried to gang rape the two men who were visiting Lot,[27] in which case the prophet describes this as the final outrage, the straw that broke the camel's back, the culmination of Sodom's sins. Thereby he describes widespread homosexual practice as something abhorrent and detestable, because of which God says, "So I removed them, when I saw it" (Ezek. 16:50).[28] Either way, this does not bode well for the "gay Christian" attempt to downplay the meaning of *to'evah*.

And note carefully Proverbs 6:16–19: "There are six things the LORD hates, seven that are detestable [*to'evah*] to him: haughty eyes, a lying tongue, hands that shed innocent blood, a heart that devises wicked schemes, feet that are quick to rush into evil, a false witness who pours out lies and a man who stirs up dissension among brothers" (NIV).

These sins hardly fall in the category of ritual taboos; instead, they speak of moral, ethical, and spiritual violations of the highest order, things that are intrinsically sinful, things that the Lord "hates"—and they are grouped under the heading of *to'evah*.

So much for the argument that *to'evah* only (or even primarily) refers to things that are not intrinsically sinful but rather are forbidden because of cultural or ritual taboos.

THE LEVITICUS PROHIBITION IS NOT LIMITED TO IDOLATRY

The prohibition against homosexual practice in Leviticus 18 and 20 is not limited to homosexual rites performed in the context of idolatry. It was this issue, namely, the connection between forbidden homosexual acts and idol worship, that Justin Lee got all wrong when he selectively quoted Professor Robert Gagnon, stating, "On Leviticus, Gagnon writes: 'I do not doubt that the circles out of which Leviticus 18:22 was produced had in view homosexual cult prostitution, at least partly. Homosexual cult prostitution appears to have been the primary form in which homosexual intercourse was practiced in Israel.'"[29] Lee then stated, "So scholars on both sides of the argument agreed that this probably had something to do with cult prostitution. That made sense to me."[30]

Yet, in fact, as Gagnon pointed out, prior to the lines that Lee quoted, he had written:

> Few today give this argument [i.e., that the Levitical prohibitions of man-male intercourse were prohibiting only cultic or idolatrous forms of male homosexual practice] much credence and for good reason. The repetition of the prohibition against homosexual intercourse in 20:13 does not follow immediately upon the references to child sacrifice in 20:2–5, but rather is sandwiched in between prohibitions of adultery and incest (20:10–12) and prohibitions of incest and bestiality (20:14–16). The link with child sacrifice in Lev 18:21 probably involves nothing more than threats to the sanctity of the Israelite family.[31]

Gagnon also noted that immediately after the lines that Lee cited, he had written:

> However, male cult prostitution was not the only context in which homosexual intercourse manifested itself in the ancient Near East generally. It was merely the most acceptable context for homosexual intercourse to be practiced in Mesopotamia, certainly for those who played the role of the receptive partner. In our own cultural context we think that the banning of male cult prostitution does not take into account consensual, non-cultic, loving homosexual relationships. In the cultural context of the ancient Near East the reasoning has to be reversed: to ban homosexual cult prostitutes was to ban all homosexual intercourse. In any case, the authors of Lev 18:22 could have formulated the law more precisely by making specific reference to the qedeshim [= 'the consecrated ones,' an ironic reference to these cult figures] (as in Deut 23:17-18), if it had been their intent to limit the law's application. That they did not do so suggests that they had a broader application in mind. Moreover, the

> *Levitical rejection of same-sex intercourse depends on Canaanite prac-*
> *tices for its validity about as much as the rejection of incest, adultery,*
> *and bestiality.*[32]

Gagnon also notes that, "Elsewhere in the book I make clear that *in the history of the interpretation of these Levitical prohibitions they are never construed as indicting only homosexual acts in the context of cult prostitution.*"[33]

You can see, then, how wrongly Professor Gagnon's work has been represented online, and it is unfortunate that some have used his book in this selective and misleading way, and for those who know better—presumably the person who first cited him in this way—it is downright dishonest.

Gagnon, then, is making a number of important points:

1. The reason prohibitions against adultery and homosexuality sandwich the prohibition against child sacrifice is because all three of these grievous violations are "threats to the sanctity of the Israelite family."

2. It is obvious that homosexual practice is not specifically linked with idolatrous practices since the prohibition against homosexual practice in Leviticus 20:13 is sandwiched between commandments against adultery and incest.

3. Since God told Israel that they must not follow the ways of the pagan nations, then listed the various sexual sins of these nations, you can no more say that homosexual practice was only wrong because the Canaanites did it than you can say that adultery or incest was wrong because the Canaanites did it.

This all becomes crystal clear as we look carefully at the relevant texts, where we see that the prohibition against sacrificing children to Molech in Leviticus 18:21 is followed by the prohibition against male-male sex in verse 22, then the prohibition against bestiality in verse 23. And so, if you want to argue that homosexual acts were only forbidden in conjunction with idolatry, you'll have to make the same case for bestiality. Anyone care to make that argument? In the same way, since the prohibition against adultery occurs in Leviticus 18:20, one verse before the prohibition against idolatrous child sacrifice in verse 21, someone could argue that adultery is only forbidden in conjunction with idolatry. Who would want to make that argument? And, to repeat Professor Gagnon's argument, what do we make of the fact that the prohibition against homosexual acts in Leviticus 20:13 is surrounded by various prohibitions against incest and adultery, with no connection to idol worship at all?

All this means that homosexual practice was *not* considered sinful because it was found in the context of pagan idolatry (or, put another way, it was *not* considered sinful only if it occurred in conjunction with idol worship). Rather, the opposite is true: according to the Old Testament, because idol-worshipping pagans were so degraded in their sexual practices, they even included homosexual acts in their temple rituals.

Sad to say, Pastor R. D. Weekly came to the totally wrong, opposite conclusion, writing with reference to Leviticus 18:22 and 20:13:

> The context of these verses clearly links the sexual behavior to the idolatry of Egypt and Canaan. Because of the connection with idolatry, the acts themselves should not be considered inherently sinful, just as planting mixed seed in the same field, working animals of two kinds, eating pork or shellfish, or wearing mixed fabrics are not inherently sinful.... Furthermore, even if these verses *were* a condemnation of all same-sex sexual activity—which they were **not**—they do not apply to Christians.[34]

If this was baseball, Pastor Weekly would have struck out in just this one paragraph since: First, the prohibition against same-sex sexual activity was not only in the context of idolatry, as seen in Leviticus 20:13. Second, the prohibition against same-sex sexual activity was not one of the particular laws meant to keep Israel separated from the nations, since it was given as a universal moral prohibition, as we noted with reference to Leviticus 18. And third, because it was deemed by God to be sinful behavior for both Israel and the neighboring pagan nations, it is absolutely forbidden for Christians today. From my heart I urge Pastor Weekly to go back to God and His Word on these life-critical issues, especially since he functions as a clergyman and believes he is called to give leadership and guidance to others.

Focusing in on the book of Leviticus, Semitic scholar Richard S. Hess writes:

> This concern, as well as the unique designation of homosexuality as "detestable" among all the laws in Leviticus, and the association of this verse with v. 21 and the clear association there with the worship of other deities, suggest that the practice of homosexuality was part of the worship of foreign deities and capitulation to the forbidden and defiling customs of other peoples.
>
> For the Christian, the unique portrayal of this practice with the strongest possible condemnation in Leviticus and its association with groups rejected by God and driven from the land provides a background for Paul to select it as one example of the moral degeneration brought about among those who turn away from the true worship of God (Rom 1:26-28).[35]

And so, to repeat, in a list of "detestable" acts (*to'evot*), only homosexual practice is singled out as "detestable" among them—making it especially heinous—and it is the only sinful act so designated that also carries the death penalty in Leviticus. (See Leviticus 20:13.) So, while we are absolutely *not* calling for the death penalty for homosexual practice (or adultery or witchcraft)—God forbid!—we must recognize how "detestable" these actions were (and are) in God's sight.

What about Leviticus 18:19 and 20:18, which speak against a man having sex with his wife during her monthly period? Well, this act was not considered worthy of the death penalty, so it is viewed with less severity than homosexual acts, and it is not mentioned in any list of sins in the New Testament. Still, the Old Testament is clear that God is not pleased with this because of the sacredness of the blood. (See also Ezekiel 18:6.) Many Christians have come to this same conclusion even without the witness of Scripture. So, yes, I believe it is wrong for a married couple to have sexual intercourse during the wife's menstrual period, but it is clearly not to be regarded as being as fundamentally wrong and offensive in God's eyes as homosexual practice.[36]

The bottom line is this: (1) The Torah puts homosexual acts in the same class as adultery, incest, bestiality, idolatry, and sacrificing children to idols, censoring them in the strongest possible terms. (2) According to Leviticus

18:24–30 God judged pagan nations for these sins. (3) According to Leviticus 20:13 God abhorred the pagan nations for committing these sexual acts. (4) The New Testament, as we will see, reinforces the seriousness of these acts, and so, for those who take the Scriptures seriously, these are weighty issues to consider.

Even Mel White's organization, Soulforce, recognized the principle of universal moral laws, stating, "Over the centuries the Holy Spirit has taught us that certain Bible verses should not be understood as God's law for all time periods. Some verses are specific to the culture and time they were written, and are no longer viewed as appropriate, wise, or just."[37] A right reading of the relevant Torah verses, however, indicates clearly that the prohibition of homosexual practice is an example of "God's law for all time periods," as reinforced clearly by the New Testament witness.

REFLECTIONS FROM GAY THEOLOGIANS

Writing in the *Queer Bible Commentary*, ancient Near Eastern scholar David Tabb Stewart noted that the word to'evah, "abomination," "is used 144 times in the Hebrew Bible and covers a number of crimes including unjust weights and measures. A fair reading of Leviticus must acknowledge that, *even if Leviticus 18.22 and 20.13 contained a general condemnation of male homosexuality, this is not the focus of chapters 18 and 20.*"[38]

But that, of course, demonstrates nothing, since bestiality was not the focus of these chapters either, although it was soundly condemned in both, along with homosexual practice. What then does this prove? Simply that these sexual sins were serious enough to be listed among the detestable acts that caused God to judge the surrounding nations—and for which He would all the more certainly judge Israel.

Writing in the Jewish-authored *Torah Queeries* volume, Rabbi Elliot N. Dorff, who helped champion Conservative Judaism's acceptance of homosexuality, acknowledged that whatever Leviticus 18:22 originally meant is "legally irrelevant because the Jewish tradition is based on the way that the classical Rabbis of the Mishnah and the Talmud [first through sixth centuries, AD] and then rabbis through the ages to our own time have interpreted the Torah (in contrast to how other Jews, Christians, Muslims, and modern biblical scholars do)."[39] And the prohibition of homosexual practice in Jewish law has been clear and consistent for millennia.

This presented a problem for Rabbi Dorff and his colleagues, since, "As rabbis committed to uphold and foster Jewish law and tradition...[we] certainly did not approach the prospect of overturning two thousand years of rabbinic precedent lightly."[40] On what basis, then, did they conclude that they could, in fact, overturn what Scripture and tradition clearly taught? "First, scientifically we now know about sexual orientation...science also has demonstrated that discrimination against gays and lesbians in our society has produced much higher rates of suicide, smoking, and depression, together with many other threats to the physical and psychological well-being of gays and lesbians."[41] (Note that Rabbi Dorff specializes in medical ethics.)

Finally, he explains that "Jewish values motivated us. Specifically, the Talmud declares that honor of our fellow human beings is so great a value for us Jews that it may supersede rabbinic legislation that undermines that honor." And so, because it is "clearly a dishonor to gay and lesbians to maintain their sexual acts are an 'abomination'...it is also both cruel and demeaning to rule that they may never engage in any sexual expression."[42]

How enlightening! First, this rabbi, who clearly cares for LGBT-identified Jews, recognizes that Jewish scholarship has consistently interpreted Leviticus 18:22 to prohibit male-male anal sex and, by rabbinic extension, "all other forms of homosexual acts."[43] This, he realizes, cannot be disputed, otherwise he would have been on the front lines of that dispute.[44]

Second, he appeals to our current understanding of "sexual orientation," which is a very recent and ambiguous concept, as if this discovery would undercut the biblical and rabbinic prohibitions—in other words, as if the ancient rabbis would have said, "Oh, now that we understand you were born this way and this is the real you, the true core of who you are, we have no problem with male-male anal sex!"—and as if the rabbis through the centuries were never confronted with Jewish (or Gentile) men who claimed to be exclusively attracted to the same sex. It is also highly questionable that fixed categories of "sexual orientation" are entirely accurate, since there are countless examples of men and women discovering their homosexuality later in life, outgrowing it, or switching back and forth between heterosexual and homosexual "orientations."[45] And is it even right to base one's entire identity on one's sexual and romantic proclivities? Does it really define who we are?

More importantly, some scientists now speak of a pedophile orientation, while others speak of GSA (genetic sexual attraction, meaning genetic attraction between siblings) as a sexual orientation. Surely Rabbi Dorff would not argue that laws concerning incest or "consensual" man-child relationships should be changed based on this.[46]

And what of the idea of divine inspiration? Did God not superintendent His Word (and, from a traditional Jewish viewpoint, the Jewish traditions) so as not to inflict so much pain and suffering on gay men through the centuries by such poorly written laws? And while it is easily demonstrated that only a misuse of Scripture allowed things like the slave trade industry, the only fair conclusion that a Jewish or Christian reader of the Bible could have come to through the centuries is that homosexual practice of any kind was forbidden. And that's why the pro-homosex reading of the Bible is something virtually unprecedented until after the sexual revolution of the 1960s.[47]

Third, Rabbi Dorff's appeal to homophobia as the cause of many health problems among homosexuals is misguided as well, since you could just as well point to the higher rates of sexually transmitted diseases among gay and bisexual males (and, according to some studies, lesbians as well),[48] not to mention some other negative health consequences for LGBT people.[49] There is also no clear evidence that lack of "homophobia" ultimately reduces rates of smoking, drinking, depression, and suicide among gays and lesbians.[50] And even if this *could* be demonstrated, wouldn't this hold true equally for other forbidden behaviors? In other words, if other sexual practices or relationships that are currently forbidden by law or frowned upon by the masses were now sanctioned by society, wouldn't that theoretically reduce suicide, depression, and drug use in those groups too? Again, what would that prove in terms of the morality of the acts or relationships involved?

Fourth, honor of fellow human beings is surely a value that all religions would affirm, but does "honor" require sanction? Doesn't it sometimes require rebuke and correction? And doesn't true love tell the truth, even when it's costly? In fact, the verse immediately before Leviticus 19:18, which famously ends with "love your neighbor as yourself," states this: "Do not hate your brother in your heart. Rebuke your neighbor frankly so you will not share in his guilt" (Lev. 19:17, NIV). That's why Proverbs 28:23 says, "The one who reproves another will in the end find more favor than the one who flatters with the tongue" (NET).

So, if I really honor someone, then with love, compassion, and humility I will tell that person the truth. In the case of homosexuality, it means telling my "neighbor," whom I am to love as myself, that God did not intend him (or her) to have sexual and romantic relationships with the same sex, and that He surely has a better way for each of them, be it fulfilled celibacy or transformation into heterosexuality.

Either way, it turns out that Leviticus 18:22 means exactly what it says, and it applies to all peoples for all times. Will we accept the words of our God?

Chapter 6

WHAT DID JESUS SAY ABOUT HOMOSEXUALITY?

The "gay Christian" argument: While Jesus spoke against divorce and adultery, He never said a word about homosexual practice, although in His teaching about eunuchs He indicated that some people are born gay and should be fully accepted by the church without being expected to change.

The biblical response: It's dangerous to use an argument from silence, but in reality, Jesus reaffirmed and deepened the sexual morals of the Law. He stated that all sexual acts outside of marriage defile us, and He stated emphatically that marriage as God intended referred to the lifelong union of one man and one woman. As for eunuchs by birth or choice or by the actions of others He was referring to those who refrained from sexual activity and marriage (or who were unable to engage in sexual activity).

C AN I ASK you an honest question? If you hold to the viewpoint stated here at the beginning of this chapter, are you willing to change your views if I can demonstrate that your position about Jesus is wrong and that He did, in fact, categorically reject homosexual practice? More importantly, are you willing to *submit* to what Jesus taught?

The reason I ask this question is because people will often argue with me about what Jesus or Paul said, or, more broadly, they'll challenge my understanding of Scripture. And when I ask them, "If I can give you a clear answer from the Word, will you accept it?", they reply, "No. I don't even believe in God."

If that's you, then there are deeper issues to discuss and other books that would be more helpful to you.[1] If, on the other hand, you accept the Scriptures as God's Word and what Jesus says really matters to you, then you're reading the right book. I simply encourage you to pray for the courage to follow God's truth wherever it leads, regardless of cost or consequence.

What, then, of the argument that Jesus never addressed homosexual practice and, if it had been so important, He would have addressed it clearly? Well, we've already seen that the reason the Bible doesn't speak a lot about homosexuality is because the Bible is a heterosexual book from beginning to end, and only heterosexual relationships are sanctioned by God and only heterosexual marriage is ordained by God.

It's the same with the teaching of Jesus. He was a first-century Jewish rabbi teaching His fellow Jews,[2] and in first-century Jewish culture homosexual practice was explicitly prohibited and forbidden. In fact, ancient Jewish texts from the last centuries BC and the first centuries have some *very negative* things to say about homosexual practice and *not one single positive* thing to say.[3] So, the fact that Jesus didn't spend a lot of time teaching against homosexual practice shouldn't surprise us at all, nor does it prove anything.

It would be like arguing, "It's clear that President Reagan thought Martians were not a real threat to America, since he never mentioned Martians once, but he did talk a whole lot about the Soviet Union." That's true in part, but the reason Reagan never spoke about Martians was because he didn't believe in Martians and so invasion from Mars was not a threat. The real threat was coming from the Soviet Union, and that's where he put his emphasis. So, it would be ludicrous to say, "Ronald Reagan thought Martians were friendly."

It is the same with Jesus and homosexual practice. He didn't have to condemn it any more than He had to condemn sins like bestiality, since every God-fearing Jew in the nation knew these things were wrong according to God's holy Torah (teaching/law). In contrast, the issue of divorce—specifically, the question of what constituted valid grounds for divorce—was a hot issue among Yeshua's Jewish contemporaries, which is one reason He addressed it on several occasions.

And that's why it's dangerous to argue from silence. Jesus didn't say a word about bestiality. Does that mean it's OK? He didn't say anything specific about rape or incest or many other sins. Does that mean all of them are OK? God forbid!

So the argument that Jesus never said anything specific about homosexuality while addressing other issues such as divorce proves nothing, unless you want to agree with Professor William Countryman, who wrote that "the gospel allows no rule against the following, in and of themselves:...bestiality, polygamy, homosexual acts...or pornography," or (apparently) adult incestuous unions, based on which Countryman claimed that we are not free to "impose our codes on others."[4] Is that where you want to go?

Does this mean, then, that I'm agreeing that Jesus had nothing to say about homosexual practice? Absolutely not. In fact, He addresses the issue at least three different ways. I'm simply explaining why He didn't make it a major focus of His teaching: it's because it was not a major issue in His day.

Remember, not only was homosexual practice completely condemned in the ancient Jewish world and clearly prohibited by the Torah and Jewish law, but also there was no such thing as gay activism in Jesus's day—no gay pride parades, no openly gay role models for the Jewish youth, no aggressive campaign for same-sex "marriage," and the like—meaning, all the more, that it was not an issue of concern in His day. You might as well suggest that Jesus was debating with the Pharisees as to whether Android smartphones were better than the Apple iPhone as suggest that homosexual issues were of major concern to Jesus and His disciples.[5]

How then did Jesus address the issue of homosexual practice? First, in Matthew 5:17–20, part of the Sermon on the Mount, He makes clear that He did not come to "abolish the Law or the Prophets...but to fulfill them," and as we read the rest of Jesus's teachings here, we see that He takes the sexual morals of the Torah (the Law) to a deeper level. For example:

> You have heard that it was said, "You shall not commit adultery."
> But I say to you that everyone who looks at a woman with lustful
> intent has already committed adultery with her in his heart. If
> your right eye causes you to sin, tear it out and throw it away. For
> it is better that you lose one of your members than that your whole
> body be thrown into hell. And if your right hand causes you to sin,
> cut it off and throw it away. For it is better that you lose one of
> your members than that your whole body go into hell.
> —MATTHEW 5:27–30

He does the same thing with divorce laws, among others, stating, "It was also said, 'Whoever divorces his wife, let him give her a certificate of divorce.' But I say to you that everyone who divorces his wife, except on the ground of sexual immorality, makes her commit adultery, and whoever marries a divorced woman commits adultery" (Matt. 5:31–32; we'll return to the issue of divorce at the end of this chapter).

This is the pattern that emerges as we continue to study the words of the Lord preserved in the Gospels, along with studying the meaning of His life, death, and resurrection. We see that He *fulfilled* the laws of sacrifices, priesthood, and the temple by offering up Himself as our perfect atonement, also becoming our great High Priest and making us into a spiritual temple.[6] So, He took these important spiritual concepts to a deeper level— *filling them to the full*—rather than doing away with them.

In the same way He took the moral laws of the Torah, which included statutes concerning marriage and sexual immorality, and took them to a deeper level—adultery included lust in the heart; murder included hatred in the heart—rather than doing away with them. And since homosexual practice was strictly prohibited in the Torah, not just for the people of Israel but for all nations (see chapter 5), when Jesus said He was *not* abolishing the Law or the Prophets but rather fulfilling them, He clearly intended that this prohibition would continue to stand as well. In fact, we could even argue that the prohibition is deepened, just as the prohibitions against adultery and murder were deepened.[7]

Second, in Matthew 15 and Mark 7 there is a discussion between Jesus and some of the other Jewish teachers about the practice of eating food with unwashed hands. The Lord's disciples did not perform the ritual hand-washings before they ate, but these zealous Jewish leaders taught that to eat food without first ritually washing the hands (presumably reciting certain prayers as well) made the food unclean. Jesus debunked this whole idea, explaining that what we eat doesn't go into our hearts but into our stomachs and from there passes out of our system. So, He explained, "to eat with unwashed hands does not defile anyone" (Matt. 15:20).

What then defiles us and makes us unclean? According to Jesus, it's not what goes into our mouths that defiles us but rather "what comes out of the mouth," since it "proceeds from the heart, and this defiles a person. For out of the heart come evil thoughts, murder, adultery, sexual immorality, theft, false witness, slander. These are what defile a person" (vv. 18–20). And note this carefully: in both Matthew 15:19 and Mark 7:21 the Greek word for "sexual immorality," *porneia*, occurs in the plural—it is literally "sexual immoralities," found in this plural form only in these two verses in the entire New Testament. This refers comprehensively to all sexual acts outside of marriage, which, as we know, consisted only of the union of a man and a woman in Jewish biblical law in Jesus's day. In fact, as we're about to see, Jesus made the strongest statement of anyone in the Bible concerning heterosexual marriage.

What then can we learn from this teaching? Jesus the Messiah—the Lord of glory and the Son of God, the express image of the Father, the one who said, "If you've seen Me, you've seen the Father" (see John 14:9)— taught explicitly that all sexual acts outside of marriage made us unclean. Yes, heterosexual fornication, homosexual acts, bestiality, incestuous acts— all of these are included by Jesus under the category of "sexual immoralities," and all of them defile us and make us unclean. And notice the other sins He listed here: evil thoughts, murder, adultery (which refers to sexually immoral acts committed by a married person), theft, false witness, and slander. Would we dare justify any of these?

Jesus spoke very clearly, not only in reaffirming the standards of sexual morality taught in the Torah but also in stating decisively that all sexual acts outside of marriage are defiling and sinful, to be listed side by side with evil thoughts, murder, theft, false witness, and slander, among others. (Mark 7:21–22 lists "evil thoughts, sexual immorality [again, this is plural in the Greek], theft, murder, adultery, coveting, wickedness, deceit, sensuality, envy, slander, pride, foolishness.")

And for those who might think my argument is circular here (namely, Jesus taught that sexual immorality was wrong, Jews in His day believed that homosexual practice was immoral, therefore Jesus taught against homosexual practice), as I stated above, every single reference to homosexual practice in the ancient Jewish world is 100 percent negative—sometimes in the strongest of terms—and there is not a single positive reference to be found.[8] Homosexual acts were considered immoral, even detestable, and they were absolutely included in the category of "sexual immorality" spoken of by Jesus.

Third, Jesus made a definitive statement about God's intent in marriage when asked by the religious leaders about His views on divorce. Before explaining that God only gave the divorce laws to Israel because of the hardness of the people's hearts—in other words, divorce was never God's ideal—Jesus laid out the foundation for marriage in the Scriptures:

> Have you not read that he who created them from the beginning made them male and female, and said, "Therefore a man shall leave his father and his mother and hold fast to his wife, and the two shall become one flesh" [quoting Gen. 2:24]? So they are no longer two but one flesh. What therefore God has joined together, let not man separate.
>
> —MATTHEW 19:4–6

In the previous chapter we saw the importance of this same account in Genesis when God established marriage as the union of one man and one woman (notice Jesus doesn't speak here of two or three or more; rather, He speaks of *two*). Jesus reiterates that here, saying that this was God's intention "from the beginning," emphasizing the unique union that comes when a man and woman are joined together—they are now "one flesh" as only a married man and woman can be—and He states that in the marital union God Himself is joining the two together. That's why divorce was not part of His original design.

In light of this, it is unconscionable to imagine that Jesus would sanction male-male or female-female unions, since, among other things, they fundamentally violate God's design and intent "in the beginning."[9] Neither would Jesus agree with efforts devoted to "eradicating gender or multiplying it exponentially,"[10] nor would He sanction teaching concepts such as "genderqueer" to children.[11] And He would not agree that the "gender binary" (meaning either male or female) is constricting.[12] For Jesus, male-female distinctions expressed aspects of the image of God and were the foundation of God's order and the basis for marriage.

To sum up, then, included within Jesus's teaching were:

1. Confirmation of the universal, moral principles of the Torah, which included a strict prohibition against homosexual practice

2. The statement that all sexual unions outside of marriage were defiling, proceeding out of the uncleanness of the human heart

3. Explicit affirmation of the male-female, divinely established order of marriage

It looks like Jesus actually had some weighty things to say about homosexual practice!

WHAT WAS JESUS REALLY SAYING ABOUT EUNUCHS?

There is one more text, however, that gay theologians are now pointing to (aside from the bizarre misapplication of the account of Jesus healing the centurion's servant, which we'll address in the next chapter), and at first glance it seems to be the worst possible text for them to use to advance their argument. I'm speaking of Matthew 19:12, which continues the discussion Jesus had with His disciples after He taught about marriage and divorce.

When they heard how strict His views were concerning divorce, they said, "If such is the case of a man with his wife, it is better not to marry" (Matt. 19:10), to which Jesus replied:

> Not everyone can receive this saying, but only those to whom it is given. For there are eunuchs who have been so from birth, and there are eunuchs who have been made eunuchs by men, and there are eunuchs who have made themselves eunuchs for the sake of the kingdom of heaven. Let the one who is able to receive this receive it.
> —MATTHEW 19:11–12

Why do I say that this is the worst possible text for "gay Christians" to use in support of their viewpoint? First, it occurs in the immediate context of the marriage discussion, where, as we just saw, Jesus explicitly taught that God ordained marriage as the lifelong union of one man and one woman—from the beginning. Second, this teaching of Jesus has to do with people *not marrying or having sex*, yet gay theologians use it to affirm homosexuality.

How do they do this? They claim that Jesus is acknowledging that people are born gay—and if they are born that way, then it follows that Jesus is endorsing who they are and what they do. I know this sounds absolutely bizarre, but it is believed so strongly that Rick Brentlinger stated emphatically in his book *Gay Christian 101* that "Jesus <u>Did</u> Address the Issue of Homosexuality,"[13] while Sandra Turnbull makes reference to "eunuch(s)" *one hundred times* in her book *God's Gay Agenda!*[14]

With his typical passion M. W. Sphero issued a warning about those who teach that *eunuchs* here in Matthew 19 actually meant *eunuchs*: "Don't let them lie to you. Trust in what Christ has said, and leave those that are nothing more than religious bigots to squander in their own intentionally deceptive filth."[15] Yes, "Those who state this [namely, that castration or a birth defect prevented some people from getting married], while being aware of ancient Greek, are again telling a bold-faced untruth straight from unfounded assumptions to attempt to deceive many for their own homophobic agendas."[16]

According to Sphero (and many other "gay Christians"):

> The word "eunuch" referred not only to castrated people, but also to homosexuals, to where Christ included both in MATTHEW 19:12. Furthermore, it is a historical fact that what people commonly referred to as "eunuchs" in those times where [*sic*] whole-bodied individuals with absolutely no "parts" missing whatsoever. Christ's listeners had no doubt about what he was talking about, and understood by his comments that gay people are not meant to marry in the conventional sense of the word, but that they should be accepted for who they are—and should likewise accept their homosexuality as it having been given to them by God from birth—as in verse 11 of the same.[17]

Is there even the slightest bit of truth in these statements? Not a chance.

First, let me state things in simple and concise terms before backing up every word with detailed scholarship. The term *eunuch* initially referred to a man who had been castrated. That's what Jesus was describing when He spoke of eunuchs who were "made that way by men." When Jesus spoke about eunuchs who were "born that way," He was speaking about men who, similar to a man who had been castrated, were born without "sexual capacity."[18] When He spoke about people "who have made themselves eunuchs for the sake of the kingdom of heaven," He was referring to those who renounced marriage (and therefore sex as well) for the sake of the gospel. In short, Jesus was referring to men who were sexually impotent (by birth), castrated (by actions of others), or celibate (by choice).

Is it true that the term *eunuch* in Hebrew (*sarîs*) and Greek (*eunuchos*) could also refer to a royal court official who was not castrated? Absolutely, since at first castrated men fulfilled certain roles in the king's court, and then, over time, the people who fulfilled those roles were simply called *sarîs* or *eunuchos*, even if they were not castrated males.[19] But that is *not* what Jesus is referring to here, since He speaks of men who were "eunuchs from birth" (speaking, again, of the lack of sexual capacity, not of being a court official!), along with those "who have been made eunuchs by men" (speaking, obviously, of men who were castrated).

Let's also remember that the whole reason this topic came up was because Jesus was talking to His disciples about never marrying—and therefore not having sex for life—and He was saying that not everyone can handle this. Some who are born without sexual capacity have no trouble with this; others, who have been castrated, have no trouble with this; still others, with God's gift of celibacy, can renounce marriage (and sex) for life by choice.

To read anything into this teaching that somehow affirms homosexual practice or to argue that "Christ's listeners had no doubt about what he was talking about, and understood by his comments that gay people are not meant to marry in the conventional sense of the word, but that they should be accepted for who they are" is to be guilty of the most gratuitous form of eisegesis imaginable. (*Eisegesis* refers to reading into the text what you want it to say; *exegesis* refers to reading out of the text what the author intended to say. Again, Sphero's explanation is a painfully obvious example of reading into the biblical text what he wants it to say.)

What about the argument that, because a Jewish man who was same-sex attracted might choose to remain celibate rather than marry, he might be included in the category of "eunuch from birth"? It is *possible* that some celibate, same-sex attracted people were included in this category—not *probable*, as gay activists often argue[20]—but again, it was only because such people did not marry and were not sexually active (since the only sexual acts sanctioned by the Torah were those of a married man and woman). So then, at the very most, it is *possible* that Jesus was including homosexual men in His teaching, but even *if* He was, He was putting them in the category of those who were sexually inactive. That's what characterized them as "eunuchs from birth," meaning, lacking the capacity to have sexual relations with women. Period.

But doesn't that mean that Jesus was still saying that some people were born gay, as many gay theologians claim?[21] Hardly. First, there was not a "homosexual" category in the ancient world—let alone a "gay" category—so Jesus could not have been saying, "Hey, I'm giving a secret shout out to all the homosexual men here! I want to acknowledge you were born that way." (To be clear, homosexual acts were known and recognized—and scorned—and there were prominent, same-sex attracted people in the ancient world; see chapter 8 for more on this. I'm simply saying that the category of "homosexual" didn't exist, and so no one thought of people being born "that way.")

Second, it is only because men with same-sex attractions *appeared* to have no sexual capacity (because they were not interested in women) that they might have been included in the category of "eunuchs" from birth. And so, *if* Jesus had included such men in this category, it would have been accidental—simply because of their behavior—and not intentional, and He would have intended nothing by it.

According to Jay Michaelson:

> It is striking that Jesus specifically recognizes, and does not judge, the presence of sexual/ gender diversity among people. Some people are eunuchs, of whatever type, and they are able to refrain from marriage. Others are not, and they are permitted to marry, though it is still better not to do so: "The one who can accept [celibacy] should accept it" (Matt. 19:12). As in the story of the Ethiopian eunuch in Acts 8:26–40, God's emissary does not withhold the gospel from the gender-variant person who desires to hear it.[22]

But, to repeat, if we apply Jesus's words to a homosexually oriented person, then He would have been saying to that person, "God has called you to refrain from marriage and sex, and you should receive that as a gift from My Father." This is the last thing on Michaelson's mind when he states that Jesus was addressing "gender-variant" people. And while it is very true that Jesus, true to form, reached out to those marginalized by society (for a precursor to this in the Old Testament, see Isaiah 56:3–4) and "did not withhold the gospel" from them, there is actually no biblical evidence at all that Jesus was including men who were same-sex attracted in His teaching about eunuchs since there is not a single verse in the Bible where a same-sex attracted person was identified as a eunuch. The argument, then, that, "In the Bible, the term eunuchs included gay men" is exaggerated out of all proportion by gay theologians.[23]

More importantly, the "born gay" argument is flatly contradicted by the context, which, to repeat, speaks of men who from birth had no sexual capacity—just as if they were castrated later in life—because of which they never married or had sexual relationships. What in the world does this have to do with gay men? Do they have no sexual capacity? Do they all agree that they cannot and should not marry?

In fact, even if someone could prove that Jesus was including gay men in His teaching—which, to repeat once more, is incredibly far-fetched— He was affirming (if not taking for granted) that all of them would practice lifelong celibacy, meaning, no marriage and no sex. Do "gay Christians" really want to quote Jesus to that effect? Do they want to argue that Jesus was saying, "Some of you are born gay, and so your lot in life is to remain celibate for life, never marrying and never having sex"? That is the only possible conclusion to draw from the claim that Jesus included homosexuals in the category of men who were born as eunuchs. To argue, as some gay theologians do, that this text supports gay marriage (!) is to be guilty of wholesale spiritual abuse—abuse of the Bible and abuse in particular of the words of Jesus.[24]

Even the statements in ancient rabbinic literature cited in some "gay Christian" books underscore the fact that all of the "eunuchs" referred to in this literature were either completely celibate (and sexless) or else married to women (but unable to perform sexually).[25] In other words, there is not a syllable in the vast corpus of rabbinic literature—so vast that it is described as the "sea of the Talmud"—that speaks of eunuchs as anything other than impotent heterosexuals.

THE EVIDENCE IS CLEAR

I'm aware, of course, that many readers don't have the ability to work through all the evidence in Hebrew and Greek and other ancient languages. And so, while the context is totally clear, as I've stated here repeatedly, I want to reinforce this by reference to the best linguistic and textual scholarship available.

The United Bible Society's handbook to Matthew, which is written to help translators convey the meaning of the Greek to people in different cultures, states this:

> Some have taken *made themselves eunuchs* to refer to self-mutilation, and others understand it to mean simply that these men renounced sexual activity. The latter is probably better, but a translation like [Barclay, "There are some who have voluntarily made marriage impossible for themselves for the sake of the Kingdom of Heaven"] does leave open both interpretations. "Have voluntarily treated their bodies as if they were unable to engage in sexual activity" is another possibility.[26]

The New Testament Greek lexicon compiled by Bauer, Arndt, Gingrich, and Danker, universally recognized as the number one New Testament Greek dictionary, states this under the entry for *eunuchos* (I have deleted some of the extensive citations from ancient literature that support their point, since for the average reader the abbreviations are meaningless, while the scholar probably has the lexicon near at hand):

> 1. **a castrated male person,** *eunuch.* **Mt 19:12b.** Eunuchs served, esp. in the orient, as keepers of a harem (Esth 2:14) and not infreq. rose to high positions in the state...

> 2. **a human male who, without a physical operation, is by nature incapable of begetting children,** *impotent male* (Wsd 3:14) εὐ. ἐκ κοιλίας μητρός **Mt 19:12a.**

> 3. **a human male who abstains fr. marriage, without being impotent,** *a celibate* **Mt 19:12c**...[27]

Again, there is no ambiguity here whatsoever in terms of the three meanings of *eunuch* in Matthew 19.

Another leading exegetical Greek dictionary has this to say about Matthew 19:12: "The text names three kinds of *eunuchs*: a) those mutilated naturally, b) those mutilated by human action, and c) those who have mutilated themselves for the sake of the kingdom of heaven. The understanding of the last of these is disputed," meaning that it could refer to self-castration (literally) or it could refer to metaphorical castration—no sex and no marriage—noting that, a "fig[urative] understanding of the text, even if it is essentially weakened, points in the same direction."[28] (In other words, whether the person physically castrated himself or simply renounced marriage and sex, the overall outcome would be the same. As for those born eunuchs, the dictionary explains it to mean "those mutilated naturally"—that is, at birth.)

According to New Testament scholar Donald Hagner in his Matthew commentary:

> Three groups of "eunuchs" (εὐνοῦχοι; the word occurs only here and in Acts 8 in the NT) are mentioned here, two literal and one metaphorical. Among literal eunuchs are those born thus (the impotent) and those made thus by others (those castrated for certain high positions in a royal court; cf. the Ethiopian eunuch of Acts 8:27). Such literal eunuchs were not allowed in the assembly of the people according to Deut 23:1 (cf. m Yebam. 8:4–6 and 6:6). A third group of "eunuchs" are those who figuratively are said to have "made themselves eunuchs" (εὐνούχισαν ἑαυτούς; the verb occurs only in this verse in the NT) "for the sake of the kingdom of heaven" (διὰ τὴν βασιλείαν τῶν οὐρανῶν; for this expression see *Comment* on 3:21). The latter phrase is to be understood in the sense of those who have renounced marriage (such as John the Baptist and Jesus himself) to give priority to the work of the kingdom (cf. 1 Cor 7:32–34)....The kingdom thus can take priority over the interpretation of Gen 1:28 as the obligation to marry and to have children. If Jesus, like John the Baptist and Paul (cf. 1 Cor 7:29, 31), expected the imminent end of the age, the idea of celibacy would take on a less objectionable aspect. ὁ δυνάμενος

χωρεῖν, "the one who is able to accept (it)," is the one to whom God grants (v. 11) the ability to accept non-marriage.[29]

Craig Blomberg, another top New Testament scholar, explains that "*Eunuchs* ('those who have renounced marriage') 'because of the kingdom of heaven' voluntarily accept a celibate life-style in order to be better able to devote their whole lives to God's work (cf. 1 Cor 7:25–38)."[30] And W. D. Davies and Dale C. Allison in their exhaustive commentary on Matthew note that:

> The verb εὐνουχίζω [*eunouxizō*] occurs twice in this verse, trans- lated the first time as "made eunuchs" and the second time as "became eunuchs." The term literally refers to castration. The second occurrence of the word in this verse is most likely figurative, though, referring to those who willingly maintain a life of celibacy for the furtherance of the kingdom.[31]

There is really no question at all about the meaning of Jesus's words, and without a doubt He is speaking in every case of those who have no sexual capacity or of those who renounce marriage and sex for the sake of kingdom of God.

According to the massive, multi-volume *Theological Dictionary of the New Testament*:

> Jesus transcends the rabbinic view by differentiating three groups of eunuchs (Mt. 19:12): those who are so from birth, those who are castrated, and those who emasculate themselves for the kingdom's sake. In the latter case the sense is obviously figurative; the refer- ence is to those who renounce sex in order to focus on the higher goal of the kingdom, as Jesus himself does. The gospel affirms the natural order but may require its denial for the sake of the new and higher order.[32]

Yes, Jesus speaks about those who "who renounce sex in order to focus on the higher goal of the kingdom," while those "who are so from birth" have no sexual capacity to renounce. They don't have it to start! Again, this is the opposite of the "gay Christian" use of this passage.

New Testament scholar Leon Morris explains what Jesus meant by eunuchs in his Matthew commentary:

> To belong to this group of people is not normally regarded as highly desirable (among the Jews eunuchs could not become priests, Lev. 21:20; they could not even enter the congregation, Deut. 23:1), but Jesus points out that there are some who *from their mother's womb* have been in this state; they have never had sexual capacity. This does not refer necessarily to literal eunuchs, men who have been physically castrated, but to those with a genetic defect. The second category does refer to castration. In the world of the first century quite a few men had been emasculated by people in high places. This might be done as a punishment, or to provide safe people to work in harems and the like. It was a fact of first-century life. Jesus goes on to point out that there are some *who made themselves eunuchs for the kingdom of heaven's sake.* Through the centuries there have always been some who have foregone the delights of marriage in order that they may discharge specific tasks for *the kingdom of heaven.* Jesus himself was not married, nor was John the Baptist. Not many have taken these words literally, as Origen did when he castrated himself. But through the centuries many have turned their backs on all that marriage means because only so could they pursue their particular vocation in the service of God. Jesus is not saying that this is a higher calling than others or that all his followers should seek to serve in this way; that would be a contradiction of his appeal to Genesis 1–2. He is simply saying that the claims of the kingdom override all other claims and that some are called to serve in the path of celibacy (just as others are called to serve in marriage). There is no one path of service, but whatever a person's calling is, grace will be given so that that calling may be fulfilled. And in this context it means that grace will be given to those called to serve God in the married state so that they will be able to fulfil their calling. He invites his hearers to *accept* the teaching as they have the ability (his word for *accept* is the same as that translated "have the capacity" in v. 11).[33]

Note again the explanation that "eunuchs from birth" would refer to those who "never had sexual capacity" because of a "genetic defect,"[34] which is decidedly *not* a description of someone with same-sex desires and attractions. What does apply, however, to "gay Christians" is the fact that, according to Jesus, "the claims of the kingdom override all other claims and…some are called to serve in the path of celibacy."

So, as hard as this word may seem, if you are a follower of Jesus who is same-sex attracted, you are called to put Him first and abstain from marriage and sexual activity unless you can find an opposite sex partner who will join you in marriage, even if your attractions don't change, or unless God changes your desires to heterosexual, which has happened for many.[35]

But here's the bottom line: it is no harder for a homosexually oriented person to follow Jesus than it is for a heterosexually oriented person to follow Him, since He requires everything from everyone who chooses to follow Him as Lord. He said repeatedly, "If anyone would come after me, let him deny himself and take up his cross daily and follow me" (Luke 9:23).

You might say, "That's easy for you to say since you're straight and have been married for almost forty years." True enough, but that doesn't change the fact that Jesus requires the same thing from all of us and, to repeat, He requires everything. As expressed by Sam Allberry, a British pastor who is still same-sex attracted but is living a celibate, holy life:

> I am to deny myself, take up my cross and follow him. Every Christian is called to costly sacrifice. Denying yourself does not mean tweaking your behaviour here and there. It is saying "No" to your deepest sense of who you are, for the sake of Christ. To take up a cross is to declare your life (as you have known it) forfeit. It is laying down your life for the very reason that your life, it turns out, is not yours at all. It belongs to Jesus. He made it. And through his death he has bought it.[36]

But isn't it harder for someone who is gay? Pastor Allberry writes:

> Ever since I have been open about my own experiences of homosexuality, a number of Christians have said something like this: "the gospel must be harder for you than it is for me", as though I have more to give up than they do. But [the] fact is that the gospel demands *everything* of *all of us*. If someone thinks the gospel has somehow slotted into their life quite easily, without causing any

Can You Be Gay and Christian?

major adjustments to their lifestyle or aspirations, it is likely that they have not really started following Jesus at all.

And just as the cost is the same for all of us, so too are the blessings.[37]

Jesus died for our entire being—spirit, soul, and body; past, present, and future—and now we live a new life in Him. And finding Him, regardless of our sexual orientation, we find all that we need, as multiplied hundreds of millions of believers can attest, from every background, lifestyle, and orientation.

What about the charge that many Christians have been guilty of hypocrisy, downplaying or ignoring the strong teachings of Jesus about divorce and remarriage and yet making a big deal about homosexuality? Those charges are true, and I have said the same thing many times myself. In fact, in many different contexts, including on national Christian TV and radio, and in meetings addressing the LGBT community, I have stated that *no-fault, heterosexual divorce in the church has done more to undermine and destroy marriage than all gay activists combined.* Please do quote me on that!

In my 1993 book *It's Time to Rock the Boat* I shared this story, as recounted by Jonathan Goforth, a missionary to China and Manchuria: "A man who had a wife and one son in We Ju [Korea] left them and became rich in another city. There he married another woman, and by her had two daughters. When his soul was revived he arranged for the support of this woman and her daughters, and went back to We Ju and was reconciled to his lawful wife."[38]

I continued:

> When Goforth shared this example in 1936 at a meeting in Ontario, Canada, he added a striking comment: *"If the Korean kind of revival ever reaches some Christian lands, where divorce prevails, there will be some startling social upheavals."* The mind reels at the thought of the social upheavals that would be produced by a real "Holy Ghost revival" in today's divorce-ridden America! And with a skyrocketing divorce rate in the Church, how can we lay claim to any kind of deep visitation of the Spirit in this hour?[39]

144

Many other Christian leaders I know share these same views, and my friend Eric Metaxas, a *New York Times* best-selling author, rightly refers to the "the scandal of evangelical silence on divorce."[40]

But once again this completely refutes the "gay Christian" argument, since our capitulation in the area of divorce and remarriage is not resolved by a further capitulation to gay activism. That would be like a heavy smoker saying to a severely overweight person, "Your gluttony and morbid obesity gives me the right to destroy my lungs with cigarettes!" Or, more to the point, it would be like the glutton saying, "Because I have been such a glutton, I might as well start smoking heavily too!" That is no different than a gay activist saying to evangelical Christians, "Because you have made such a mess of marriage through no-fault divorce, you should now completely redefine it to include same-sex couples."

Both are terribly wrong—with tragic consequences for the family and society as a whole—and both must be renounced. And with that, I turn the tables and say to my "gay Christian" friends, join me in upholding the standards of marriage by renouncing no-fault divorce, remarriage without biblical grounds, and all forms of homosexual practice.

Can we stand together on this? Can we stand with Jesus?

Chapter 7

THE HEALING of the CENTURION'S SERVANT

The "gay Christian" argument: When Jesus healed the servant of a Roman soldier, it is clear that He was affirming their homosexual relationship, since the Greek words used indicate clearly that the servant was the soldier's lover.

The biblical response: Nothing could be further from the truth. There is nothing in the Greek text that supports this, and it is contradicted by the clear testimony of the rest of the New Testament. What it reveals is how some "gay Christians" twist the meaning of the Bible to conform to their lifestyle and beliefs, creating a Jesus in their own image.

I T IS ONE thing to claim that the Bible does not prohibit homosexual practice. It is another thing to claim that Jesus sanctioned it or, more extreme still, actively encouraged it, or, worse yet, used His healing power to enable a man to continue engaging in same-sex activities with his young male slave.

As horrific as this notion is, it is now a commonplace in "gay Christian" literature and openly proclaimed on "gay Christian" billboards that announce that "Jesus affirmed a gay couple."[1]

If anything should stand as a warning sign to sincere LGBT people wanting to find affirmation for their sexuality in the Bible, it is this profane rewriting of the sacred Scriptures—really, this blasphemous re-creating of Jesus as the enabler of a master-slave same-sex relationship (possibly even a pederastic one). Where in the world did "gay Christians" get this idea?

Because this "gay Christian" misinterpretation of a biblical passage is so revealing, we'll devote this entire chapter to looking at the text in question, which appears to be quite straightforward. It is found in Matthew 8:5–13 (and Luke 7:1–10), where Jesus heals the paralyzed servant of a Roman soldier:

> When Jesus had entered Capernaum, a centurion came to him, asking for help. "Lord," he said, "my servant lies at home paralyzed and in terrible suffering." Jesus said to him, "I will go and heal him."
>
> The centurion replied, "Lord, I do not deserve to have you come under my roof. But just say the word, and my servant will be healed. For I myself am a man under authority, with soldiers under me. I tell this one, 'Go,' and he goes; and that one, 'Come,' and he comes. I say to my servant, 'Do this,' and he does it."
>
> When Jesus heard this, he was astonished and said to those following him, "I tell you the truth, I have not found anyone in Israel with such great faith. I say to you that many will come from the east and the west, and will take their places at the feast with Abraham, Isaac and Jacob in the kingdom of heaven. But the subjects of the kingdom will be thrown outside, into the darkness, where there will be weeping and gnashing of teeth."
>
> Then Jesus said to the centurion, "Go! It will be done just as you believed it would." And his servant was healed at that very hour.
>
> —Matthew 8:5–13, niv

There is nothing mysterious in this account, and any reference to sex in general, let alone to homosexual practice, is nowhere to be found. All the more, then, it is surprising to find this account used by gay authors. Even more surprising—or should we say shocking?—is that Jay Michaelson claims there is "an unmistakable same-sex subtext to this story."[2] Unmistakable?

Here's what gay partners Rev. Jeff Miner and John Tyler Connoley have to say about this account:

> Just another miracle story, right? Not on your life!
>
> In the original language, the importance of this story for gay, lesbian, and bisexual Christians is much clearer. The Greek word used in Matthew's account to refer to the servant of the centurion is *pais*. In the language of the time, *pais* had three possible meanings, depending upon the context in which it was used. It could

mean "son or boy"; it could mean "servant," or it could mean a particular type of servant—one who was "his master's male lover." Often these lovers were younger than their masters, even teenagers.

...In that culture, if you were a gay man who wanted a male "spouse," you achieved this, like your heterosexual counterparts, through a commercial transaction—purchasing someone to serve that purpose.[3]

The authors then proceed to "prove" that, in this context, the word *pais* must mean the centurion's purchased, young male lover, stating, "For objective observers, the conclusion is inescapable: In this story Jesus healed a man's male lover. When understood this way, the story takes on a whole new dimension."[4]

Really? This is the "inescapable" conclusion for "objective observers"? Or, to quote Michaelson again, the "same-sex subtext to this story" is "unmistakable"? Miner and Connoley answer with a resounding yes, claiming that "all the textual and circumstantial evidence in the Gospels points in one direction."[5] Seriously?

Then why didn't one single commentator or interpreter of the Gospels from the first century until the twentieth century—among whom there have been multiplied thousands—dream up such an outlandish interpretation before the birth of the gay liberation movement? Gay scholars such as John Boswell have argued that through much of church history, some same-sex relationships were approved, a theory that has been thoroughly refuted by historians.[6] Further refutation can be found by reviewing the interpretation of Matthew and Luke over the centuries. Boswell claimed that there was often a positive attitude to "sanctified" same-sex relationships, yet not one single interpreter recognized the alleged same-sex dimensions of this Gospel account. It's because those dimensions are simply not there!

And that is why, in all the massive lexicographical research that has been devoted to every word of the New Testament, with brilliant scholars of different faith (and non-faith) persuasions examining the Greek vocabulary in meticulous detail, not one single biblical dictionary or encyclopedia suggested the same-sex implications that are supposedly so obvious in this passage.[7] In light of that glaring absence, "gay Christian" leader Rick Brentlinger noted, "Oddly, one of the most important ancient meanings of *pais, beloved or same sex lover,* is not listed in many standard lexicons."[8] I wonder why!

Michaelson summed up the standard "gay Christian" interpretation of the passage with typical dogmatism:

> The servant for whom the centurion pleads is more than just an ordinary servant; one would not expect a Roman centurion to intercede—let alone "beg" *(parakaloon)*—on behalf of a mere cook or housekeeper. Rather, *as any contemporary reader would know* [my emphasis], the relationship between a centurion and his favored servant is assumed to be a romantic one. The centurion's servant is a *pais,* a boy companion, not a *doulos,* a mere slave. And it was common practice for Roman centurions to have younger male servants who acted as concubines as well.... In other words, Jesus is being asked to heal not just the centurion's servant, but also his lover.[9]

Yes, based on this perversion of the text, Jesus is being asked to enable a slave owner (possibly a pederast at that) to continue having sexual relationships with his young slave. And I repeat: this is a widely accepted interpretation in "gay Christian" circles.[10]

Those responsible for the billboard campaign mentioned at the beginning of this chapter stated that, "In this story, Jesus restores a gay relationship by a miracle of healing and then holds up a gay man as an example of faith for all to follow." And Jesus allegedly did this despite the fact that, "*To our modern minds, the idea of buying a teen lover seems repugnant.*"[11] Yet these "gay Christians" still feel compelled to offer this gratuitous rewriting of the biblical text.

Once more I say with genuine love and concern: this alone should demonstrate that "gay Christians" are reading (and even rewriting) the Bible through the lens of their sexuality rather than submitting their sexuality to the Word of God. Let every LGBT reader take heed.

Remarkably, Brentlinger comes to the opposite conclusion, stating, "Jesus did not rebuke the sexuality or the slavery implicit in this relationship. What we learn from this passage, beyond its lesson of faith, is that *our modern view of same sex relationships is informed more by twenty-first century culture than by the scriptures.*"[12] He has this completely upside down!

And Brentlinger is not alone. To many gay readers, the sexual meaning of the text is undeniably clear, as noted by Michaelson: "Now, the text does not record the nature of this relationship, so it is subject to interpretation. However, consider for a moment how *crystal clear* this relationship would have been to someone hearing the story in the first century, or witnessing it firsthand."[13]

Yes, it was so "crystal clear" that no one dreamed of such an interpretation of the text until after the rise of an out and proud "gay Christianity." How telling! Nonetheless, Brentlinger can claim, without any linguistic, textual, cultural, or contextual proof that, "*Every first century Greek reader of Matthew's Gospel* would have picked up on the *pais* reference which almost every twenty-first century English reader misses. *Pais* and *paidika* were used by writers in ancient times to refer to a lover in a homosexual relationship."[14]

An accurate statement would have been this: "In some ancient texts outside the Bible, *pais* and *paidika* were used to refer to a lover in a homosexual relationship. However, there's not a single instance of this in the entire Bible, where the word always means son, child, or servant, without any sexual implication of any kind. This would have been totally clear to any first-century reader of the Gospels." (For more on the biblical use of the word *pais*, keep reading.)

Yet there's more from Michaelson, once again summing up a well-known "gay Christian" reading of the text and demonstrating (unknowingly) how this very reading refutes itself:

> And consider, too, the radical act of healing the centurion's servant/lover: Jesus is extending his hand not only to the centurion but to his partner as well. In addition to Jesus's silence on homosexuality in general, it speaks volumes that he did not hesitate to heal a Roman's likely same-sex lover. Like his willingness to include former prostitutes in his close circle, Jesus's engagement with those whose conduct might offend sexual mores even today is a statement of radical inclusion, and of his priorities for the spiritual life.[15]

Yes, Jesus included "former prostitutes in his close circle," not practicing prostitutes. And after forgiving the woman caught in adultery, Jesus said to her, "Go and sin no more." (See John 8:1–11.)[16] But when it came to homosexual sex between a Roman soldier and his same-sex slave lover, not only did Jesus not rebuke them, but He also empowered them! This is really a blasphemous perversion of the nature of our Savior and Lord.

AN OUTRIGHT FABRICATION

All this, however, does not stop Miner and Connoley from offering an outright fabrication of the Gospel account:

> …the centurion approaches Jesus and bows before him. "Rabbi, my…," the word gets caught in his throat. This is it—the moment of truth. Either Jesus will turn away in disgust, or something wonderful will happen. So, the centurion clears his throat and speaks again, "Rabbi, my *pais*—yes my *pais* lies at home sick unto death." Then he pauses and waits for a second that must have seemed like an eternity. The crowd of good, God-fearing people surrounding Jesus became tense. This was a gay man asking a televangelist to heal his lover. What would Jesus do?
>
> Without hesitation, Jesus says, "Then I'll come and heal him."
>
> It's that simple! Jesus didn't say, "Are you kidding? I'm not going to heal your *pais* so you can go on living in sin!" Nor did he say, "Well, it shouldn't surprise you that your *pais* is sick; this is God's judgment on your relationship."
>
> Instead, Jesus' words are simple, clear, and liberating for all who have worried about what God thinks of gay relationships. "I will come and heal him."[17]

Talk about rewriting the Bible! Talk about reading one's own ideas into the text and about understanding the Bible based on homosexuality rather than understanding homosexuality based on the Bible. This is absolutely classic, and it is really very sad.

So then, from this simple account of healing, and based on an inexcusably gratuitous interpretation of the word *pais* (after all, in Matthew's Gospel Jesus is called the *pais* of God, His Father!), we now "know" that: (1) the Roman soldier was gay, (2) his servant functioned as his gay lover (more specifically, a purchased teen lover), (3) Jesus knew all this, and (4) rather than rebuking him or refusing to heal the man's slave-lover, He worked a miracle and made him whole.

Jesus, therefore, according to this "interpretation," set an example by accepting homosexuals without condemnation and by fully condoning homosexual practice. And, as just stated, it is striking that the same Jesus who forgave the woman caught in adultery but said to her, "Go and sin no more" (see John 8:11), said no such thing to the Roman soldier and his (bought and owned) boy sex toy. Instead, according to the gay version of the story, He basically said, "Be healed and keep up the (pederastic?) love-fest!" (Let's remember that Jesus never asks how old the servant is, so he could well have been a fairly young boy if his primary function was that of a concubine, as alleged by these gay interpreters.)

It would appear then that, according to gay biblical interpretation, Jesus disapproved of adultery but sanctioned the practice of purchasing a young slave for same-sex intercourse. Can moral evaluations like this be called anything less than queer—and in the most negative sense of the word?

Seeking to soften the force of this, Brentlinger claims that, "...*pais* in the context of Matthew 8 and Luke 7, does not indicate illicit love between an adult male and a child. No decent person would condone such behavior and neither Matthew nor Jesus condoned child abuse in these passages."[18] Instead, Matthew and Jesus allegedly empowered same-sex activity between a Roman soldier and his (probably) teenaged concubine slave. This too is nothing less than a perversion of the Bible and the Savior.[19] (And I ask again, since Jesus doesn't inquire as to the age of the *pais*, how did He know it was not "illicit love between an adult male and a child"?)

This whole interpretation is actually so baseless that it's not even mentioned in the *Study New Testament for Lesbians, Gays, Bi, and Transgender.*[20] And, to repeat, the Greek word *pais* is found in the Greek Scriptures (the Septuagint and the New Testament) approximately ninety times, and *never once* does it have any sexual overtones, in contrast with its usage in some nonbiblical contexts. In every single case it simply means "son" or "servant," and thus, not a single scholarly Greek lexicon recognizes a sexual meaning of *pais* in the Bible at all.

REREADING SCRIPTURE

Writing in the book *Religion Is a Queer Thing*, John McMahon cites a 1991 article written by a gay pastor, Rev. Dr. Robin H. Gorsline. In the article "Let Us Bless Our Angels: A Feminist-Gay-Male-Liberation View of Sodom," Gorsline stated:

> Gay liberation is deeply suspicious of attempts, however well intentioned, to address the issue of homosexuality in the Bible. The issue is not of homosexuality and whether the Bible sustains, condemns, or is neutral about it. Neither canonical testament [i.e., neither the Old Testament nor the New Testament] carries any authority for gay liberation on the subject of homosexuality. *Gay liberation interprets scripture, not the other way around.*[21]

Let every sincere "gay Christian" stop for a moment and reread this revealing comment: "Gay liberation interprets scripture, not the other way around." And that is exactly what has happened here in this biblical account.

What it means is this: if you embrace this new same-sex affirming "Jesus," one who might have even been empowering pederasty but who, at the very least, empowered the use of a slave as a same-sex concubine, you are rejecting the Jesus of the Bible. Put another way, you are rejecting the Lord. Still, for the sake of those readers who are genuinely confused about the passage, let's take a few more minutes and review the details of the account, which make totally clear that the master-slave, same-sex concubine interpretation is untenable.

Professor Robert Gagnon, the foremost academic authority on the Bible and homosexual practice, made some salient observations about the text. He noted first that, *"Sex with male slaves [was] not a universal phenomenon. Not every provincial or Roman officer was having sex with his slave so Jesus could hardly have assumed such behavior was going on. This is especially true in Luke's version where the centurion is portrayed as a paradigmatic 'God-fearer.'"*[22]

Exactly! It is utterly gratuitous to assume that this particular Roman soldier was engaging in sexual acts with his younger male servant and even more gratuitous to think that Jesus simply assumed the soldier and his servant were sexually involved. Why would He? And as we'll see shortly, there is nothing in the account to suggest any sexual activity was going on.

Think of a pastor coming to Jesus and saying, "Lord, my secretary is very sick and on the verge of death. She's very special to my ministry, having served our church for many years, and I'm begging You to come and heal her."

Should Jesus assume that because some pastors have had affairs with their secretaries that this particular pastor was having an affair with his secretary and that he was asking Jesus to heal her so they could go on living in adultery? It would be the same in the case we are reviewing, since there was no reason for Jesus to assume that there was sexual activity going on between the Roman soldier and his servant.

"But," some may protest, "it was far more common for Roman soldiers to be having sex with their younger male servants than it was for a pastor to be having sex with his secretary. Plus, in Luke's version of the story, the soldier said this servant was *entimos* to him, meaning especially valuable. They obviously had quite a relationship going on!"

Really? Is there no other reason that the centurion could be so concerned about his servant? Isn't that a very sex-obsessed way of thinking? Also, as observed by one of the top Lucan scholars in the world, the word *entimos* "here means 'honoured, respected' ([Luke] 14:8; Phil. 2:29), rather than 'precious, valuable' (1 Pet. 2:4, 5), and indicates why the centurion was so concerned over him; Luke's own concern for the inferior members of society is perhaps also reflected."[23] He was an excellent servant, highly respected by his master, rather than a hot sex toy.

More importantly, as Gagnon observed, "the centurion is portrayed as a paradigmatic 'God-fearer,'"[24] also known as a righteous Gentile. That's why he was able to send Jewish elders to Jesus to intercede on his behalf, since, in their own words, "This man deserves to have you do this, because he loves our nation and has built our synagogue" (Luke 7:4–5, NIV). He is an upright man, they were saying, a man who fears the God of Israel, and he "is worthy to have you do this for him." This does not sound like a man who was regularly violating his younger male slave!

In contrast, according to the gay rewriting of the text, the Jewish leaders beseech Jesus on the centurion's behalf, saying to him, "Please, this is a good man who actually built a synagogue for us, so please heal his sex-toy so he can continue to indulge himself." Can any objective reader take this seriously? As Gagnon notes:

> *The Jewish elders in Luke 7 could not have supported a homosexual relationship.* Luke adds the motif that Jewish elders interceded on the centurion's behalf (7:3–5). Should we argue that these Jewish elders had no problem with same-sex intercourse, when every piece of evidence that we have about Jewish views of same-sex intercourse in the Second Temple period and beyond is unremittingly hostile to such behavior (*The Bible and Homosexual Practice*, 159–83)?[25]

In addition, Gagnon writes:

> *Jesus would have had to have been endorsing rape in this case.* We know that the form which much master-slave homoeroticism took in the Greco-Roman world included not only coerced sexual activity but also forced feminization, up to and including castration. By the reasoning of those who put a pro-homosex spin on the story, we would have to conclude that Jesus had no problem with this particularly exploitative form of same-sex intercourse inasmuch as he did not explicitly tell the centurion to stop doing it.[26]

These arguments are really quite conclusive to all but those with a personal agenda driving their interpretation. "But what about that word *pais?*" some may ask. "Doesn't that prove that the relationship was sexual?"

Absolutely not. Outside of these accounts in Matthew and Luke, the word is used a total of nineteen times in the New Testament, and in every case *pais* simply means "servant," "son," or "child," and nothing more. Here is the data so you can see for yourself:

+ Matthew 2:16—*pais* refers to the baby boys in Bethlehem whom Herod killed.

+ Matthew 12:18—the Father calls Jesus "my servant" (*pais*).

+ Matthew 14:2—*pais* refers to King Herod's attendants.

+ Matthew 17:18; Luke 9:42—*pais* refers to a man's son who was healed by Jesus.

+ Matthew 21:15—*pais* refers to children praising God in the temple.

+ Luke 1:54—Israel is called God's servant (*pais*).

+ Luke 1:69—David is called God's servant (*pais*).

+ Luke 8:51, 54—*pais* refers to Jairus's daughter, whom Jesus raised from the dead.

+ Luke 12:45—*pais* refers to a man's household servants.

+ Luke 15:26—*pais* refers to a Jewish man's servant.

+ John 4:51—*pais* refers to a Roman nobleman's son, whom Jesus healed.[27]

+ Acts 3:13, 26—Jesus is God's *pais* (meaning either servant or Son).

+ Acts 4:25—David again is called God's servant (*pais*).

+ Acts 4:27, 30—Jesus is called God's servant (*pais*).

+ Acts 20:12—*pais* refers to a young man whom Paul raised from the dead.

Not one of these contexts has even the slightest hint of any sexual connotation, and this nonsexual usage is typical for *pais* throughout the Septuagint, the Greek translation of the Old Testament as well. (The Septuagint includes the apocryphal books, which are found today in Catholic Bibles.)

In short, *not one time in the entire Bible does* pais *refer to a servant with any sexual connotation*, and it is used approximately ninety times in the Septuagint and New Testament writings. That's why it never dawned on a single commentator or lexicographer in all of church history—meaning for almost two thousand years—that Jesus was enabling a Roman soldier to continue having sex with his younger male slave. To repeat: this is a perversion of the Word of God and the God of the Word.

Only one more point needs to be made. Some commentators have suggested that the word *pais* should be translated "boy," used as a loving term by a concerned master, also underscoring the servant's youthfulness, but with nothing sexual implied. Based, however, on the twisted, "Jesus, please heal my boy toy" reading of the text proclaimed on gay activist billboards and from same-sex-affirming pulpits, it would suggest that the relationship was likely pederastic in nature.[28]

God forbid we entertain such blasphemy even for a second, and God forbid that any of us allow our sexuality to demean the beautiful and glorious Savior in such ugly terms. Idolatry can be defined as creating a God in our own image. That is exactly what has happened here.

Chapter 8

PAUL and HOMOSEXUALITY

The "gay Christian" argument: When Paul condemned homosexual practice in Romans 1, he was speaking of sensual acts that took place in idolatrous temples, possibly even referring to idol-worshipping, sexually inflamed heterosexuals whom God gave over to homosexuality. And the Greek words he used in 1 Corinthians 6 and 1 Timothy 1 have nothing to do with monogamous, loving same-sex relationships.

The biblical response: Paul looked at homosexual practice as a direct result of humankind's rejection of God, something contrary to His created order, and he listed it along with many other sinful practices. And while there may be debate about the precise meaning of the Greek words he used in 1 Corinthians and 1 Timothy, there is absolutely no doubt that he was condemning homosexual practice. The good news is that he declared that the blood of Jesus could save people from homosexual sin.

I T WOULD SEEM that Paul's views on homosexual practice are quite clear—and quite clearly negative. After all, in 1 Corinthians 6:9 he explained that "passive homosexual partners" and "practicing homosexuals" (NET) will not inherit the kingdom of God, while in Romans 1 he explained how God gave sinful people over "to dishonorable passions. For their women exchanged natural relations for those that are contrary to nature; and the men likewise gave up natural relations with women and were consumed with passion for one another, men committing shameless acts with men and receiving in themselves the due penalty for their error" (vv. 26–27). This seems pretty clear!

How do gay theologians respond? First, they tell us that the words just cited in 1 Corinthians 6:9 refer to homosexual prostitutes and pederasts, so Paul is not addressing monogamous, gay relationships (or consensual, committed gay sex). In fact, we are told the two Greek words translated by the New English Translation as "passive homosexual partners" and "practicing homosexuals" might not even be related to homosexual acts of any kind, since there is wide debate about what the words in question mean.

Second, gay theologians argue that the passage in Romans 1, which seems to be so clear, connects homosexual practice with idolatry, meaning that it is the debased sexual acts that took place in pagan temples that Paul was talking about, not two Christian men or women who love God and love each other and join together sexually. Some even argue that Paul is actually talking about sexually inflamed, idol-worshipping *heterosexuals* whom God gave over to homosexuality, *contrary to their heterosexual nature.*

Is there any truth to these "gay Christian" interpretations? Before answering that question, let me ask some questions of my own, especially to those who do believe that the "gay Christian" reading of these texts is correct.

1. Do you think it's significant that no commentators came up with some of the "gay Christian" readings of Romans 1 until after the sexual revolution of the 1960s and the rise of the gay liberation movement, despite the fact that there were thousands of books written about Paul by a wide variety of scholars, many of whom were anything but fundamentalists?

2. Do you think it's significant that every major dictionary of New Testament Greek or Classical Greek understood Paul's key vocabulary (in particular, the word *arsenokoitēs*) to refer to men engaging in homosexual acts, despite the fact that many of these lexicographers were anything but fundamentalists and were simply experts in Greek?

3. Do you think it's significant that some leading gay scholars recognize that Paul categorically rejected homosexual practice?

Let's think about each of these points for a moment, recognizing that Paul's writings—at most, thirteen letters, or even fourteen, if he wrote Hebrews—have been subjected to intensive scholarly scrutiny for many centuries, and those studying his writings have ranged from devoted followers of Jesus to skeptics and mockers. The range of interpretative differences between these scholars has often been massive, and some of the interpretations they have offered have been absolutely preposterous. Yet before the sexual revolution and the rise of gay activism, none of these scholars came up with these pro-gay reading of his writings.

Some might say, "That's because Paul didn't know anything about monogamous, same-sex relationships, nor did he have any concept of homosexual orientation. The same can be said for all interpreters of Paul who lived before we learned things about sexual orientation in the last forty to fifty years."

But then wouldn't that mean Paul wasn't inspired in what he wrote? Wouldn't that mean he was guilty of condemning the innocent with his words?

Gay religious teachers would likely say, "Not at all. He was only condemning homosexual acts that took place in abusive or immoral situations, like pederasty and prostitution, or that took place in the context of idol worship in pagan temples. The interpreters of Paul before the gay liberation movement didn't grasp this. They only saw homosexuality through the lens of their limited understanding, and they had no concept of loving, committed, long-term relationships between people who were born gay. So, you simply can't apply Paul's words to loving, gay relationships today."

As Union Seminary professor Robin Scroggs expressed (speaking about the Bible as a whole, but including Paul's writings), "*Biblical judgments against homosexuality are not relevant to today's debate. They should no longer be used...not because the Bible is not authoritative, but simply because it does not address the issues involved....No single New Testament author considers [homosexuality] important enough to write his own sentence about it.*"[1]

But these objections are quite weak and, in reality, fatally flawed, since it can easily be demonstrated that Paul *did* know about people in long-term, same-sex sexual relationships in his day (or in the classical Greek literature that he would have learned as an educated Greek citizen).[2] More importantly, his condemnation of homosexual acts—both male and female—is so comprehensive that under no circumstances could anyone fairly imagine that he would countenance these acts (or relationships) in any setting, even if he recognized such a thing as "gay identity." And that's why a number of leading gay and gay-friendly scholars agree that Paul condemned homosexual practice, period, which leads us back to the question: Isn't it curious that no one thought of these new, pro-homosex interpretations of Paul before the sexual revolution?

Let's remember that John Boswell, professor of history at Yale University before his death by AIDS at the age of forty-seven, argued that for much of church history, homosexual relationships were accepted and even blessed by the church, which would mean that there were many prominent "gay Christians" through the centuries.[3] Why then didn't it occur to any of them that Paul was not against homosexual practice?

The answer, of course, is that Boswell's claims are utterly false—in fact, other scholars have demolished his claims[4]—which is why no reputable scholar thought of denying that Paul condemned homosexual practice before the gay liberation movement. And so these new readings do not arise from the biblical text; instead, they have been read back into the text by gay theologians against the backdrop of the moral deterioration of our society.

When it comes to lexicographers, the scholars who compile dictionaries, they base their work on decades of meticulous study of texts and words, trying to avoid theological debates and doing their best simply to explain the meaning of the words in their specific contexts. It is painstaking, detailed work. My doctoral dissertation focused on one Hebrew root in its ancient Near Eastern context, and I have written a number of word study articles for major theological dictionaries. For this reason my respect for these top lexicographers is massive. It takes a lot of hard work to do what they do, and they often devote a good part of their lives to completing their lexical projects.

They can't have axes to grind, any more than a mathematics teacher can have an axe to grind when teaching students the multiplication tables. And while it is true that there are often disputed texts and hard-to-translate words, when you see all the major dictionaries agreeing on the meaning of a specific word, that's because the meaning of that word is clear (rather than being the result of some lexicographical conspiracy!). When it comes to Paul's vocabulary about homosexuality, in particular the word *arsenokoitēs*, there is fundamental agreement on the meaning of the word. This is very significant too.

But here's the real kicker (and it has to be discouraging for those who want to argue that God in the Scriptures blesses monogamous, same-sex relationships): some of the top gay and gay-friendly scholars in the world recognize that Paul categorically rejects homosexual practice, which would be like a defense attorney in a court of law turning to the judge and jury and saying, "My client is pleading innocent, but I'm here to say he's guilty." You know you are in trouble then.

As noted by Pim Pronk, a gay biologist, theologian, and philosopher (and again, speaking of the Scriptures as a whole, including the writings of Paul):

> To sum up: wherever homosexual intercourse is mentioned in Scripture, it is condemned. With reference to it the New Testament adds no arguments to those of the Old. Rejection is a foregone conclusion; the assessment of it nowhere constitutes a problem. It obviously has to be repeated from time to time, but the phenomenon as such nowhere becomes the focus of moral attention. It is never condemned in isolation but always in association with other major sins: unchastity, violence, moral corruption, and idolatry.[5]

Bernadette Brooten is a lesbian feminist and a learned professor who authored an important work on lesbianism in the ancient world titled *Love Between Women: Early Christian Reponses to Female Homoeroticism.* She wrote in that book, "I see Paul as condemning all forms of homoeroticism."[6]

Louis Crompton was a "noted scholar of nineteenth-century British literature and a pioneer of gay studies."[7] In his book *Homosexuality and Civilization* he wrote:

According to [one] interpretation, Paul's words were not directed at "bona fide" homosexuals in committed relationships. But such a reading, however well-intentioned, seems strained and unhistorical. Nowhere does Paul or any other Jewish writer of this period imply the least acceptance of same-sex relations under any circumstance. The idea that homosexuals might be redeemed by mutual devotion would have been wholly foreign to Paul or any other Jew or early Christian.[8]

Walter Wink was a biblical scholar and theologian active in "progressive Christianity" and famous for liberal, pro-gay, antiwar views. In the *Christian Century Review* he wrote, "The Bible is negative toward same-sex behavior, and there is no getting around it.... Paul wouldn't accept [a nonexploitative homosexual] relationship for a minute."[9]

Even Professor Dan Via, in a debate with Professor Robert Gagnon (whom, you will recall, is often regarded as the top "antigay" biblical scholar by gay theologians), stated, "Professor Gagnon and I are in substantial agreement that the biblical texts that deal specifically with homosexual practice condemn it unconditionally. However, on the question of what the church might or should make of this we diverge sharply."[10]

This is not looking good for the "gay Christian" position!

But it gets worse still for those claiming that, based on a fair and honest reading of the Scriptures, God is not against committed, same-sex relationships. Even the GLBTQ online encyclopedia, which bills itself as "the world's largest encyclopedia of gay, lesbian, bisexual, and queer culture," and which fully embraces standard, gay activist positions, states:

> The bad news from the Christian Bible is that it condemns same-sex desire and same-sex acts without qualification of age, gender, role, status, consent, or membership in an ethnic community.
>
> This may seem less drastic when we recall that Paul outlawed all sex except that between married couples and preferred celibacy to marriage for himself.[11]

Do you now understand why I gave the analogy about the defense attorney telling the judge and jury that his client is actually guilty as charged? This is almost identical!

PAUL'S MESSAGE WAS CLEAR

Speaking about Paul's writing, this GLBTQ online encyclopedia states, "Verses from two of Paul's epistles are important for gay men and lesbians. From the earliest days of the new religion, they shaped the attitudes of Christians to male and female homosexuality. It would be difficult to overestimate the importance and influence of these texts."[12]

With regard to Romans 1:26–27, the article notes that:

> Writing in 58 C.E. to the Christians in Rome, Paul broadened the prohibitions of the Hebrew Bible to include same-sex acts of women.... That Paul meant to condemn female homosexuality along with male is confirmed by the first Latin commentator, a still unidentified author writing about 370 and known as Ambrosiater or Pseudo-Ambrose.[13]

Yes, this gay encyclopedia states, "Paul's language will reverberate, directly or indirectly, in almost every later Christian reference to male and female same-sex eros."[14] Rightly so.

And what of the disputed Greek words in 1 Corinthians 6:9–10? Note carefully what the article on Paul explains—and I have to commend the author of this article for his candor:

> The meanings of these Greek nouns have been the subject of lively debate, largely provoked by gay authors anxious to show that Paul and the early church had not intended to condemn homosexuality per se as harshly as has been traditionally supposed, but only a degraded type of pederasty associated with prostitution and child abuse.
>
> Recent scholarship has shown conclusively that the traditional meanings assigned to these words stand. So do the traditional translations: the Latin translation "commonly used in the church," and therefore known as the Vulgate, and the English King James Version (KJV).[15]

Some of that is worth repeating: The debate about the meaning of these words (which, as noted above, was hardly disputed in the major Greek dictionaries) was "largely provoked by gay authors anxious to show that Paul and the early church had not intended to condemn homosexuality per se as harshly as has been traditionally supposed." Unfortunately for them, "Recent scholarship has shown conclusively that the traditional meanings assigned to these words stand."

Dear reader, please don't let anyone trick you into believing that Paul was not speaking against homosexual practice in general. Even the world's largest online GLBTQ encyclopedia says that he was, as confirmed by top gay and gay-friendly scholars, as seen immediately above.

But to remove all doubt, let's look at the key texts in more depth, beginning with 1 Corinthians 6:9–11, which I'll cite here in the New English Translation (NET):

> Do you not know that the unrighteous will not inherit the kingdom of God? Do not be deceived! The sexually immoral, idolaters, adulterers, passive homosexual partners [*malakoi*], practicing homosexuals [*arsenokoitai*], thieves, the greedy, drunkards, the verbally abusive, and swindlers will not inherit the kingdom of God. Some of you once lived this way. But you were washed, you were sanctified, you were justified in the name of the Lord Jesus Christ and by the Spirit of our God.

Some translations, such as the English Standard Version, group these two Greek words, *malakoi* and *arsenokoitai*, together, understanding them to mean "men who practice homosexuality" (similarly, the most recent edition of the New International Version renders the words together as "men who have sex with men"), but most translations render each word separately. Here's a representative sampling:

- King James Version: effeminate; nor abusers of themselves with mankind

- New King James Version: homosexuals; sodomites

- New American Standard Bible: effeminate; homosexuals

- Complete Jewish Bible: who engage in active or passive homosexuality

- Revised Standard Version: sexual perverts (rendering both words together)

+ New Revised Standard Version: male prostitutes; sodomites

+ Holman Christian Standard Bible: anyone practicing homo-sexuality (rendering both words together)

Going back to the second to third century AD, the Peshitta version, which is the oldest translation of the Greek New Testament into Aramaic, renders the words with "corrupt [ones]" and "men who lie with males"; the Latin Vulgate, dating back to the fourth century AD, renders with *molles* (technically, the receptive partner in anal intercourse) and *masculorum concubitores*, "men who lie with males."

It is totally clear, then, that while there may be minor differences in the rendering of these Greek words, there is absolutely no question that they speak categorically against homosexual practice, despite what some gay theologians claim. And Paul says those who practice these things will not inherit God's kingdom—and remember that he had already mentioned fornicators (speaking of all sexual immorality outside of wedlock) and adulterers (speaking of sexual immorality committed by married people) in his list in 1 Corinthians 6:9, and so there would be no need to mention two more categories of sexual sinners unless they were to be distinguished from these first two classes.

In short, the first word *malakos* (plural, *malakoi*) literally means "soft," and it is used in that sense in verses such as Proverbs 25:15 (a soft answer, in the Septuagint) and Matthew 11:8 (soft clothes). Elsewhere in ancient Greek, however, the term is commonly used for the receptive partner in homosexual sex as well as for men who dressed and acted like women (hence the rendering "effeminate" in the King James, but clearly not meaning a man who simply had some unintentional effeminate mannerisms).

The second word, *arsenokoitēs* (plural, *arsenokoitai*), is composed of two Greek words meaning "men who lie with males," and it is most likely derived from the Septuagint, the Greek translation of the Hebrew Scriptures (Old Testament) completed nearly two centuries before the time of Jesus. There, the Greek translation of the Hebrew words for "lying with a male" in Leviticus 18:22 and 20:13 include the words *arsen* (male) and *koites* (bed), leading to the compound word *arsenokoitēs*, a man who lies with a male.

Significantly, when the two words *malakos* and *arsenokoitēs* are used side by side, the sexual connotations are undeniable, which is why there is virtually unanimous agreement in all major dictionaries and translations, despite some minor differences in the exact nuances of the words. And that's one of the reasons gay scholars like Professor Brooten, cited previously, could say, "I see Paul as condemning all forms of homoeroticism." For Brooten, the logical conclusion was to reject the authority of Paul for the church![16]

Now, I could cite all the discussions in the major lexicons to support these points in detail, but I will allow the online GLBTQ encyclopedia to speak for itself:

> *Malakoi* (Latin Vulgate: *molles*) should have caused no problem. There is ample evidence that in sexual contexts, in both classical and post-classical times, *malakos* designated the receptive partner in a male same-sex act, a meaning decisively reconfirmed in late antiquity by the physician Caelius Aurelianus when he tells us that the Greeks call *malakoi* males whom the Latins call *molles* or *subacti*, males, that is, who play the receptive role in anal intercourse.
>
> *Paul's malakoi, we can say with certainty, are males—boys, youths, or adults—who have consented, either for money or for pleasure, for some perceived advantage or as an act of affectionate generosity, to be penetrated by men* [emphasis added].
>
> *Arsenokoitai*
> The word is a verbal noun, and its earliest attestation is in this verse of Paul's. It is a compound of *arsen* = "male" and *koités* = "a man who lies with (or beds)." And so we have, describing Oedipus, *metrokoités,* "a man who lies with his mother," *doulokoités,* "a man who lies with maidservants or female slaves," *polykoités,* "a man who lies with many," and *onokoités,* "a man who lies with donkeys," said of Christians in a graffito from Carthage of about 195.
>
> *Arsenokoitai* are therefore "men who lie with males," and the Vulgate's *masculorum concubitores* (where *masculorum* is an objective genitive), renders the Greek exactly to mean "men who lie with males," "men who sleep with males," "men who have sex with males."
>
> ...The dependence of Paul's *arsenokoitai* on the Levitical *arsenos koitén* [from Leviticus 18:22] demonstrates unequivocally

its source and confirms his intended meaning. The word was almost certainly coined by Greek-speaking Jews.[17]

This part of the article concludes by saying, "Understood in the context of what we know about role playing in most ancient same-sex relationships, *malakoi* are the receptive parties and *arsenokoitai* the inserters in male-male anal intercourse."[18] And this, again, is from a GLBTQ reference work, reminding us of how futile it is to suggest that Paul would have been OK with men having sex with men as long as it was in the context of a loving, committed relationship. Not a chance! Such acts were contrary to God's intentions for His creation, especially for those who wanted to serve Him and please Him.

Interestingly, the *Study New Testament for Lesbians, Gays, Bi, and Transgender: with extensive notes on Greek word meaning and context*, compiled by the linguist Dr. A. Nyland, does not translate these Greek words into English, rendering the first with *cinaedi* and leaving *arsenokoitēs* untranslated.[19] This begs the question: If the words clearly do *not* refer to homosexual practice, why not make that clear in the translation? She then explains the meaning of the words in the notes, writing first about "The Cinaedi" and stating: "*malakos*, 'receptive male homosexual promiscuous cross dresser' or 'coward', usually considered in this context to mean the former due to its proximity to the following word *arsenokoitēs*.'"[20]

As for *arsenokoitēs*, Dr. Nyland explains, "The word does not mean 'homosexual', but rather its semantic range includes one who anally penetrates another (female or male), rapist, murderer, or extortionist. When used in the meaning 'anal penetrator', it does not apply exclusively to males as the receptors, as it was also used for women receptors."[21]

What this means is that even in a study Bible written and edited specifically for LGBT readers and with obvious, pro-gay biases in the notes, the translator cannot get away from the fact that *malakos*, when found next to *arsenokoitēs*, most likely means "receptive male," "homosexual," or "promiscuous cross dresser," while *arsenokoitēs* itself refers to "one who anally penetrates another" (or to a "rapist, murderer, or extortionist," meanings that have been rightly discarded here by virtually all major translations, ancient and modern, as well as all major Greek dictionaries).[22]

Nyquist even notes in her discussion of *malakoi* that, "Such men (and the *cinaedi* were mature men, not boys) were portrayed as effeminate cross dressers, many depicted with ringlets, women's jewelry, and cosmetics; with women's tastes in general."[23] This almost sounds like a condemnation of those who identify as transgender today, dressing and acting like the opposite of their biological sex, and it is straight out of the notes of a LGBT study New Testament.

The *Queer Bible Commentary* argues that Paul's list of "the unrighteous" in 1 Corinthians 6:9–10, which also includes fornicators, adulterers, drunkards, idolators, and swindlers, "is not *specifically* descriptive of nor directed towards homosexual activity, nor, indeed, sexual activity in general."[24] But this is clearly grasping at straws, based on gay presuppositions rather than dispassionate, unbiased scholarship. The linguistic and exegetical evidence is completely against it.[25]

What about the argument that it is quite a jump from first-century Corinth to the contemporary world, especially in terms of our understanding of sexuality? Professor Anthony Thiselton, one of the world's top Corinthian scholars and the author of a 1,492-page commentary on the Greek text of 1 Corinthians, puts that notion to rest:

> The claims often made that "the issue of 'homosexuality'—psychosexual orientation—simply was not a biblical issue" are confused. Paul addresses every form of "desire," whether heterosexual or materialistic, and distinguishes between passionate longing and action (cf. [1 Cor] 7:9). It is true that "homosexual orientation" does not feature as a phenomenon for explicit comment, but to dismiss the parallel, e.g., between heterosexual desire and an illicit habituated heterosexual relationship is itself to isolate same-sex relations from other ethical issues in a way which such [gay and gay friendly] writers as Furnish, Scroggs, Boswell, and Nelson rightly deplore. Many also argue that abusive pederasty was the standard form in which Paul encountered male intimacy. But Wolff shows that this is far from the case. Paul witnessed around him *both* abusive relationships of power or money *and* examples of "genuine love" between males. We must not misunderstand Paul's "worldly" knowledge.[26]

Thiselton then concludes:

On the basis of the distance between the first and twentieth centuries, many ask: "Is the situation addressed by the biblical writer genuinely comparable to our own?" The more closely writers examine Graeco-Roman society and the pluralism of its ethical traditions, the more the Corinthian situation appears to resonate with our own.[27]

As noted by Amy Orr-Ewing, and speaking about the Bible as a whole:

Although both the Old and New Testaments were given in eras which found homosexual activity culturally and morally acceptable, the texts are countercultural and call for a moral standard among believers different from that of the world around. While recognizing that what the Bible says about homosexual practice may seem controversial and unpopular, it is important to remember that *it would also have seemed so at the time it was written.*

So although the Bible may seem "out of date," the culture in which it was written was not so dissimilar from our own.[28]

This is an important point! Paul's teaching went against the cultural norms in his day as well, especially in the ancient Greco-Roman world, which witnessed both long-term same-sex relationships and rampant male homosexuality. As explained by Professor Eva Cantarella in her book *Bisexuality in the Ancient World*:

As regards Greece, everything that we have seen confirms that for a Greek man, from the earliest times that the sources allow us to examine, homosexual relationships were part of a life experience regulated by a series of social norms which laid down the time scales and etiquette of these relationships, and their alternation with heterosexual relationships.[29]

And, she noted, "Like the Greeks, the Romans also felt that it was normal for a man to have sexual relationships with other men as well as with women."[30] It was against this backdrop that Paul laid out this new lofty ethic of life in the Spirit for followers of Jesus.

Finally, returning to the meaning of *malakoi* and *arsenokoitai*, Professor Thiselton, in the midst of a very thorough discussion of the relevant issues in his article "Can Hermeneutics Ease the Deadlock" (in the careful and compassionate volume, *The Way Forward? Christian Voices on Homosexuality and the Church*), acknowledged that, "The translation of the Greek words *malakoi* and *arsenokoitai* has become notoriously controversial,"[31] but the controversy, of course, has been driven by the concerns of gay theologians and their allies. The reality, however, is simple:

> No amount of lexicographical manipulation over *malakoi* can avoid the clear meaning of *arsenokoitai* as the activity of males (*arsēn*) who have sexual relations, sleep with (*koitēs*) other males.
>
> [Also], the view that one or both Greek words refer only to pederasty or to male prostitution for payment, as advocated by Kenneth Dover, Robin Scroggs, and others, cannot withstand the battery of detailed linguistic arguments brought against by a number of historical and linguistic specialists. Moreover, it positively violates the contextual theme which has emerged of a general grasping beyond ordained boundaries in the face of what God assigns as the self's due which characterises every other habitual act in the list, culminating in Paul's rejection of the Corinthian slogan within the church "I have the right to do anything" or "all things are lawful."[32]

So, it appears that very little has changed. What Paul wrote was clear and direct both then and now, yet professing Christians today, just as in Paul's day, respond with, "I'm free in Jesus! I'm not under the law! I have the right to do anything!" We will come back to this subject in the last chapter of the book.

HOMOSEXUAL PRACTICE AND ROMANS 1

As we turn to Romans 1, it would seem that Paul's condemnation of homosexual practice is even clearer since, in contrast with the single words listed in 1 Corinthians 6:9–10, Paul's discussion in Romans 1 actually describes homosexual acts, both male and female, as contrary to nature, sexually depraved, and the result of God's judgment. To give the larger context, we see that Paul begins this section in Romans 1:18, where he declares that "the wrath of God is revealed from heaven against all ungodliness and unrighteousness of men, who by their unrighteousness suppress the truth."

And note carefully that he is speaking of the human race as a whole here (as opposed to focusing on idol worshippers in the city of Rome).

Paul then explains that God's revelation in nature is so clear that people who deny Him are without excuse (vv. 19–20), and thus, despite knowing of God's reality, they foolishly denied Him, worshipping the creation rather than the Creator (vv. 21–23). "Therefore," Paul writes, "God gave them up in the lusts of their hearts to impurity, to the dishonoring of their bodies among themselves, because they exchanged the truth about God for a lie and worshiped and served the creature rather than the Creator, who is blessed forever! Amen" (vv. 24–25). Again, Paul is not speaking about former monotheists in Rome who turned away from God to worship idols, as a result of which God gave them over to sexual impurity between themselves. He is speaking of the descent of the human race into sin.

Next Paul writes, "For this reason God gave them up to dishonorable passions. For their women exchanged natural relations for those that are contrary to nature; and the men likewise gave up natural relations with women and were consumed with passion for one another, men committing shameless acts with men and receiving in themselves the due penalty for their error" (vv. 26–27). This would seem to be the most direct, comprehensive condemnation of homosexual practice in the Bible, and it is one that has troubled "gay Christians" through the years.

In reply, gay theologians would say: first, these verses must be interpreted in the context of idol worship, and we are clearly not idol worshippers. Second, we did not follow this pattern of descent into depravity, beginning with idolatry, then heterosexual lust then degenerating further into homosexual lust. We have always been romantically attracted to the same sex, and the love we have for each other is no different from the love two heterosexual Christians have for each other. Third, it is not contrary to our nature to be homosexual, but it would be contrary to nature for a heterosexual to engage in homosexual acts, and that's obviously what Paul was talking about.

As expressed by Matthew Vines, a professing "gay Christian" in his early twenties whose video teaching on this subject has gone viral:

> Both the men and the women started with heterosexuality—they
> were naturally disposed to it just as they were naturally disposed
> to the knowledge of God—but they rejected their original, natural

inclinations for those that were unnatural: for them, same-sex behavior. Paul's argument about idolatry requires that there be an exchange; the reason, he says, that the idolaters are at fault is because they first knew God but then turned away from Him, exchanged Him for idols. Paul's reference to same-sex behavior is intended to illustrate this larger sin of idolatry. But in order for this analogy to have any force, in order for it to make sense within this argument, the people he is describing must naturally begin with heterosexual relations and then abandon them. And that is exactly how he describes it.

But that is not what we are talking about. Gay people have a natural, permanent orientation toward those of the same sex; it's not something that they choose, and it's not something that they can change. They aren't abandoning or rejecting heterosexuality—that's never an option for them to begin with. And if applied to gay people, Paul's argument here should actually work in the other direction: If the point of this passage is to rebuke those who have spurned their true nature, be it religious when it comes to idolatry or sexual, then just as those who are naturally heterosexual should not be with those of the same sex, so, too, those who have a natural orientation toward the same sex should not be with those of the opposite sex. For them, that would be exchanging "the natural for the unnatural" in just the same way. We have different natures when it comes to sexual orientation.[33]

How can we fairly and honestly reply to these objections? Let's continue reading Romans 1 before coming back to these questions. Paul concludes the chapter with these words:

> And since they did not see fit to acknowledge God, God gave them up to a debased mind to do what ought not to be done. They were filled with all manner of unrighteousness, evil, covetousness, malice. They are full of envy, murder, strife, deceit, maliciousness. They are gossips, slanderers, haters of God, insolent, haughty, boastful, inventors of evil, disobedient to parents, foolish, faithless, heartless, ruthless. Though they know God's righteous decree that

those who practice such things deserve to die, they not only do them but give approval to those who practice them.

—ROMANS 1:28–32

Now, one thing is immediately apparent, and it confirms what I have already pointed out. Paul is not simply referring to sins that people commit in the context of idol worship in a pagan temple. He is referring to the sins of the human race as a whole, which, he explains, are the result of our rejection of the one true God, who consequently gave us over to sins of the flesh and sins of the heart. Stop for a moment and reread the verses just cited. Is there any doubt that Paul was speaking of the universal nature of human sin? And is there anything on this list—from heterosexual promiscuity to homosexual acts (male and female) to "evil, covetousness, malice" and "envy, murder, strife, deceit, [and] maliciousness" to people being "gossips, slanderers, haters of God, insolent, haughty, boastful, inventors of evil, disobedient to parents, foolish, faithless, heartless, ruthless"—is there anything listed here that is *not* sinful wherever it is found, whether in the context of idolatry or in the context of everyday life? Obviously not.

The offshoot of this is clear: Paul was not specifically speaking about homosexual acts that took place in pagan temples as the people worshipped idols and engaged in sexual promiscuity.[34] He was speaking generically about homosexual acts, both male and female, and denouncing them as sinful in the strongest possible terms. This also means that he was not claiming that every person who engaged in these acts did so because they were inflamed with lust and depravity. Rather, he was explaining how these things became part of the human race: They are the result of God giving us over to our own ways, and our own ways are never the best ways.

A similar analogy can be made regarding sickness and disease, which are always, in and of themselves, negative, not positive conditions.[35] Sickness entered our world because of human sin, and it sometimes affects us individuals as the direct result of sinful choices we make. But many times sickness and disease are unrelated to choices we make (think of a handicapped baby born to godly parents who live healthy lifestyles). And so, while it is right to say that sickness is in the world because of sin, it would be wrong to say that all sickness is the result of specific sin. At the same time, we still recognize sickness as bad and try to treat it and prevent it rather than celebrate it.

In the same way, if not for human sin and the fall of Adam, there would be no homosexual desires in the world, even though the great majority of people experiencing same-sex attraction did not make conscious choices (or commit specific sins) in order to attain those attractions. Similarly, if not for human sin and the fall of Adam, we would not have a natural propensity to laziness, gluttony, oversleeping, or selfishness, nor would the average, happily married, heterosexual man have to exercise discipline not to lust after other women. The bottom line, again, is that homosexual acts are contrary to God's order and design and are only in the world because of our fallen, broken nature.

This becomes even clearer when we break down the two key verses in this chapter, starting with verse 26: "For this reason God gave them up to dishonorable passions. For their women exchanged natural relations for those that are contrary to nature." Professor James D. G. Dunn, one of the world's foremost Pauline scholars and the author of a major commentary on Romans, explains the second half of this verse to mean, "For their females changed the natural function into what is contrary to nature." He then explains, "Both θήλειαι and ἄρσενες (v 27), 'females, males,' are used presumably because Paul has in mind particularly their sexual relationship, and indeed sexual compatibility (cf. Mark 10:6//Matt 19:4; Gen 1:27; Gal 3:28)."[36]

Do you understand the significance of this? Paul is *not* saying that heterosexual women engaged in lesbian sex contrary to their heterosexual nature, a concept that is not only contrary to the Greek usage and the context (as we will demonstrate) but is also based on contemporary conceptions about sexual orientation that would have been foreign to Paul. After all, it is gay theologians who constantly remind us that Paul knew nothing about "sexual orientation" or about people being "born gay"—although, as we noted previously, he certainly knew about long-term, same-sex partners.[37] No, the Greek is speaking of women abandoning the natural function of their bodies—made for men rather than for women—a thought that Paul continues in the very next verse. As translated by Dunn, "Likewise also the males gave up the natural function of the female" (Rom. 1:27).[38] Paul's point is quite clear!

The fact is, it doesn't take an advanced degree in biology to recognize that God carefully designed men for women and women for men (see also chapter 4), that only a man and woman can come together in sexual intimacy, face-to-face, and consummate their relationship sexually; that only a man and woman can produce a child; and that only a woman can carry that child and uniquely nurture the baby who has been born.

As I pointed out in my debate with "gay Christian" activist Harry Knox, "There is something to looking at your spouse in an embrace of love, joining together in sexual union, and then experiencing the miracle of a child that uniquely combines the two lives. A homosexual couple can never possibly experience this, and to me, this is a cause for pain, not thanksgiving."[39]

I then offered this illustration to back up the point I was making:

> The LA Times reported in December of last year [2007] about two gay men who desperately wanted to have a child. Their attempt "to bring a child into the world involved a woman they barely knew. After fertilizing her eggs in vitro using both men's sperm, another woman would carry the resulting embryos to term. They had no idea whose DNA would carry the day. [The birth of their son Jansen] marked the end of a four-year journey that involved three egg retrievals, 65 eggs, seven fertilization attempts, three surrogates and more than $200,000 in expenses."
>
> ... The Times reported that when they finally succeeded and produced a baby boy, "As for the identity of the biological father, they prefer not to know....
>
> "As the new family settles in its Atlanta home, the surrogate continues to pump and freeze breast milk for Jansen. Each week she ships bottles from Massachusetts to Georgia packed in dry ice."
>
> I don't doubt that these two men are doting fathers, but the whole story underscores clearly that God does not bless His human creation with homosexuality. And what about those who can't afford $200,000 to produce a child? And what of the fact that a child has been brought into the world by human choice that is guaranteed not to have a mother or even to know for sure who his father is? This is a blessing? Can't you see the beauty, wisdom, and simplicity of male-female complementarity?[40]

I once watched a TV documentary featuring a gay couple who already had one child and wanted a second one. They seemed like really nice guys, and they certainly appeared to love the child they were raising. Now it was time for baby number two.

So these two men met with a lesbian couple, and the four of them sat across the table and talked about their plan: one of the men would provide his semen to artificially impregnate one of the women, who would then carry the baby and give it to the gay men for adoption at birth. (For the record, the lesbian couple seemed very sweet as well.) So they talked through the whole plan (slightly awkwardly, as I recall), and then they discussed what the price would be—did the mother want somewhere around seventy thousand dollars?—and they agreed to move forward.

And as I watched this show with my wife, Nancy, I said to her (with pain), "This is obviously not what God intended!"

After all, the normal thing is for the man to marry the woman he loves, have sexual relations with her, and produce a child that is the unique product of their sexual union and their two lives joined together, rather than for a man to sit across a table from a woman who will be the biological mother of his child (only to have no connection with that child for the rest of her life) and have her impregnated through a medical procedure (even though both of them are perfectly healthy and physically able to produce a child between them through natural means), and then pay a large sum of money for her to carry the baby.[41] To repeat: this is not what God intended for His male-female creation.

Paul underscores this by using the Greek words for "male" and "female" rather than the more common words for "man" and "woman." In fact, Paul only uses the terms "male" and "female" here in Romans 1:26–27 and then in Galatians 3:28,[42] whereas he often uses the Greek nouns for "man" and "woman" in his writings.[43] And note this carefully: the first time the terms "male" and "female" occur in the Greek Bible are in Genesis 1:27, "So God created man in his own image, in the image of God he created him; male and female he created them."

Yes, Paul is talking about God's created order, about the natural functions of male and females, not about people individually doing what was (allegedly) contrary to their normal sexual attractions, as some gay theologians argue. (Again, no one in recorded history ever came up with this far-fetched and utterly false idea until after the sexual revolution of the 1960s.)

But there's more: the only other time in the New Testament that the

Greek words for "male" and "female" are found is in on the lips of Jesus when He affirmed His Father's intent for marriage—namely, one man and one woman joined together for life—and where He quoted from Genesis 1:27, which I just cited. (See Matthew 19:4; Mark 10:6). And so, without a doubt, when Paul speaks of females and males doing what was contrary to nature and abandoning their natural function, he was saying that *homosexual acts are contrary to God's created order.*

As explained in the *New International Dictionary of New Testament Theology,* "*physis* [nature] stands further for the regular order of nature, which determines the distinction between the sexes. God has given up the idolaters, so that they have exchanged natural (*physiken*) sexual intercourse between man and woman for unnatural (*para physin,* Rom. 1:26)."[44] To cite Romans 1:26–27 again (but this time clarifying these key Greek words in the brackets), "God gave them over to shameful lusts. Even their *women* [females] exchanged natural relations for unnatural ones. In the same way the *men* [males] also abandoned natural relations with *women* [females] and were inflamed with lust for one another. *Men* [males] committed indecent acts with other *men* [males], and received in themselves the due penalty for their perversion" (NIV). To say it once more: Paul is teaching that *females* "exchanged natural relations for unnatural ones"—not heterosexuals exchanged natural relations for unnatural ones. "In the same way," he writes, "the *males* also abandoned natural relations with *females.*"

But there's one more thing that Paul says to drive this point home. Beginning just a few verses earlier, in Romans 1:20, Paul points back to the creation: "For since the creation of the world God's invisible qualities—his eternal power and divine nature—have been clearly seen, being understood from what has been made, so that men are without excuse" (NIV). Then, as noted by Professor Gagnon, there is an unmistakable connection between Romans 1:23 and Genesis 1:26 (in the Septuagint). Just look at these two verses side by side.

- Romans 1:23: "And they exchanged the glory of the immortal God for the likeness [*homoiomati*] of the image [*eikonos*] of a mortal human [*anthropou*] and of birds [*peteinon*] and of four-footed animals [*tetrapodon*] and of reptiles [*herpeton*]" (translation by Robert A. J. Gagnon).

+ Genesis 1:26 (in the Septuagint): "Let us make a human [*anthropon*] according to our image [*eikona*] and according to our likeness [*homoiosin*]; and let them rule over the fish of the sea, and the birds [*peteinon*] of the air, and the cattle [*ktenon*], and over all the earth, and over all the reptiles [*herpeton*] which creep upon the earth."[45]

The overlap in the vocabulary is undeniable, continuing with the use of *arsen* (male) and *thelus* (female) in Genesis 1:27 and Romans 1:26–27, which cements the connection between Genesis 1 and Romans 1 and makes absolutely clear that Paul is saying that homosexual acts (be they male or female) are contrary to God's natural, intended order for His creation—and that applies whether they are promiscuous or monogamous. They are wrong in God's sight either way, in every situation and setting.[46]

In the words of the (nonfundamentalist) German theologian Ernst Käsemann, "Moral perversion is the result of God's wrath, not the reason for it."[47] Or, as expressed by another (nonfundamentalist) German theologian, Wolfhart Pannenberg: "The biblical assessments of homosexual practice are unambiguous in their rejection." And "the entire biblical witness includes practicing homosexuality without exception among the kinds of behavior that give particularly striking expression to humanity's turning away from God."[48]

CONSUMED WITH PASSION

Isn't it best to swallow this tough pill and go to the Father for help and grace rather than to live in denial and twist the Scriptures? Perhaps some of you reading this book have been trying to convince yourself that the gay interpretations of Romans 1 were correct, but deep down you had questions that you couldn't resolve. Now you know why! But don't despair. Our heavenly Father is waiting to take you in His arms and pour out His love for you, and through His Son Jesus you will find everything you need.

And since I am being as candid and up front as possible, but, I pray, with mercy, grace and compassion, I need to broach one more difficult subject. Can we continue on this journey together?

I'm fully aware that there is massive, perverted, out-of-control, sexual sin *among heterosexuals*, and that's why through the decades, as a heterosexual,

I have preached against heterosexual lust, adultery, pornography, and no-fault divorce, using the many illustrations from Scripture, history, and contemporary society that are so readily available. And I'm fully aware that there are constant scandals involving female school teachers and their male students; in fact, we have an epidemic of these sinful, heterosexual unions in America today. So, to be perfectly clear, homosexuals do not have a monopoly on sexual sin, and I have no doubt that there are homosexual couples who try to live morally (believing that monogamous, committed gay relationships are blessed by God) and heterosexual couples who live quite immorally.

But it is also undeniable (and well documented) that gay and bisexual men are, on average, much more promiscuous than their heterosexual counterparts (and much more prone to engage in anonymous sexual encounters, some even pointing to this sexual "liberty" as a positive), while even lesbians are, on average, more promiscuous than their heterosexual counterparts.[49]

Writing in my book *A Queer Thing Happened to America*, I asked some questions to help explain why this is so:[50]

> First, is it true that men, in general, are more focused on sex than women? I think there is widespread agreement that this is true.[51] Second, do women have a domesticating, tempering effect on men when they are in a committed relationship together? Again, I think this is generally recognized to be true as well.[52] As Christian apologist Frank Turek asks, "How many married men do you know who rove neighborhoods in street gangs?"[53]
>
> So, putting these two questions together, if men are more overly focused on sex than women, and if gay men do not experience the tempering effects of a long-term, committed relationship with a woman, isn't it likely that gay men will be especially promiscuous? This is not because they are especially evil; it is simply a logical corollary of being a gay male, as noted boastfully by gay sex columnist Dan Savage, "Gay people know more about sex than straight people do, have more sex than straight people do, and are better at it than straight people are."[54]
>
> Let's take this a little further. Heterosexual sex is inherently procreative in nature, even if every instance of sex doesn't result in children, so there is a major procreative side to sex for heterosexuals,

in addition to the intimate and sensual side. In contrast, the procreative dimension of sex is inherently absent in homosexual relationships, in every instance, without exception. Thus, along with the intimate side of a sexual and romantic relationship, sex itself can easily take on a more dominant role in gay relationships. Wouldn't this aspect of sexuality within homosexual relationships naturally lead to more promiscuity and to a broader emphasis on sex itself?

And as far as gay men are concerned, they don't have partners who have to deal with various aspects of womanhood and motherhood, both of which also have a tempering effect on married, heterosexual relationships. This too places the emphasis more squarely on sex itself, as explained by gay activist and author Michael Bronski, who stated approvingly that "homosexuality offers a vision of sexual pleasure completely divorced from the burden of reproduction: sex for its own sake, a distillation of the pleasure principle."[55]

A comprehensive 1987 study, the Multicenter AIDS Cohort Study, indicated that more than three-quarters of the nearly 5,000 gay men interviewed "reported having 50 or more lifetime sexual partners, and over 80 percent had engaged in receptive anal intercourse with at least some of their partners in the previous two years."[56] A 1997 survey of 2,583 sexually active homosexual men in Australia—and thus almost twenty years after AIDS was recognized—revealed that, "Only 15% of the men reported having fewer than eleven sex partners to date, while on the other end of the spectrum 15% had over 1000 sex partners. A whopping 82% had over 50 partners and nearly 50% had over 100."[57]

A major study titled "Sex in America" indicated that gays and lesbians, combined as one group, had *twelve times* as many lifetime sexual partners as heterosexuals and *seven times* as many sexual partners in the twelve months prior to the study. Even more striking was the fact that heterosexual couples were *forty-one times* more likely to be monogamous than homosexual couples.[58] In fact, in the 1984 volume *The Male Couple* by D. McWhirter and A. Mattison, the authors, themselves a gay couple, found that:

> ...of the 156 couples studied, only seven had maintained sexual fidelity; of the hundred couples that had been together for more

than five years, none had been able to maintain sexual fidelity. The authors noted that "The expectation for outside sexual activity was the rule for male couples and the exception for heterosexuals."[59]

To be sure, some gay activists have criticized this study, calling it outdated or inaccurate, but more recent studies and articles have confirmed this trend,[60] some of them including candid admissions that homosexual couples—especially male—play by a different set of rules. Typical is a 2003 study that found three-quarters of gay men in Canada who had been in relationships longer than a year were not monogamous. Researcher Barry Adam, a gay professor at the University of Windsor in Canada, interviewed seventy gay men who were part of sixty couples. He found that those who were monogamous were more likely to be younger and to have been in relationships for less than three years.

> "One of the reasons I think younger men tend to start with the vision of monogamy is because they are coming with a heterosexual script in their head and are applying it to relationships with men," Adam said. "What they don't see is that the gay community has their own order and own ways that seem to work better."[61]

Yes, the gay community has its own order and its own ways, including a new definition of monogamy, which includes things like, "We are monogamous. We only have three-ways together and are never sexual with others apart from each other."[62] Others, like Dan Savage, advocate being "monogamish," arguing that true monogamy is actually harmful to the great majority of couples, be they gay or straight.[63] All this is confirmed in a 2009 article in the *International Journal of STD and AIDS*, based on surveys of 5,168 men in the UK from 1999–2001, reporting that, "For the preceding 5 years the median numbers of partners for heterosexual, bisexual and exclusively homosexual men were 2, 7 and 10, respectively. Thus bisexuals and exclusively homosexual had 3.5 and 5 times, respectively, as many partners as the heterosexual men."[64]

All this means that Paul's words in Romans 1:27 have an abiding relevance, as he stated that "the men likewise gave up natural relations with women and were consumed with passion for one another, men committing shameless acts with men and receiving in themselves the due penalty for their error."

This also helps to explain why gay and bisexual men today account for a massively disproportionate percentage of STDs in general and HIV infection in particular. (To be blunt, it is *not* homophobic to report this—really, even the thought of this being "homophobic" is outrageous—anymore than it is obesophobic to report that obesity is unhealthy and leads to many serious health consequences.) Most recently (and continuing a common trend), the Centers for Disease Control and Prevention (CDC) reported that from 2008 to 2011 some 94 to 95 percent of HIV cases among boys and young men aged thirteen to twenty-four were linked to homosexual sex, despite the fact that these boys and young men make up just 3 percent of the population.[65] God simply didn't design men to be with men, and this is one of the sad consequences.[66] There are even indications that negative health consequences exist for lesbians as opposed to heterosexual women, one reason being that most of them will never get pregnant, and there are actually health benefits to pregnancy over the course of a lifetime.[67]

I'm sure that many "gay Christians" seek to live holy lives before the Lord based on their view that they can be "holy homosexuals"—to use the title of gay pastor Mike Piazza's book[68]—and I am certainly not saying that AIDS is divine judgment on homosexuals.[69] (Statistically, especially in Africa, far more heterosexuals have died of AIDS than homosexuals, although in Africa as well, the percentage of homosexual STDs per capita is massively higher than the percentage of heterosexual STDs.[70])

But I am saying that God designed men and women to have vaginal sex, not anal sex (all the more did He not design men to have anal sex with other men), which is one reason there are more health risks associated with these acts. After all, the anus is part of the body's digestive and disposal system, not the reproductive system, and it is designed to expel feces rather than to accept penetration, let alone play any role in reproduction. This in stark contrast with a women's sexual organs, which are designed for intercourse and reproduction.[71]

In addition to this aspect of divine intent in our physical design, there is also a unique chemistry between a man and a woman that cannot be duplicated when people of the same-sex join together in committed relationships. (See chapter 4 for more on this.)

In sum, then, in Romans 1 Paul is outlining the general, downward progression of the human race in ancient history—idolatry, heterosexual immorality, homosexual acts, and then "every kind of wickedness, evil, greed, and depravity." These are all aspects of our fallen nature, the result of worshipping created things rather than the Creator, and so Paul is not saying that all homosexual acts are the result of a downward, sinful tendency in every individual's life but rather evidence of the fallen state of the human race. And so there is no possible way to imagine that Paul would sanction any type of same-sex act, be it in a committed relationship or in an anonymous sexual encounter. Such acts are contrary to God's created order, and God's ways are best.[72]

And this leads us to a very important point, and one we must approach with real sensitivity. When addressing Paul's words in Romans 1, we have seen that gay theologians consistently say, "But Paul is speaking against homosexual acts that took place in the context of idolatry, and we are not idol worshippers. In fact, we love God and believe in Jesus Christ."

To be sure, in this chapter we exposed the fallacy of this interpretation, but there's something important I must say, since I know that it is far better to be truthful, even when the truth hurts, than to compromise the truth for the sake of popularity and acceptance. In short, there *is* an idolatry that many "gay Christians" engage in, and in a sense it is the ultimate idolatry, the idolatry of self, and it goes like this: "I have wrestled with what the Bible says about homosexual practice, and I'm not 100 percent sure what to make of it. But I am 100 percent sure that I'm gay—that's who I am to the core of my being—and therefore I will interpret the Word through the lens of *me*—through the lens of who I am."

Yes, this too is idolatry, putting ourselves and our desires and our needs in the place of God, interpreting the Word based on who we are rather than interpreting who we are based on the Word. This is a surefire path to deception. In stark contrast with this, to follow Jesus means to realize that we are not our own, that we have been bought with a price, that we are to deny ourselves and take up the cross and follow Him (see chapter 5), and that we live for another Lord and Master—and in so doing, we find abundant life.[73]

As expressed in somewhat academic terms by Professor Thiselton, looking at both of the passages we have been discussing (namely, 1 Corinthians 6:9

and Romans 1:26–27), "What is clear from the connection between 1 Cor 6:9 and Rom 1:26–29 and their OT backgrounds is Paul's endorsement of the view that idolatry, i.e., placing human autonomy to construct one's values above covenant commitments to God, leads to a collapse of moral values in a kind of domino effect."[74]

So, what will it be? Your will or His? Exalting self or surrendering self? Human autonomy or divine rule? One leads to death, the other to life. What will it be?

Chapter 9

EVERYTHING REPRODUCES
AFTER ITS OWN KIND

The "gay Christian" argument: "Gay Christianity" produces wonderful, holy fruit, comparable to the best, holy fruit produced by heterosexual believers, and aside from welcoming same-sex couples, "gay Christians" read the Bible just like the rest of the church.

The biblical response: God has ordained that everything produces after its own kind, and since the root of "gay Christianity" is not pure, it produces an impure reading of the Scriptures and impure values.

A CCORDING TO THE Creation account in Genesis 1, God made plant and animal life to reproduce after its own kind: "Then God said, 'Let the land produce vegetation: seed-bearing plants and trees on the land that bear fruit with seed in it, according to their various kinds.' And it was so. The land produced vegetation: plants bearing seed according to their kinds and trees bearing fruit with seed in it according to their kinds. And God saw that it was good" (Gen. 1:11–12, NIV).

It was the same for the animal kingdom: God made everything reproduce after its own kind. And so, cows reproduce cows, elephants reproduce elephants, owls reproduce owls, and so on. This is because the seed for reproduction is within the species itself, and so it can only reproduce what it is.

The same also applies to the spiritual kingdom: complacency reproduces complacency, carnality reproduces carnality, fear reproduces fear. In contrast, purity reproduces purity, godliness reproduces godliness, compassion reproduces compassion. To use the language of the Scriptures, we will always reap what we sow.[1] This is a principle found throughout the Bible.[2]

Now, proponents of "gay Christianity" will argue that the church's traditional teaching about homosexuality produced fear and bondage, oppression and depression, and even suicide, whereas the new, gay-affirming message produces liberty, joy, freedom, and spirituality. In part, I agree with that assessment, although my perspective and approach are quite different, as I'll share in the next chapter. But what I find undeniable is that there is a strong sexual, even perverted, trajectory that "gay Christianity" inevitably takes, leading to spiritual destruction and deception. This is what is ultimately reproducing "after its own kind."

Some critics of my book *A Queer Thing Happened to America* accused me of grossly misrepresenting "gay Christianity" in the chapter titled "Queer Theology, a Translesbigay Bible, and a Homoerotic Christ." They claimed that I painted a distorted—indeed, twisted—picture of what "gay Christians" really believed and that I took the worst and most extreme quotes from the most fringe gay theologians, thereby making all "gay Christians" look bad.

In that chapter I spoke of the "inevitable direction in which 'gay Christianity' develops," noting that, "Jesus taught that we could judge a tree by the fruit it produces." This led to the question: "What kind of fruit does this 'gay Christian' tree produce?" I answered this by saying, "In some respects, it resembles the traditional, biblical faith; in other respects, it is shockingly—and tellingly—different."[3]

Then, after citing some of the writings of a leading gay theologian, Rev. Robert E. Goss, writings so profane that I hesitated to quote them in the book, I noted, "Of course, there are conservative 'gay Christians' who would be appalled by such sexual depictions, yet the sad fact is that 'gay Christian' literature has a strong sexual fixation that is marked by extremely frequent references to sexual orientation and sexual issues."[4] Was this a fair assessment?

I'm fully aware that many conservative "gay Christians" would completely renounce this sexual-theological trash—in fact, I assume that many have never heard of it—and yet the point I was making still stands. There really is an inevitable direction in which "gay Christianity" develops, and it is the direction of sexual fixation mingled with theological interpretation, leading to profane readings of the Word and blasphemous depictions of the Lord.

The fact is, I didn't go looking for these sexual, often perverse, interpretations (contrary to the accusations of the critics). I found them everywhere I looked in the leading "gay Christian" writings as I began to research the literature and listen to the messages. These texts found me more than I found them. (For a case in point, see chapter 7, "The Healing of the Centurion's Servant.")

And so, the reason I quoted Robert Goss (now using the name Robert Shore-Goss) was because he was a highly respected leader in the largest "gay Christian" denomination, the Metropolitan Community Churches (MCC), and because his writings were often cited in "gay Christian" literature. To my shock, Goss wrote things that could only be called sexually perverse—and he did this while speaking of Jesus![5]

And when I went online to look at the program for the biannual conference of the Metropolitan Community Churches, I was shocked to find topics such as these (alongside seminars on church planting and other practical ministry issues):

+ Building Closets or Opening Doors (Polyamory)

+ Finding God in Your Erotic Experience

+ Our Gay Gaze: Using Your Eyes in Whole New Ways to Get What You Want (part of the blurb for this seminar said, "Whether you're cruising for sex, intimacy, or spirit, this experiential, intimate session will open your eyes about how to use your gaze to get what you most need. You won't ever see gay men the same way again.")[6]

These are seminars at a *church conference*?

Not surprisingly, this same sex-driven mind-set was present at the annual "Creating Change Conference" held by the National Gay and Lesbian Task Force, one of the major gay activist events of the year. The theme of the 2010 conference, held in Dallas, Texas, was "Live Large. THINK BIG." Yet the front cover of the conference program book featured two prominent captions: "ACTION is HOT," and "Power is sexy."[7] How common is this for a civil rights/equality conference?[8]

A welcome letter from Dallas Mayor Tom Leppert (dated February 3, 2010) stated that, "The Creating Change Conference has a long history of nurturing political skills and leadership within the LGBT community, and we are pleased that you chose Dallas for this year's event."[9] Yet this conference devoted to "nurturing political skills and leadership within the LGBT community" has some very peculiar elements to it.

Really now, how many political activist conferences print out warnings against sexual harassment for conference attendees? But the NGLTF found it necessary to do so, listing these specific examples of "unwelcome behavior of a sexual nature" in their program book:[10]

+ Touching someone without their permission (grabbing, hugging, petting)

+ Sexual propositions

+ Sexually offensive pictures, magazines, notes, calendars, cartoons, or jokes

+ Unwanted flirtations or advances

+ Graphic comments about an individual's body or dress

+ Verbal abuse (including sexual insults and name-calling)

+ Repeated pressure or requests for sexual activities

+ Rewards for granting sexual favors or the withholding of rewards for refusing to grant sexual favors

And remember: this is a major, political, gay activist conference, yet it is understood that unwelcome sexual behavior could very well be an issue too. After all, this *is* about sex and sexuality, at least on some unavoidable level. (On a more minor level, note that in order to acknowledge the needs of transgender people, all restrooms are designated as "gender neutral," the program book explaining, "Regardless of what bathroom you are in, please let everyone pee in peace."[11])

How many other political activist conferences feature a Saturday night "Mas-Queer-Ade Ball?"[12] How many offer fourteen different workshops under the heading of "Sexual Freedom"? Some of the workshops offered include:[13]

- Creating Communities of Resistance/Change Through Innovative Sex Organizations and Businesses

- Sexual Liberation as a Framework for Change

- Young and Poly

- Mapping Your Desire

- Kink, Race and Class

- Our Common Cause—A place for polyamorous/non-monogamy communities in the LGBTIQA movement

- Polyamory/Nonmonogamy Caucus

- Sex Workers' Caucus

- Leather Caucus

And yet we are told that LGBT issues are simply matters of social justice and *not* sexually focused (or, often, sexually aberrant) matters as well. This is simply not true, as evidenced by the subject matter of just this one workshop (a workshop, I remind you, that is *not* being offered at a gay sex fair somewhere but rather at perhaps the most prestigious political activist conference in the entire LGBT movement). Note the subject matter well, and then note who is presenting it:

Leather Caucus: Sexual Freedom

Whatever your kink—come meet your peers—fetishists of every stripe, the tippity tops, the brash bottoms, the doms and dommes, the bois, the high femmes, the givers and takers, the lovers of pain and pleasure. We'll all be here, queer and fabulous.

Presenters: Jaime M. Grant, Director of the Policy Institute, National Gay and Lesbian Task Force, Washington DC.[14]

Grant is obviously a mainstream player in a mainstream (indeed, flag-ship) LGBT political organization, and at this conference he was giving a presentation on bizarre sexual practices, including sado-masochism—but, we're told, it's not about sex!

The Creating Change Conference even has an annual Leather Leadership

Award, in 2010 awarded to Hardy Haberman, "a member of many BDSM/Fetish organizations including Leather Rose Society, National Leather Association-Dallas, Discipline Corps and a founding member of Inquisition-Dallas."[15] (Remember that BDSM stands for "bondage, discipline, sadism, masochism." As for Inquisition-Dallas, it bills itself as "exclusive adult dating for the BDSM, bondage, kink & fetish community.") This is what the NGLT awards and celebrates?

Yes, I understand that this is a political organization rather than a ministry organization, but the point I'm making is clear: gay activism and "gay Christianity" *are* often largely about sex, and ultimately some of what drives "gay Christianity" is the desire to have God-approved, God-blessed sex with people of the same gender.[16]

Returning to my studies in gay theology and gay biblical scholarship, with real interest, I purchased the *Queer Bible Commentary*, the only work of its kind to date and the combined efforts of some of the top LGBT scholars in the world. There too I found interpretations of Scripture that were sexually perverse, along with bizarre theological propositions like this one from Robert Goss, speaking of God's role in the virgin birth: "...God is more akin to queers, the sexual outlaws who break cultural codes of decency and sexual restrictedness. God is a 'faggot,' for God creatively pursues the conception of Jesus outside the bounds of vanilla religiosity. But Mary is queer as well..."[17]

Some leading Jewish thinkers, most of them LGBT, authored a series of essays on the weekly Torah portions (meaning, the weekly synagogue readings covering the Five Books of Moses in one year). I ordered that book, titled *Torah Queeries*, as soon as it was available, and to my dismay, once again I found sexually perverse readings of God's Word, including the idea that when the fire of God burned up Aaron's two sons Nadab and Abihu in Leviticus 10, it was an act of sexual passion:

> God accepts the men and takes them into his innermost sanctum, and he consumes them in an act of burning passion.... This text offers an example of homoerotic attraction between human males and the male God of the Bible. Each desires to come closer to the other. Nadav and Avihu strip themselves literally and figuratively— they strip themselves of their clothing, their societal expectations,

of confining rules—and they come forward. God meets them in a passion of fire, taking them in completely.[18]

Words fail to describe such a horrific reading of sacred Scripture, and yet it is reflective of some of the top gay Jewish scholarship. Need we ask why?

GROSS MISREADINGS OF SCRIPTURE

Before buying that volume, I had purchased a collection of essays on Old Testament themes written by respected gay scholars, only to find material so grotesque that I could only quote it in abbreviated form in *A Queer Thing Happened to America*, and I will not repeat it here.[19]

That's how I compiled the material in the chapter, material that was so offensive and grievous that I literally broke down in tears when talking with my wife, Nancy, after completing the chapter. Yet the material was reflective of what was commonly found in gay biblical interpretation. It was not cherry-picked to make "gay Christians" look bad. It was found in work after work that I read and researched.

In the last couple of years I began to notice the name of Patrick Cheng through his columns in the online *Huffington Post*. He is a former lawyer, now theologian, who holds a PhD in systematic theology from Union Theological Seminary in New York and is associate professor of historical and systematic theology at the Episcopal Divinity School in Cambridge, Massachusetts. He is openly and proudly gay and is a licensed minister with the MCC.[20]

In August 2012 Cheng participated in the Human Rights Campaign's (HRC) Summer Institute for Religious and Theological Study, speaking to "15 lucky students, leading theologians, scholars and activists" and serving as "a resident mentor and scholar encouraging and supporting the next generations of students in bringing their ideas about sexuality, religion, theology, race and identity into the wider arena."[21] (For those unfamiliar with the HRC, it is the world's largest gay activist organization, so influential that President Obama has spoken at some of their fund-raising dinners in Washington DC.)

Sharon Groves, director of the HRC's Religion and Faith Program, hailed Cheng as "a leading scholar on LGBT issues and faith," also heaping praise on his 2012 book *From Sin to Amazing Grace: Discovering the Queer*

Christ.[22] Speaking of his 2011 volume *Radical Love: An Introduction to Queer Theology,* James H. Cone, the Charles Augustus Briggs Distinguished Professor of Systematic Theology at Union Theological Seminary, said, "Patrick Cheng's *Radical Love* is not only an excellent introduction to LGBT theology but an important contribution to the discipline of theology and the life of the church. It is a must read for anyone who cares about the health of the church and theology today."[23]

Does Patrick Cheng qualify as a respected "gay Christian" leader? Here are some representative excerpts from *Radical Love.*[24] (If you are easily upset when the things of the Lord are mishandled and abused, you might want to skip the rest of this chapter. For those who continue to read, be prepared to have your heart broken and your sensibilities shocked. It was very painful for me to type these words out, and I had to ask the Lord to cleanse me from the filth of them as I typed.)

Describing how Jesus allegedly crossed "gender boundaries," Cheng wrote:

> Kittredge Cherry, a lesbian writer and Metropolitan Church minister, has portrayed Jesus Christ as a bisexual-transgender person who has sexual relationships with the apostle John, Mary Magdalene, as well as a "pan-gendered, omni-erotic" Holy Spirit. In her novel, *Jesus in Love,* Jesus speaks in the first person about his multiple sexual identities: "My nature can't be captured in the confines of human language, either. I switch between being gay, straight, lesbian, bisexual, trisexual.... If you want to get technical about my love life, it's masturbation as much as incest, since we're really all one Being. But none of the labels really fit." For Cherry, this bisexual-transgender Christ is "too queer for most churches, but too Christian for most queers."[25]

Does it scare you to read such blasphemy? It comes from the pen of one the foremost young gay theologians on the scene today.

Speaking of the work of the Spirit, he writes:

> [The] fundamental connection between the Holy Spirit, the desire for God, and sexual passion is illustrated by a humorous story that Robert Williams tells about his friend, another openly gay minister, who, at the moment of a particularly intense orgasm during

an anonymous sexual encounter on a beach, started inexplicably to engage in glossolalia, or the charismatic practice of speaking in tongues....As Williams' friend explained, "No longer could I differentiate between the sexual experience and my prayer life...." Indeed, who hasn't invoked—or heard—the divine name during a particularly intense orgasm or sexual experience?[26]

As a charismatic Christian myself—meaning that I too speak in tongues as a language of prayer and praise—it is hard for me to imagine anything more God-mocking than a gay minister speaking in tongues at the climax of his anonymous sexual encounter with another man on a beach. Who can find words to describe such profaning of the sacred things of the Holy Spirit?

Somehow Cheng even manages to pervert the very concept of holiness, which, he claims, is the "second mark of the church." (The first mark he delineated was "oneness.") He cites lesbian theologian Elizabeth Stuart, who describes holiness as:

> ...where the divine meets the human, or where God's grace is manifested on earth. For Stuart, the holy occurs whenever we attempt to give back to God what God has done for us. Specifically, what God has done for us is characterized by the sheer gift of grace, which can only be "repaid" in our own radical generosity and hospitality to others. Thus, a community marked by holiness is one that exhibits radical generosity and hospitality to others.[27]

To be sure, this is a limited definition of holiness, but that is not what is troubling. Rather, it is the illustration of hospitality as holiness that is so grievous. Cheng continues:

> Kathy Rudy has written about how anonymous sexual encounters actually can be a form of hospitality and welcome to others. What Rudy proposes is an ethic of hospitality, which is essentially the reverse of the Sodom and Gomorrah narrative. Indeed, the early Christian church was marked by its generosity of welcoming those who were outsiders. As such, this ethic of hospitality should be the overriding norm for all issues, including sexuality. As a result, certain sexual acts—including anonymous or communal sex—would

not be forbidden *per se*, but rather measured by the degree to which the actions are welcoming and hospitable.[28]

What? Cheng claims that "anonymous sexual encounters actually can be a form of hospitality and welcome to others," and thus an expression of the holiness that is a mark of the church? Talk about calling good evil and evil good.

But Cheng is not only a theologian. He is a practical teacher, wanting to explain exactly how this works itself out:

> As a result of this ethic, according to Rudy, "all genders are collapsed into Christian, and all Christians go about this seamless work of God." The only distinction that ultimately matters is whether one is "working toward the new creation" (that is, "church") or not (that is, "the world"). Thus extrapolating from Rudy's ethic of hospitality, queer people—indeed, all people—might very well find ecclesial holiness in a variety of unorthodox places, including a circuit party, a gathering for nude erotic massage at the Body Electric School, or a sex party. This, indeed, would be a manifestation of church as radical love.[29]

Yes, in this twisted theological world—to use Cheng's word, this "queer" world—we "might very well find ecclesial holiness in a circuit party [where thousands of gay men come together for a night and day of dancing, drugs, and sex], a gathering for nude erotic massage at the Body Electric School, or a sex party." To quote the words of Jesus again, judge the tree by its fruit!

What about Cheng's 2012 volume, *From Sin to Amazing Grace*, the book so highly recommended by the faith arm of the HRC?[30] Part two of the book is called "Discovering the Queer Christ," with the first chapter titled "Model One: The Erotic Christ." Once again, he cites Kittredge Cherry:

> Kittredge Cherry, a lesbian minister with the Metropolitan Community Churches, also has written extensively about the Erotic Christ. Cherry has published a book, *Art That Dares*, in which she reproduces images of contemporary art that depict the Erotic Christ. For example, some of these images include a queer interpretation of the Stations of the Cross by the New York City painter Douglas Blanchard in which a gay Jesus Christ

is arrested, tortured, and executed. Other images include Becki Jayne Harrelson's "Judas Kiss," which depicts a nearly naked Jesus and Judas in a passionate embrace. Many of these images—and other works—can be found on Cherry's website and blog, "Jesus in Love."[31]

But, of course, there's more stomach-turning trash:

> Gay male theologians—especially those who grew up Roman Catholic—also have written about the Erotic Christ, most commonly in terms of Jesus Christ being an object of erotic desire. For example, Donald Boisvert, a gay professor of religion at Concordia University, wrote a chapter on the Erotic Christ in his book *Sanctity and Male Desire*. In that chapter, Boisvert talks about his own "special enthrallment" from a young age with the corpus of the crucified Jesus Christ. For Boisvert, the "handsomely glorious body of Jesus [that] hung from the cross" creates a space in which he and other gay men could "enter into an act of erotic and spiritual intimacy with their lord."[32]

Can this be described as anything less than perverse?

I was criticized for citing the aforementioned Robert Goss (now Shore-Goss) in a similar context, but Cheng makes reference to him as well in this identical context:

> As a Jesuit priest, Shore-Goss envisioned Jesus as a lover. Shore-Goss writes that he had "sexual intercourse with Jesus" many times while masturbating, and it was a natural progression for Shore-Goss to evolve as a "lover of Jesus" to "falling in love with a man." Later, when Shore-Goss had sex with his first lover, Frank, he experienced lovemaking as communion. He writes: "I saw Christ's face within Frank's face as I penetrated him in intercourse" and "[a]s I was penetrated, I felt penetrated by Frank and Christ."[33]

I truly apologize for having to share these things, but one of the functions of light is that it exposes darkness and makes all things visible (Eph. 5:11–13), as unpleasant as it is.

In the chapter on "The Out Christ" Cheng cites other gay theologians who suggest that Jesus was gay or bisexual and even involved in a homosexual relationship with Lazarus (and/or other men). Similarly, when writing about "The Transgressive Christ," Cheng refers to a wide range of "gay Christian" literature that argues that "the Transgressive Christ can be seen in bisexual, transgender, and intersex christologies that respectively challenge binary thinking with respect to sexuality, gender identity, and biological sex." He notes further that "transgender theologians such as Justin Tanis have written about a transgender Christ who challenges the gender binaries of masculine and feminine."[34] And on and on it goes.

To cite just one more example out of many that could be cited, in the chapter on the "The Self-Loving Christ" Cheng notes that "gay Christian" scholar "Mark Jordan has written about how a fully embodied corpus [meaning, physical body] of Jesus Christ, complete with realistic genitals, might be one way in which LGBT people can encounter the Self-Loving Christ."[35] We can certainly judge the tree of "queer theology" by its fruit.

You might say, "But Patrick Cheng is an example of liberal gay theology, not conservative gay theology."

I'm fully aware of that. But the fact is that: (1) Cheng is a respected leader in the largest "gay Christian" denomination, the MCC; (2) he is recognized as a leading gay theologian by the largest gay activist organization, the HRC; (3) he is a regular contributor to the "Gay Voices" division of the religion section of the *Huffington Post*; (4) throughout his writings he cites many other "gay Christian" leaders; (5) he supports all the standard arguments for "gay Christianity"; (6) it is only in "gay Christian" literature that such blasphemous writings are commonly found; and 7) "gay Christians" are not renouncing these blasphemous interpretations and calling for the censure of those putting them forth. To the contrary, they are celebrating these theologians.

To repeat: I didn't have to go searching for these writings. I found them over and over again as I read the works of respected gay theologians, pastors, and leaders.

PUTTING SEXUALITY FIRST

It is also undeniable that many conservative "gay Christians" hold to some inexcusably sexual interpretations of the Scriptures, such as the claim that Jesus healed the boy-toy of a Roman soldier so they could continue their sexual relationship. (See chapter 7.) Others allege that Jesus had a sexual relationship with the apostle John or that the biblical characters Ruth and Naomi had a lesbian relationship.[36] This is the inevitable trajectory of "gay Christianity," given enough time.

Why is this the case? It is because sexuality comes first and the Bible second, or, put another way, "gay Christians" start with the perspective of, "I am 100 percent sure that I am gay (or bisexual or transgender), but I am not sure what the Scriptures say about homosexuality (or bisexuality or transgenderism). This much I do know: I cannot deny who I am, and I must be true to myself. So I will now read the Bible through the lens of my sexual identity."

And so, rather than starting with the sure foundation that God and His Word are unchangeably true while everything else—including our sexuality—must be interpreted by God's standards, "gay Christians" interpret God and His Word through their sexuality, whether consciously or unconsciously. Once that is done, no matter how sincere the "gay Christian" may be, deception is inevitable. And as someone once said, the problem with deception is that it is very deceiving! That's why Jesus, Paul, James, and others in the Word often warned their hearers and readers about the danger of being deceived.[37]

Ultimately the Bible ends up being submitted to homosexual (or bisexual or transgender) identity rather than homosexual (or bisexual or transgender) identity being submitted to the Bible. And because there is an inordinate focus on sexual identity among "gay Christians," the Bible is often read with a disproportionate emphasis on sexual questions. It is not surprising, then, that gay theologians "discover" sexual references in scores of places where they certainly do not exist.[38]

Finally, because of the power of the sexual drive, combined with the deep human desire for intimacy, being "true to yourself" and satisfying your sexual and romantic desires becomes a spiritual act—something God somehow smiles on—even when it means engaging in sexual perversion. In the words of transgender theologian Justin Tanis, cited by Cheng, "We who are sexual deviants—defiantly and gladly different than the neighbors—need the freedom to be who we are."[39]

Who is Justin Tanis? Tanis was born female and then underwent sex-change surgery, subsequently becoming an ordained minister with the

MCC and earning advanced degrees from Harvard Divinity School and San Francisco Theological Seminary. Tanis has also been active—proudly so—in BDSM circles (standing for bondage, discipline, sadism, masochism).

On a BDSM web page introducing Tanis as the author of *Trans-Gendered: Theology, Ministry, and Communities of Faith*, this bio (dating to 2003) is used:

> **Justin Tanis** has been exploring BDSM since he finally convinced someone to tie him up and do wonderfully mean things to him 18 years ago. He graduated from the Journeyman II Academy (an 18-month leather training program) in 1997 and is currently the newsletter editor for the Leather Archives & Museum publication, *Leather Times*. He lives in Los Angeles and is looking forward to wherever his next adventure leads him.[40]

And none of this is hidden. When I did a Google search for "Justin Tanis," trying to find out what his original name was, this website, containing an interview with "Sensuous Sadie," was the sixth one listed.

Remarkably, according to Tanis, sexually deviant interests like this are common among members of his "gay Christian" denomination:

> **Sadie:** Your church has a strong contingent from the leather community. What in Christianity speaks to this very special group?

> **Justin:** People of Leather Among You is probably the largest affinity group within Metropolitan Community Churches. Our founder, Troy Perry, was interviewed in the 2001 Folsom Street Fair program and has a chapter in Mark Thompson's wonderful book *Leatherfolk* if your readers would like more background about that. There have been leatherfolk in MCC throughout our history and in many of our churches. One of MCC's greatest strengths is that we have people from many different spiritual perspectives—from radical to very conservative—so we have a wide range of people who will have their own spiritual reasons for being part of a Christian church. I would venture a guess that MCC speaks to this particular group of people because it is in MCC that they are free to pursue a spirituality that feels right to them without (or with less) of a judgment than they would experience in other

communities of faith and because their personal spiritual practice is strengthened through participation in a community.[41]

Once again, I didn't go looking for this information; it was there for the world to see, boldly, proudly standing as a testament to the justification of all kinds of sexual practices and perversions in the name of gay spirituality. And note that there is not the slightest shame in mentioning that "gay Christian" pioneer Troy Perry (mentioned also in chapter 10) was attending the infamous Folsom Street Fair in San Francisco, where male nudity is everywhere and sex acts are performed in broad daylight on the streets.[42]

Note also that Tanis explains that the MCC has "people from many different spiritual perspectives—from radical to very conservative." What unites them, then, is not so much their biblical convictions as much as their sexuality. They are "GAY Christians" more than they are "gay CHRISTIANS," otherwise they could not possibly be part of the same denomination.[43] Can you imagine any other setting where one church member feels that in order to please God he must remain celibate (because he is gay), while another church member finds spiritual release in anonymous same-sex encounters or proudly participates in public sadomasochistic acts?

Yes, everything reproduces after its own kind, and this is the undeniable fruit being proudly produced by "gay Christianity," certainly not among its most conservative adherents, but quite commonly among many adherents—and without shame at that. This is an inevitable trajectory once it is claimed that God makes people gay, that He is not opposed to homosexual practice and gender distinctions are not essential, and that Jesus even affirmed homosexual practice.

The Lord Jesus gives us the remedy: "Make the tree good, and its fruit [will be] good also." (See Matthew 12:33.) The question is how exactly we are to do this. That's what we'll take up in the next—and last—chapter of this book.

Chapter 10

BALANCING GRACE and TRUTH

The "gay Christian" argument: The Word of God and our own experiences both tell us that following Jesus and homosexual practice are perfectly compatible, as long as we are in committed relationships.

The biblical response: While it is possible to have same-sex attractions and be a devoted follower of Jesus, living a holy life and not yielding to those attractions or affirming them, it is impossible to follow Jesus and engage in same-sex practice at the same time.

I N THE FIRST chapter of this book, I quoted a powerful passage from Jewish scholar Jay Michaelson's important volume *God vs. Gay?* in which he, in turn, quoted the words of a New Testament scholar who said that "any interpretation of scripture that hurts people, oppresses people, or destroys people cannot be the right interpretation, no matter how traditional, historical, or exegetically respectable."[1]

That New Testament scholar was Professor Dale Martin, himself openly gay. It's important that we hear the full context of Professor Martin's words, since he brings a serious challenge. I encourage you to read it carefully:

> I take my stand with a quotation from an impeccably traditional witness, Augustine, who wrote, "Whoever, therefore, thinks that he understands the divine Scriptures or any part of them so that it does not build the double love of God and of our neighbor does not understand it at all" (Christian Doctrine 1.35.40).
>
> By this light, any interpretation of Scripture that hurts people, oppresses people, or destroys people cannot be the right interpretation, no matter how traditional, historical, or exegetically

respectable. There can be no debate about the fact that the church's stand on homosexuality has caused oppression, loneliness, self-hatred, violence, sickness, and suicide for millions of people. If the church wishes to continue with its traditional interpretation it must demonstrate, not just claim, that it is more loving to condemn homosexuality than to affirm homosexuals. Can the church show that same-sex loving relationships damage those involved in them? Can the church give compelling reasons to believe that it really would be better for all lesbian and gay Christians to live alone, without the joy of intimate touch, without hearing a lover's voice when they go to sleep or awake? Is it really better for lesbian and gay teenagers to despise themselves and endlessly pray that their very personalities be reconstructed so that they may experience romance like their straight friends? Is it really more loving for the church to continue its worship of "heterosexual fulfillment" (a "non-biblical" concept, by the way) while consigning thousands of its members to a life of either celibacy or endless psychological manipulations that masquerade as "healing"?

The burden of proof in the last twenty years has shifted. There are too many of us who are not sick, or inverted, or perverted, or even "effeminate," but who just have a knack for falling in love with people of our own sex. When we have been damaged, it has not been due to our homosexuality but to others' and our own denial of it. The burden of proof now is not on us, to show that we are not sick, but rather on those who insist that we would be better off going back into the closet. What will "build the double love of God and of our neighbor"?[2]

In reality, since the Scriptures plainly condemn same-sex practice as sinful, the burden of proof remains on people like Professor Martin, especially when we consider that there are countless thousands of believers who came out of homosexual lifestyles and who are blessed and content today. In fact, many of them claim that it was living as gay men and women that caused so much pain in their lives.

One man posted this on my Facebook page:

When I was in the "gay" deathstyle in the 80s, I TOO was a strong believer in/preacher of what is called "gay theology". Full of holes.

Full of mindless segways. Lacking wisdom. And lacking true love of God and neighbor. But boy, it sure FELT good! I was led (and led others) into a system of false gods and a lot of Michael Joncas sing-alongs. Ask Saint Augustine to join you in your prayer to our Lord Jesus to send His Holy Spirit to break their hearts of stone.[3]

One of my friends is a pastor in New York City, and he has a tremendous love for the LGBT community. A few years ago his church started a new outreach to gays and lesbians, and he told me with tears how broken and lost so many of them were and how many of them hated the life they were living. And this was not due to some alleged self-loathing because of societal homophobia. It was due to the fact that the way they were living caused them great pain. Thankfully quite a few of them have given their lives to the Lord and have experienced a deep transformation and are overflowing with a newfound joy and hope.

What does Dale Martin say to people like this? Or what does he say to a man who posted this comment on a website in response to one of my articles?

> I will use myself as an example on why this article is so correct. I have had same-sex attractions since I was a young boy. I started to go to church as a teenager and became a Christian. For years, I have prayed for (and been prayed for) these tendencies to go away, but they have not. In spite of that, I got married many years ago and have children and grandchildren. My wife knows of my struggles, although because I knew it was sin, I have never acted on my feelings. Is it easy all the time? No, although with time it has gotten easier. But I have made a choice that I will be faithful to God and to my family. Was I born this way? I don't know, but that does not matter. I would never choose to dishonor God by living out my desires. I love my wife very much although she understands that I am conflicted inside, but not to the point where I could ever be untrue to her. THAT would be "living a lie." Am I to be admired? No. Many Christians deal with tendencies which are contrary to God's Word, but I hope to be an encouragement to someone out there that thinks they cannot "stay the course." By God's grace, you can and should.[4]

And this brings us again to the root of the problem: Professor Martin's whole perspective, as powerful as it sounds and as sincerely motivated as it appears to be, is based on the false premise that your identity is defined by your sexual desires and romantic attractions and God is somehow obligated to affirm that identity. Consequently, he believes that the only options the church has are either to (wrongly) condemn who you are or (rightly) affirm who you are. All this is patently false, as this testimony here makes plain.

It was actually an Orthodox Jewish friend of mine who sent me Professor Martin's quote, a man whom we'll call Adam. He has struggled since puberty with same-sex attractions, and it was his homosexual desires that drove him to study in-depth everything he could on the subject, wanting to know if there really was scientific evidence that people are born gay (there is no such evidence), wanting to know if there really was evidence of people moving along the continuum from homosexual toward heterosexual, according to both the scientific literature and according to reliable testimony (there is such evidence), and if it was even reasonable to assume based on the scientific data we have about childhood development that altering one's sexual feelings was theoretically possible. In other words, he wondered if it was outlandish even to make such a claim based on what we know about childhood development and sexuality.

Adam knew, of course, that as an Orthodox Jew, homosexual practice was forbidden, and when he confided in different rabbis about his struggles, he was met with compassion and understanding. But he has lived with these deep-seated desires firsthand and has interacted with those from both sides of the debate, "ex-gays" and "ex-ex-gays" (in other words, those who tried to change and then went back to homosexual practice), so I asked him how he would respond to Martin's words.

He explained:

> First, if you adopt the sociopolitical version of "gay" identity, it's virtually a self-fulfilling prophecy that you'll despise yourself, feel oppressed, depressed, lonely, sick and whatever else, and that you'll feel people who don't affirm your "gay" identity hate you and want to hurt you and destroy you. If you shed that identity and victimhood status, and open yourself up to the love, compassion, and understanding of people who you formerly thought hated and despised your very core, you'll open up a whole new world

you never thought possible, and half your problems will be solved. Being single really isn't the worst thing in the world, even if it is difficult. We all have difficulties.

Some have unthinkable difficulties that make same-sex attractions pale in comparison, and plenty of straight people will stay single for the rest of their lives. Also, it is true that some have been mean and unkind, insensitive and such, and they should stop, apologize, and earnestly change their ways, but that isn't an argument in favor of homosexuality. It's just an argument that those people should do some serious soul-searching, and be nicer to their fellow human beings.[5]

Exactly! So, rather than saying, "I'm gay, and so everything else will be interpreted through that sexual identity paradigm," a person should say, "I'm a man (or woman) who experiences same-sex attraction," proceeding from that starting point. Then, according to my friend, who is living this out himself, "half your problems will be solved."

Why define your entire identity based on your romantic attractions and sexual desires?[6] Why not find your identity in the Lord and give your life unconditionally to Him, saying, "Father, I belong to You, and I'm trusting my whole life to You; so I'm believing that You'll help me find my way in dealing with these attractions and desires." This is a mind-set of hope and life, not despair and death.

Adam continued:

The idea that not "being gay" or engaging in efforts to alter one's sexual feelings in reconstructing personality is hogwash. The only objective and scientifically measurable component of same-sex attractions are sexual feelings and acts. Everything else is sociopolitical subjective additions to those objective facts, subjective additions that have only been around very recently. It's true that not all human goods can be measured objectively, but no gay person has made a solid argument that "gay" is in fact "who you are" and a definitive part of your identity if you experience same-sex attractions. So, if you've swallowed all that, then yes, it might be a difficult kind of "reconstruction."

What I mean is that many gay-affirmative people will say their sexuality is "who they are" and "essential to their being" and their "very core." They state all these like they are given, obvious and factually true. I wanted to counter this by saying that there is no objective evidence for any of these. All of it is subjective. The only objective thing is that you experience attractions, they are arousing to you, and that you can act on them. Both of these can be measured by scientists and proved by scientists, objectively. The rest cannot. This is what I meant.[7]

Is this making sense to you? Are you following what my Jewish friend is saying?

The other day, a "gay Christian" accused me of not understanding what I was talking about since I hadn't lived through what he had experienced. To an extent he's right, no matter how empathetic I try to be. But he can't say that to Adam, nor can he say that to Christian friends of mine who are ex-gay.

These ex-gay Christian friends know what it's like to grow up feeling different, then to realize they're actually attracted to the same-sex, then to accept (or embrace) the fact that they are gay (to use the contemporary understanding), then to come out of the closet, then, after living homosexually for some time—in some cases, for decades—to have a life-changing experience in the Lord and to realize that they are *not* in fact "gay" but rather flawed and broken children of God, just like the rest of us, all in need of the Great Physician.

The Word of God is clear on this: "All we like sheep have gone astray; we have turned—every one—to his own way; and the LORD has laid on him the iniquity of us all" (Isa. 53:6). As Paul explains, it is our very nature that is corrupt, and so, in a real sense, without Jesus all of us are rotten to the core:

And you were dead in the trespasses and sins in which you once walked, following the course of this world, following the prince of the power of the air, the spirit that is now at work in the sons of disobedience—among whom we all once lived in the passions of our flesh, carrying out the desires of the body and the mind, and were by nature children of wrath, like the rest of mankind.

—EPHESIANS 2:1–3

It is only our modern, post-sexual-revolution mentality that has defined one's entire personhood by one's homosexual desires. And it is reminiscent of the chaotic situation that prevailed during the Book of Judges, when "everyone did what was right in his own eyes" (Judg. 21:25).

That's why we now have an almost endless list of sexual identities (cited in chapter 2), along with more and more people like "Sally [who] considers himself a gender outlaw, playing outside the traditional definitions of man and woman. Sally runs his business as a man and has not had sex change surgery but considers himself a woman."[8]

And that's why we have more and more people like Renata Razza, who "was born female and came out as a lesbian at 15" but, a few years later, decided she wanted to take testosterone. Yet Razza "doesn't identify as male, nor does he [sic] want to live life as a man. Instead, Razza wants to live in a space between male and female. His identity of choice? Gender-queer. If bisexuals defy the notion that a person can be attracted only to one gender, gender-queers explode the concept that a person has to be one gender."[9]

Or, as one individual commented on the Ex-Gay Watch website:

> Being attracted to both genders it has not been a clear cut decision for me to seek a complete sex change. My therapist advised me that some people in my situation choose to live as "she-males", taking hormone therapy but not actually having the surgery. I have seriously considered this "third sex" option....I would love to be a genetic female but I can't force the public to accept me as such. I don't feel I should have to force fit myself into black and white roles [meaning male or female] just because other people need to categorize me in that way.[10]

What? Being a she-male? Considering a "third sex" option? Or being multiple genders at the same time? At the root of this thinking is the idea that if I'm attracted to both genders, then that's who I am (as in, "I'm bi") and I should give full expression to my desires. There are even Christians who claim to be bisexual believers, the ultimate expression of non-self-denial.[11] My heart goes out to these people!

Dale Martin explains that gay people "just have a knack for falling in love with people of our own sex."[12] (What a way of describing homosexuality!)

Well, it's also true that many married people have a knack for falling in love with people they're not married to, and polyamorous people have a knack for falling in love with several people at the same time, and, according to some researchers, siblings who have been separated as young children have a knack for falling in love with each other when they meet later in life due to what is called genetic sexual attraction.[13] Does any of this define who we are or justify our choices? Does the fact that we have strong, even overwhelming feelings mean that it's fine to act on those feelings?

Rev. Jerry Falwell had some poignant things to say in his response to Dr. Mel White. (If you recall, Dr. White was the Fuller Seminary professor and ghost writer for Jerry Falwell who has become a leading "gay Christian" activist. And Dr. White openly published his correspondence with Rev. Falwell, leading to Falwell's public response.) Jerry Falwell wrote:

> I do not question your claims that you have struggled with the temptations of homosexuality for much of your life.
>
> Every believer is similarly challenged in some area of life, according to Hebrews 12:1 "...Wherefore...let us lay aside every weight, and the sin which doth so easily beset us, and let us run with patience the race that is set before us."
>
> Every believer has a particular sin which "doth so easily beset him," be it homosexuality, dishonesty, heterosexual promiscuity, selfishness or ten thousand other transgressions of God's Law. While I do not believe these sins (including homosexuality) are genetically received, that is irrelevant. Inherited or learned, the Scriptures demand that sin be laid aside.
>
> You have written of your many attempts to conquer your inordinate affections early in your life. I do not doubt your sincerity nor the pain you have endured in the process. But this is also irrelevant. "The spirit of the prophet is subject to the prophet." *Moral behavior, like all human conduct, is a choice.*[14]

Before telling me that Falwell was lacking in compassion (which I personally don't sense here in the least), and before you challenge me with, "So, you want some gay man to marry your straight daughter and pretend to have a real marriage?", may I ask a simple question? Is what Rev. Falwell wrote true or false? Is moral behavior, like all human conduct, a choice?

He continued:

> Millions of godly and pure individuals have chosen to be single and celibate for life. They have determined to have no sexual relationship, heterosexual or homosexual, for a lifetime. Millions more have been widowed early in life and have chosen to remain unmarried and chaste for the remainder of their lives. *Because we are human beings, and not animals, we have the God-given capacity to govern our conduct, regardless our passions and feelings.*
>
> Therefore, Mel, there can be no justification for you allowing your passions and feelings to cause you to abandon your wife and family for a male lover, as you have done. The fact that your dear wife is "understanding," and does not hate you, in no way vindicates what you have done to her. This simply speaks to her character and the genuineness of her personal relationship with Christ....
>
> I personally know former homosexuals who have been delivered from the gay lifestyle and, with their spouses and children, now serve Christ as pastors and Christian workers.
>
> This is not to say that these former homosexuals have not been tempted over and over again. Some have, no doubt, reverted to immoral behavior at times, repented and started over. But, they have recognized the sinfulness of their sin and have decided to spend a lifetime trusting, obeying and serving God according to His Word. They have determined not to allow "the sin that doth so easily beset them" to destroy them and bring shame to their Lord and families.[15]

So rather than saying, "I'm gay, and Jesus died to help me fulfill my sexual identity," they should say, "I struggle with the sin of homosexuality, but by God's grace I will not be defined by it or ruled by it."

To reiterate, when I speak of people struggling with these issues, wherever they identify on the LGBT-and-beyond spectrum, there's not an ounce of condemnation or criticism in my heart toward them, and I only feel compassion for them in the midst of their challenges. But this underscores the fact that if we start with Dale Martin's paradigm (which begins with how the person feels about his sexuality and gender) combined with a false conception of what "sexual identity" means, and then we define reality based on those perceptions and reinterpret the Bible based on them, we end up with the tragically confused world I have been describing.

And lest you think I'm painting an exaggerated picture, I'll let Mel White speak for himself. He wrote:

> While throughout [my book] *Religion Gone Bad* I use "gay" and "gay and lesbian" or "lesbian and gay," I want to make it clear up front that I'm not just talking about gay men and lesbians but about all my lesbian, gay, bisexual, transgender, transsexual, intersex, queer, and questioning sisters and brothers. The "LGBT" alphabet soup option is an ugly abbreviation for a beautiful community. It leaves out other important sexual and gender minorities.[16]

To be sure, Jesus gave His life for every single person in the LGBTQ+ "community" Dr. White describes, but He does not affirm us in our confusion and struggles, nor does He die for us so we can fulfill our sexual and romantic attractions, as Professor Dan Via claimed. Instead, He gives Himself for us so we can experience new life and wholeness in Him, and it is only right and fair that we hear from the many men and women today who say, "That was me! Dr. White described who I used to be, but in Jesus I have found a brand-new life, and it is wonderful beyond words." Let's not mute their testimonies!

A FALSE CHOICE

Returning to my Jewish friend's response to Professor Martin, Adam takes exception to his statement that, "If the church wishes to continue with its traditional interpretation it must demonstrate, not just claim, that it is more loving to condemn homosexuality than to affirm homosexuals." As Adam rightly notes, "There is no 'condemning of gay people.' And the opposite of condemnation isn't necessarily praise. We could just as easily alter our tone or change the way we treat the issue. There isn't only one answer to this debate, condemn or affirm. It's a false choice. So the very assumption is wrong before you even answer it!"[17]

Exactly so. Let me illustrate this with a Facebook post by a pastor in California named Kris Vallotton:

I grew up in a Spanish home where affection for one another was normal. Everybody hugged and kissed one another; men hugged and kissed men, women did the same. My father drowned when I was three years old, leaving a great big hole in my heart for male attention and affection. My two stepfathers didn't like me (frankly I don't think they liked themselves), which served only to increase my need to feel loved and accepted by men. Actually I was starving for male attention and affection. Therefore I was attracted to men and loved when they put their arm around me or gave me a hug. I have no idea what would've happened in those formative years if someone would've taught me that these desires might make me a homosexual. But thankfully that never happened; instead I was taught that men have a special affection for other men that was different than a woman's affection for men (as was the same for women).

(This story is told with Jason's permission.) When my youngest son, Jason, was around eight years old, he committed a homosexual act with his friend. It took him a while to tell me about it, as he was living in a lot of shame. When he finally did, I told him, "Son, you were just being dumb and experimenting as young boys often do. Don't worry about it. Just ask God to forgive you and go on with life; it's no big deal." I'm not sure what would've happened if he would have been in a school system that taught that some people are born as homosexuals, bisexuals, and transsexuals. But thankfully he was never exposed to those options, and to this day he's never been sexually attracted to the same gender.

When we came to Bethel [the church in Redding, California, where Kris is a pastor], I was our main counselor for the first three years. Although I grew up on the streets, I realized in those years of counseling that I lived a pretty sheltered life. I was already exposed to the fact that there were people who were sexually attracted to the same gender from the time they were children, so that did not surprise me when they came in for help. My heart would break for them as I listened to their stories, the shame they carried, and the ridicule they endured. When you walk in somebody's shoes, you see things from a different perspective. And although my convictions on homosexuality have never changed, my compassion for people struggling with these desires has radically increased after many sessions of weeping with them over their pain.[18]

At this point, I should interject that Bethel Church is often criticized for putting *too much emphasis* on God's goodness and grace, so there's absolutely no way that anyone who knows them could call them "condemning" or "judgmental."[19] Yet that was one of the false premises of Dale Martin's position, namely, that the church has only two choices: to condemn or affirm someone's homosexuality. As my friend Adam pointed out, that is simply not true.

Pastor Kris continues:

> But what I was surprised to discover during my sessions at Bethel is how many people have sexual attractions (many from their youth) to all kinds of extreme perversions. The amount of people who are sexually attracted to little children and even babies would probably shock most of the population. Others are compelled to rape; the idea of sexually forcing themselves on somebody who resists them literally plagues some people. For the sake of the sensitivity of my readers I will leave it at that…but this doesn't even begin to touch stories told behind closed doors. Many of these people never carried out these acts but were literally tormented by the temptation to do the worst sexual acts imaginable. Others, of course, did give in to these temptations and live with tremendous guilt and self-hatred.
>
> *These experiences have taught me that when you define yourself by your temptations or your passions (instead of managing your appetite and resisting temptations), there is no bottom to that cesspool! The truth is that we all have temptations and appetites that are not healthy and must be managed or we will live with a deep sense of shame no matter what values our culture tries to validate, because God has written His own values on our hearts.*
>
> I have no desire to shame anybody who is struggling with temptation whether it be a homosexual or a person who struggles in any other way. I do think I have a unique insight into the pain they go through because I have mourned with many of them and to this day have the privilege of calling them my friends (some of them have chosen to embrace that lifestyle despite my help).

That being said, I also am concerned that the young Krises and Jasons of the world are being deceived into thinking that there's something wrong with them because of their temptations or their experience. It's for this reason I will continue to make my voice heard at the risk of being called a hater, which God knows I am not![20]

So we return to the basic question of this book, Can you be gay and Christian? If by that you mean, can you be committed to Jesus and serve Him faithfully while still having homosexual attractions—recognizing those attractions as contrary to God's design and resisting them as sinful—then the answer is yes, of course! You would join the ranks of some very committed, sensitive, devoted disciples of the past and present.[21] And you would join every other true follower of Jesus in the world, since all of us have aspects of our lives, sometimes to the core of our being, that we recognize as contrary to God's design and reject as sinful. And, as we have shared repeatedly through this book, being a disciple begins with denying ourselves and taking up the cross.

On the other hand, if by being gay and Christian you mean, can you be committed to Jesus and serve Him while practicing homosexuality—embracing your homosexual attractions as a gift from God and acting on them, thereby affirming your "gay" identity—then the answer is absolutely not. The Word of God is clearly against it.[22]

Personally, I am convinced that if you gave the Bible to one million people who had never read it before, and if they could read the original texts in Hebrew, Aramaic, and Greek, if you left them alone to study God's Word for one year, virtually none of them would come away with the idea that God approved of homosexual relationships or would ever endorse same-sex "marriages." It is only when the Bible is read through the eyes of same-sex desires or through contemporary understandings of sexuality in the aftermath of the sexual revolution that anyone would come away with the notion that homosexuality was a gift from God or that He approved of men having sex with men or women having sex with women. And it is only when we start with "self"—how I feel about things; who I perceive myself to be; what I like or don't like—that we effectively turn the gospel on its head, as if Jesus is here to do our will rather than us being here to do His will.

You might say, "But why do you keep bringing up the issue of sex? Being gay is far more than having sex with someone of the same gender." As one "gay Christian" once wrote to me:

> You somehow think that this is just about sex. Is your sexuality just a sexual act? Is that all your marriage to your wife is about? As your friend Andrew Marin once said, "Christians reduce being gay down to a sexual act and then blame them for it." I know gay couples that have relationships that many couples in the evangelical church could learn a great deal from.[23]

Oh, I certainly understand that being gay is not "just about sex," just as being heterosexual is not just about sex (although homosexuality is still commonly more focused on sexual issues, sexual identity, and often sex itself). And I'm sure there are many gay couples who are deeply committed to each other, and their relationships are not centered on sex. But are you telling me that sexual activity is *not* included in being gay? That you are perfectly happy to separate sexual relationships from the discussion? That having sex is not a normal part of being in an intimate relationship? That you would be perfectly willing to continue in a close friendship with your current partner (if you have one) and leave sex out of the picture? Or, to come at this from another angle, if God clearly opposes same-sex sexual relationships, are you willing to lose your relationship with God over sex?

One of the most disturbing things I observed in reading the stories of "gay Christians" is that the sexual ethic seems to be, "If it's gay, it's OK," by which I mean: even if the act was clearly immoral—meaning, if the homosexual union constituted adultery for a married man or fornication for an unmarried man—it was still considered to be fine, because the person was simply being true to who he or she was.

For example, in his autobiography the late Rev. Troy Perry, founder of the Metropolitan Community Churches, the world's largest "gay Christian" denomination, describes his first homosexual encounter with another boy at the age of nine, and he does so in glowing terms:

> I was nine when another young boy and I went into Tallahassee's Bird's Words to cut our own Christmas trees, and I had my first sexual encounter. The two of us sat in a forest clearing and played

with tumescent flesh that I had never previously shared with anyone. The stimulation we enjoyed was magical, a gift at the earliest onset of puberty. There was no fear or shame—there was only delight, the wonderful pleasure and happiness of a harmless and minor transgression. For me, those were the greatest years, the innocent time of religious and sexual discovery.[24]

How revealing this account is, especially when you realize that it comes from one of this generation's most prominent "gay Christian" leaders. Could you imagine a heterosexual Christian leader describing his first youthful sexual encounter with a little girl as an "innocent time of religious and sexual discovery"?[25]

Later in the book Perry describes how when he was a paid, traveling evangelist, both the young women and their boyfriends and brothers all liked him, "and occasionally the male attraction led to pleasant sexual interludes that never went beyond the state of tender exploration in which most healthy boys engage."[26] What? This is how a traveling preacher who belonged to a holiness denomination describes his sexual encounters with other young men? Even if these acts stopped short of intercourse, his description is quite telling, especially when he next explains that as for the women he was dating, "compromising acts of love were easily avoided, because of the strong Pentecostal belief that sexual intercourse outside of marriage is a terrible sin."[27] How ironic!

Then, newly married to his wife, Pearl, he had full-blown sex with another man, knowing it was what he wanted to do but with "nagging anxieties," saying to himself, "God, I'm a married man—with a wife in the next room! What will happen if I disregard a lifetime of inhibition?"

Still, he explains, "Eventually, I came to realize that what we were doing seemed right for me. No force was employed during that long night. Everything was different from anything I had known. It stopped short of being love, but was a marvelous education."[28] A "marvelous education"? It was what "seemed right for me"? This is how he describes committing homosexual adultery while his wife slept in the next room?

Perry's wife tried to forgive him, and they eventually had two boys (although he claims she had no interest in having sex with him, leading to even more sexual frustration). When she finally realized he was homosexual, she even suggested that they have a platonic marriage in which he would be allowed to have some nights out with the boys (seriously!). She still wanted to work things out. Perry, however, declined, saying, "The time has come for me to stand up and find me. I've got to know who I am."[29]

How eloquently—and unknowingly—Troy Perry expressed the root of the problem: "I've got to stand up and *find me*. I've got to know *who I am*."[30] A true disciple is actually called to do the exact opposite: I have to *find God* and know *who He is*, and by losing myself I find myself.

The route that Perry took—one filled with pain and challenges and courage (but, unfortunately, courage to do the wrong thing)—led to the wrong kind of fulfillment, one that destroyed a marriage, separated him from his sons, and led him into many homosexual encounters. And so, after he and Pearl broke up and he had sex with numerous other men, he eventually formed the MCC denomination.

Without exaggeration, you could say that this is a "Christian" denomination founded on sexual desires, with a theology driven by desire.[31] In fact, Perry actually contributed a chapter to the book *Leatherfolk* in which he speaks of his own "journey into leather," which, by definition, includes sado-masochism. Yes, the gay magazine *Frontiers* (October 1, 1999, 51) referred to Perry as a "big ol' leather queen"![32] And do you remember some of the seminars offered at past MCC conferences, which I mentioned in the last chapter, including sessions devoted to polyamory and gay cruising? But should we really be surprised? This is what I mean when I speak of a the-ology that is "driven by desire."

I have no doubt that the churches back then had no idea how to help Troy Perry, and even though he speaks of falling in love with his wife, I'm not saying that it was wise for them to get married. And I absolutely affirm the idea that when we yield ourselves to God, dying to our will and desires, we find who we really are, and with that, we find a deep fulfillment. As expressed by Olympian and then missionary Eric Liddell in the movie *Chariots of Fire*, "I believe God made me for a purpose, but He also made me fast. And when I run I feel His pleasure."[33]

But Liddell was referring to a holy pleasure of divine affirmation rather than a carnal pleasure of "This is who I am." One promotes the glory of God, leading to holiness, character, and discipline. The other promotes the flesh and is contrary to God's holiness, character, and discipline.

In an article titled "Why Happiness Isn't a Feeling," philosophy professor

216

J. P. Moreland contrasted the contemporary understanding of happiness with the classical understanding, illustrating his claims with a seven-point chart.[34] Quoting the first and last points of the chart, according to the contemporary understanding, happiness is "Pleasure and satisfaction," it is "Achieved by self-absorbed narcissism," and so, "success produces a celebrity." In contrast, according to the classical understanding of happiness—really, the biblical understanding of true happiness—it is "Virtue and character," it is "Achieved by self-denying apprenticeship to Jesus," and so "success produces a hero."[35] Well said!

What kind of happiness are you seeking? The self-centered "God, please satisfy my desires" happiness, or the happiness that comes from a godly and virtuous character and from a life bound up with the Lord and marked by a "self-denying apprenticeship" to Him?

Moreland then explains the meaning of Jesus's words in Luke 9:23–25:

> And he said to all, "If anyone would come after me, let him deny himself and take up his cross daily and follow me. For whoever would save his life will lose it, but whoever loses his life for my sake will save it. For what does it profit a man if he gains the whole world and loses or forfeits himself?"

What was Jesus saying? According to Moreland:

> The issue is finding one's self vs. losing one's self. More specifically, to find one's self is to find out how life ought to look like and learn to live that way; it's to become like Jesus, with character that manifests the fruit of the Spirit and the radical nature of Kingdom living; it's to find out God's purposes for one's life and to fulfill those purposes in a Christ-honoring way.
>
> Eternal life as defined in the New Testament isn't primarily about living forever, it's about having a new kind of life, a new quality of life so distinct that those without it can, in a real sense, be called dead. It's life lived the way we were made to function, a life of virtue, character and well-being lived for the Lord Jesus.[36]

That's where true happiness is found, and it often means going against the grain of some of our most fundamental, deeply rooted desires. But if we go the way of the cross, we will also experience the new life of the resurrection. That's what Paul meant when he wrote, "I have been crucified with Christ. It is no longer I who live, but Christ who lives in me. And the life I now live in the flesh I live by faith in the Son of God, who loved me and gave himself for me" (Gal. 2:20). Beginning a new life in Jesus means the end of the old life—in many more ways than we could imagine when we first put our faith in Him.

As missionary Amy Carmichael once explained, to be dead to self and alive to God means "dead to all one's natural earthly plans and hopes, dead to all voices, however dear, which would deafen our ear to His."[37] Is that what you desire? A life fully in tune with God and given wholly to Him?

WHAT'S WRONG WITH TWO MEN LOVING EACH OTHER?

I once had dinner with a "gay Christian" couple, and one of the men said to me, "If someone commits adultery, they hurt another person. Or if they steal or lie or murder, they hurt another person. But my relationship with my partner doesn't hurt anyone."

In response I asked the two of them, "What about two adult brothers who fall in love? They're not hurting anyone and they can't produce children together, so there can be no concern about the incestuous relationship producing unhealthy children. So would that be OK?"

They replied, "That is just wrong! No way is that right! That is just icky!"

I said to them, "But you have no basis for saying that, especially if you disregard the Scriptures. And, really, I don't want to offend you, and I'm not comparing you to two blood brothers, but to me, what you two do together is icky."

Ultimately, they had to accept the force of the argument, which undermines the whole premise of their argument. More importantly, if God says something is wrong, then when we participate in it with another person, we *are* hurting that person, even if we love him and are devoted to the individual.

I know that some gay theologians (and even my friend and debating colleague Rabbi Shmuley Boteach) cite Genesis 2:18, where the Lord said, "It is not good that the man should be alone." They feel this justifies homosexual relationships, since it is the only way they can have intimate companionships. But as much as I am deeply sensitive to the emotional power of the argument, not wanting anyone to be deprived of intimacy and love, I'm also fully aware that we cannot read the Lord's words in Genesis 2:18 without reading the second half of the verse, where the Lord said, "I will make him a helper fit for him"—namely, a woman!

And so I urge every reader who is same-sex attracted to cast yourself on the Lord, saying, "You understand my struggles, and You promised to help me in my times of deepest need, so I'm asking You to help me overcome every impulse and desire that is contrary to Your will. And I'm asking You to provide whatever I need to live for You." He will not let you down. He will either satisfy You with His presence, He will provide you with godly friends and companions, or He will help to bring change in your attractions so you can marry a fitting, lifelong companion.

But of this you can be sure. He will not leave you as an orphan (John 14:18), and in Him you will find everything you need for life and godliness (2 Pet. 1:3–4).

But Isn't This Message Driving Homosexuals Out of Church?

During this same dinner one of the men said to me, "But when you preach what you preach, people like us leave your churches—or, if we know you preach this, we will never set foot in your churches. So wouldn't it be better to modify your message on sexuality and keep us in the church, since we really want to follow the Lord?"

Of course, as much as I understood his point, it was ultimately very weak, since the same reasoning could apply to a host of other sins—if we only modified our message here or there, so many other people would join us!—not to mention a host of other beliefs, as in, "Why be so exclusive in your faith? If you welcomed people from other religions and told them that Jesus was not the only way to God, they would feel much more affirmed!" Where, then, do we draw the line? We obviously draw it where God draws it in His Word, which is why we need to submit humbly to what He has said, doing our best to understand it on His terms, not ours.

But, as good as these answers would have been, that's not the primary way I responded. Instead I told him that my goal was for him to have such a real and radical encounter with Jesus that he would joyfully abandon everything in this world just to know Him. To quote Paul again, "But whatever gain I had [meaning the life he was living as an emerging leader in the Jewish community], I counted as loss for the sake of Christ. Indeed, I count everything as loss because of the surpassing worth of knowing Christ Jesus my Lord. *For his sake I have suffered the loss of all things and count them as rubbish, in order that I may gain Christ*" (Phil. 3:7–8). Ultimately he considered it nothing to lose his own life as long as he could finish the task the Lord gave him. (See Acts 20:24.)

For me as a Jew, to follow Jesus means that many of my own people hate me and call me an apostate. And if I had been raised in an ultra-religious Jewish home, I would have been excommunicated for my beliefs and my parents would have had a funeral service for me. Either way, it is worth it all for the Lord!

Since 1993 I have gone to India once a year to minister, and I have literally washed the feet of a martyr's widow, a woman whose husband was killed by Hindus upset with his ministry. And she continues to serve the Lord with joy along with her children, knowing that even losing her husband was a small price to pay in the light of eternity.

I also prayed with men who had been beaten to the point of death—one was in a coma for six days before the Lord miraculously healed him—and after his recovery, he went back to preach to the same people who tried to take his life. And he was full of joy as he shared his resolve to continue to bring the good news to his people, whatever his fate in this world might be.

Closer to home, in 2012 a young Christian man who graduated from our ministry school was killed by Muslim terrorists, leaving behind a wife and two young children. He had moved to a very dangerous part of the world to preach the gospel, and he and his wife actually talked about the possibility of losing their lives as they worked in an impoverished Muslim community, serving the people there and trying to meet their needs. Some months after he was brutally killed, I spoke with his wife and asked her if she had any regrets about the choices she had made—marrying him and then going on the mission field with her family. With a vibrant smile that I can see as I write these words (even as I type with tears in my eyes) she said to me, "No regrets." Even his own brother, himself a missionary working against human trafficking overseas, after hearing the shocking news that his brother and best friend had been killed, said, "This is what we signed up for"—meaning, whatever the cost, whatever the consequence, we will follow Jesus.

And this, in fact, is what He requires of us. He said, "Whoever loves father or mother more than me is not worthy of me, and whoever loves son or daughter more than me is not worthy of me. And whoever does not take his cross and follow me is not worthy of me. Whoever finds his life will lose it, and whoever loses his life for my sake will find it" (Matt. 10:37–39).

But it is not some kind of morbid, depressing act of religious servitude that He requires, like a medieval monk wearing sackcloth under his shirt or whipping himself to pay for his sins. Instead it is the response of love and joy, since in finding Him we find everything we need. As Jesus taught:

> The kingdom of heaven is like treasure hidden in a field, which a man found and covered up. Then in his joy he goes and sells all that he has and buys that field. Again, the kingdom of heaven is like a merchant in search of fine pearls, who, on finding one pearl of great value, went and sold all that he had and bought it.
> —MATTHEW 13:44–46

Isn't that what really matters? When we look back one billion years from now, won't we say that a life spent in the service of the Lord was a life well spent?

So let me say it once more: You are not defined by your attractions, and you are not a slave to your desires. You can even live without sex or be single (if that is God's will, although He has the power to change your attractions), but you cannot live without Him. And so, rather than focusing on whether you are gay or bi or trans (or something else), why not focus on finding that one glorious, beautiful pearl of great price, that incredible, mind-boggling hidden treasure in the field: Jesus, the Lord and Savior.

It's worth selling all you have—to use the language of His parables— to have an intimate relationship with Him. As missionary Henry Martyn once said after realizing that he would never marry the love of his life and would instead give his life on the mission field to reach the lost, "May I turn away forever from the world and henceforth live forgetful of all but God. With Thee, O my God, is no disappointment. I shall never have to regret that I have loved Thee too well."[38]

Let that be your starting point: If you cast yourself on Him with all your heart and all your soul, giving yourself for Him the way He gave Himself for you, He will never disappoint you. In fact, others will look at your life and want what you have. As the psalmist declared, "You make known to me the path of life; in your presence there is fullness of joy; at your right hand are pleasures forevermore" (Ps. 16:11).

Isn't this enough?

SELECT BIBLIOGRAPHY

Aarons, Leroy. *Prayers for Bobby: A Mother's Coming to Terms With the Suicide of Her Gay Son*. San Francisco: Harper One, 1996.

Allberry, Sam. *Is God Anti-Gay? And Other Questions About Homosexuality, the Bible and Same-Sex Attraction*. N.p.: The Good Book Company, 2013.

Althaus-Reid, Marcella. *The Queer God*. New York: Routledge, 2003.

Anderson, Kerby. *A Biblical Point of View on Homosexuality*. Eugene, OR: Harvest House, 2008.

Bahnsen, Greg. *Homosexuality: A Biblical View*. Grand Rapids, MI: Baker, 1978.

Bawer, Bruce. *Stealing Jesus: How Fundamentalism Betrays Christianity*. New York: Three Rivers, 1997.

———, ed. *Beyond Queer: Challenging Gay Left Orthodoxy*. New York: Free Press, 1996.

Besen, Wayne R. *Anything But Straight: Unmasking the Scandals and Lies Behind the Ex-Gay Myth*. New York: Harrington Park Press, 2003.

Bettendorf, Craig. *A Biblical Defense Guide: For Gays, Lesbians and Those Who Love Them*. Victoria, BC: Trafford Publishing, 2005.

Boswell, John. *Christianity, Social Tolerance and Homosexuality*. Chicago: University of Chicago Press, 1980.

Botha, Peet H. *The Empty Testament: Four Arguments Against Gay Theology*. Victoria, BC, Canada: Trafford Publishing, 2008.

———. *Same-Sex Unions in Premodern Europe*. New York: Vintage Books, 1994.

Bradshaw, Timothy, ed. *The Way Forward? Christian Voices on Homosexuality and the Church*. Grand Rapids, MI: Eerdmans, 2004.

Brannum-Harris, Rod. *The Pharisees Amongst Us: How the Anti-Gay Campaign Unmasks the Religious Perpetrators of the Campaign to be Modern Day Pharisees*. N.p: N.p., 2005.

Brawley, Robert L. *Biblical Ethics and Homosexuality: Listening to Scripture*. Louisville, KY: Westminster John Knox, 1996.

Brentlinger, Rick. *Gay Christian 101: Spiritual Self-Defense for Gay Christians*. Pace, FL: Salient Press, 2007.

Brooten, Bernadette J. *Love Between Women: Early Christian Responses to Homoeroticism*. Chicago: University of Chicago Press, 1996.

Brown, Michael L. *A Queer Thing Happened to America: And What a Long, Strange Trip It's Been*. Concord: EqualTime Books, 2011.

———. *Hyper-Grace: Exposing the Dangers of the Modern Grace Message*. Lake Mary, FL: Charisma House, 2013.

———. *In the Line of Fire: 70 Articles From the Front Lines of the Culture Wars*. Concord, NC: EqualTime Books, 2012.

Brownson, James V. *Bible, Gender, Sexuality: Reframing the Church's Debate on Same-Sex Relationships*. Grand Rapids, MI: Eerdmans, 2013.

Brunson, Hal. *Lesbos, Narcissus, and Paulos: Homosexual Myth and Christian Truth*. New York: iUniverse, 2006.

Budziszewski, Jay. *True Tolerance: Liberalism and the Necessity of Judgment*. Brunswick, NJ: Transaction Publishers, 2000.

Butterfield, Rosaria Champagne. *The Secret Thoughts of an Unlikely Convert: An English Professor's Journey Into Christian Faith*. Pittsburgh: Crown & Covenant, 2012.

Campbell, W. P. *Turning Controversy Into Church Ministry: A Christlike Response to Homosexuality*. Grand Rapids, MI: Zondervan, 2010.

Chambers, Alan, ed. *God's Grace and the Homosexual Next Door: Reaching the Heart of the Gay Men and Women in Your World*. Eugene, OR: Harvest House, 2006.

Chapman, Patrick M. *"Thou Shalt Not Love": What Evangelicals Really Say to Gays*. New York: Haiduk Press, 2008.

Chappelle, Lucia. "Silent Night, Raging Night." *DeColores MCC Hymnal*. Los Angeles: N.p., 1983.

Chellew-Hodge, Candace. *Bulletproof Faith: A Spiritual Survival Guide for Gay and Lesbian Christians*. San Francisco: Jossey-Bass, 2008.

Cheng, Patrick S. *Radical Love: An Introduction to Queer Theology*. New York: Seabury Books, 2011.

———. *From Sin to Amazing Grace: Discovering the Queer Christ*. New York: Seabury Books, 2012.

Chu, Jeff. *Does Jesus Really Love Me? A Gay Christian's Pilgrimage in Search of God in America*. New York: Harper, 2013.

Cohen, Richard. *Coming Out Straight: Understanding and Healing Homosexuality*. Winchester, VA: Oakhill Press, 2000.

Corvino, John. *What's Wrong With Homosexuality?* New York: Oxford University Press, 2013.

Cunningham, James D. *Gay Christian Survivors. Refuting Anti-Gay Views With the Word of God*. N.p.: N.p., 2001.

Dailey, Timothy J. *Dark Obsession: The Tragedy and Threat of the Homosexual Lifestyle*. Nashville: Broadman & Holman, 2003.

Dallas, Joe. *The Gay Gospel? How Pro-Gay Advocates Misread the Bible*. Eugene, OR: Harvest House, 2007 (rev. and expanded edition of *Strong Delusion*).

Dallas, Joe and Nancy Heche, eds. *The Complete Christian Guide to Understanding Homosexuality: A Biblical and Compassionate Response to Same-Sex Attraction.* Eugene, OR: Harvest House, 2010

Davidson, Richard M. *Flame of Yahweh: Sexuality in the Old Testament.* Peabody, MA: Hendrickson, 2007.

Davies, Bob and Lela Gilbert. *Portraits of Freedom: 14 People Who Came Out of Homosexuality.* Downers Grove, IL: InterVarsity Press, 2001.

Dean, Kenda Creasy. *Almost Christian: What the Faith of Our Teenagers Is Telling the American Church.* New York: Oxford University Press, 2010.

De Young, James B. *Homosexuality: Contemporary Claims Examined in Light of the Bible and Other Ancient Literature and Law.* Grand Rapids: Kregel, 2000.

Diamond, Lisa M. *Sexual Fluidity: Understanding Women's Love and Desire.* Cambridge, MA: Harvard University Press, 2009.

Drinkwater, Gregg, Joshua Lesser, and David Shneer. *Torah Queeries.* New York: New York University Press, 2009.

Dunnam, Maxie D. and H. Newton Malony, eds. *Staying the Course: Supporting the Church's Position on Homosexuality.* Nashville: Abingdon, 2003.

Dwyer, John F. *Those 7 References: A Study of the 7 References to Homosexuality in the Bible.* N.p.: N.p., 2007.

Edser, Stuart. *Being Gay and Christian: You Can Be Both.* Wollombi, Australia: Exisle Publishing, 2012.

Eldridge, Erin. *Born That Way? A True Story of Overcoming Same-Sex Attraction With Insights for Friends, Families, and Leaders.* Salt Lake City, UT: Deseret Book Company, 1994.

Emmanuel, Tristan. *Warned: Canada's Revolution Against Faith, Family, and Freedom Threatens America.* Canada: Freedom Press, 2006.

Erzen, Tanya. *Straight to Jesus: Sexual and Christian Conversions in the Ex-Gay Movement*. Berkeley, CA: University of California Press, 2006.

Faris, Donald L. *Trojan Horse: The Homosexual Ideology and the Christian Church*. Burlington, Ontario: Welch Publishing, 1989.

Ferguson, David, Fritz Guy, and David Larson, eds. *Christianity and Homosexuality: Some Seventh-Day Adventist Perspectives*. Roseville, CA: Adventist Forum, 2007.

Fox, E. Earle and David W. Virtue. *Homosexuality: Good and Right in the Eyes of God?* Alexandria, VA: Emmaus Ministries, 2003.

Gagnon, Robert A. J. *The Bible and Homosexual Practice: Texts and Hermeneutics*. Nashville: Abingdon, 2001.

Geis, Sally B. and Donald E. Messer, eds. *Caught in the Crossfire: Helping Christians Debate Homosexuality*. Nashville: Abingdon, 1994.

George, Robert P. and Jean Bethke Elshtain, eds. *The Meaning of Marriage: Family, State, Market, and Morals*. Dallas: Spence Publishing, 2006.

Godfrey, Floyd. *A Young Man's Journey: Healing for Young Men With Unwanted Homosexual Feelings*. N.p.: CreateSpace, 2012.

Goss, Robert E. *Jesus Acted Up: A Gay and Lesbian Manifesto*. San Francisco: HarperSanFrancisco, 1993.

———. *Queering Christ: Beyond Jesus Acted Up*. Cleveland, OH: Pilgrim Press, 2002.

Goss, Robert E. and Mona West, eds. *Take Back the Word: A Queer Reading of the Bible*. Cleveland, OH: Pilgrim Press, 2000.

Gold, Mitchell and Mindy Drucker, eds. *Crisis: 40 Stories Revealing the Personal, Social, and Religious Pain and Trauma of Growing Up Gay in America*. Austin, TX: Greenleaf Book Group Press, 2008.

Goldberg, Arthur. *Light in the Closet: Torah, Homosexuality and the Power to Change*. Beverly Hills, CA: Red Heifer Press, 2008.

Gomes, Peter J. *The Good Book: Reading the Bible With Heart and Mind.* San Francisco: HarperSanFrancisco,1996.

Greenberg, Steven. *Wrestling With God and Men: Homosexuality in the Jewish Tradition.* Madison, WI: University of Wisconsin Press, 2004.

Grimsrud, Ted and Mark Thiessen Nation. *Reasoning Together: A Conversation on Homosexuality.* Scottdale, PA: Herald Press, 2008.

Guest, Deryn, Robert E. Goss, Mona West, and Thomas Bohache, eds. *The Queer Bible Commentary.* London: SCM Press, 2006.

Haley, Mike. *101 Frequently Asked Questions About Homosexuality.* Eugene, Oregon: Harvest House, 2004.

Haller, Tobias Stanislas. *Reasonable and Holy: Engaging Same-Sexuality.* New York: Seabury Books, 2009.

Hamilton, Julie Harren and Philip J. Henry, eds. *Handbook for Therapy for Unwanted Homosexual Attractions.* N.p.: Xulon Press, 2009.

Harvey, John F. *The Truth About Homosexuality: The Cry of the Faithful.* San Francisco: Ignatius Press, 1996.

Heimbach, Daniel R. *True Sexual Morality: Recovering Biblical Standards for a Culture in Crisis.* Wheaton, IL: Crossway, 2004.

Helminiak, Daniel. *What the Bible Really Says About Homosexuality.* Updated and expanded edition. New Mexico: Alamo Square Press, 2000.

Heyer, Walt. *Gender, Lies, and Suicide: A Whistleblower Speaks Out.* N.p.: N.p., 2013.

High, Brenda, compiler. *Bullycide in America: Moms Speak Out About the Bullying/Suicide Connection.* Darlington, MD: JBS Publishing, 2007.

Hill, Wesley. *Washed and Waiting: Reflections on Christian Faithfulness and Homosexuality.* Grand Rapids, MI: Zondervan, 2010.

Himbaza, Innocent, Adrien Schenker, and Jean-Baptiste Edart, eds. *The Bible on the Question of Homosexuality*. Eng. trans., Benedict M. Guevin. Washington DC: The Catholic University Press of America, 2011.

Hirshman, Linda. *Victory: The Triumphant Gay Revolution*. New York: Harper, 2012.

Holland, Erik. *The Nature of Homosexuality: Vindication for Homosexual Activists and the Religious Right*. New York: iUniverse, 2004.

Hopko, Thomas. *Christian Faith and Same-Sex Attraction: Eastern Orthodox Reflections*. Ben Lomond, CA: Conciliar Press, 2006.

Jennings, Theodore W., Jr. *Jacob's Wound: Homoerotic Narrative in the Literature of Ancient Israel*. New York: Continuum Press, 2005.

————. *The Man Jesus Loved: Homoerotic Narratives From the New Testament*. Cleveland, OH: Pilgrim Press, 2003.

Jennings, Theodore W., Jr. and Tat-Siong Benny Liew. "Mistaken Identities but Model Faith: Rereading the Centurion, the Chap, and the Christ in Matthew 8:5–13," *Journal of Biblical Literature* 123 (2004): 467–494.

Johnson, Toby. *Gay Spirituality: The Role of Gay Identity in the Transformation of Human Consciousness*. Repr. Maple Shade, NJ: Lethe Press, 2004.

Johnson, William Stacy. *A Time to Embrace: Same-Gender Relationships in Religion, Law, and Politics*. Grand Rapids, MI: Eerdmans, 2006.

Jones, James H. *Alfred C. Kinsey: A Public/Private Life*. New York: W. W. Norton & Co., 1997.

Jones, Stanton L. and Mark A. Yarhouse. *Ex-Gays: A Longitudinal Study of Religiously Mediated Change in Sexual Orientation*. Downers Grove, IL: IVP Academic, 2007.

Jordan, Mark D. *Blessing Same-Sex Unions: The Perils of Queer Romance and the Confusions of Christian Marriage*. Chicago: University of Chicago Press, 2005.

———. *The Invention of Sodomy in Christian Theology*. Chicago: University of Chicago Press, 1997.

Klein, Walter. *God's Word Speaks to Homosexuality*. Enumclaw, WA: Winepress Publishing, 2007.

Konrad, Jeff. *You Don't Have to Be Gay: Hope and Freedom for Males Struggling With Homosexuality or for Those Who Know of Someone Who Is*. Revised edition. Hilo, HI: Pacific Publishing, 1992.

Kundtz, David J. and Bernard S. Schlager. *Ministry Among God's Queer Folk: LGBT Pastoral Care*. Cleveland, OH: Pilgrim Press, 2007.

Langteaux, James Alexander. *Gay Conversations With God: Straight Talk on Fanatics, Fags and the God Who Loves Us All*. Scotland, UK: Findhorn Press, 2012.

Laycock, Douglas, Anthony R. Picarello Jr., and Robin Fretwell Wilson, eds. *Same-Sex Marriage and Religious Liberty: Emerging Conflicts*. Lanham, MD: Rowman & Littlefield, 2008.

Lee, Justin. *Torn: Rescuing the Gospel From the Gays-vs.-Christians Debate*. New York: Jericho Books, 2012.

LeVay, Simon. *Gay, Straight, and the Reason Why: The Science of Sexual Orientation*. New York: Oxford University Press, 2011.

Loader, William. *Making Sense of Sex: Attitudes Towards Early Jewish and Christian Literature*. Grand Rapids, MI: Eerdmans, 2013.

Lovelace, Richard F. *Homosexuality: How Should Christians Respond?* Repr. Eugene, OR: Wipf and Stock, 2002.

Marcus, Eric. *Is It a Choice? Answers to 300 of the Most Frequently Asked Questions About Gay and Lesbian People*. San Francisco: HarperSanFrancisco, 1999.

Marks, Jeremy. *Exchanging the Truth of God for a Lie: One man's spiritual journey to find the truth about homosexuality and same-sex partnerships.* 2nd ed. Glasgow, Scotland: Bell & Bain, 2009.

Magnuson, Roger. *Informed Answers to Gay Rights Questions.* Sisters, OR: Multnomah, 1994.

Marin, Andrew. *Love Is an Orientation.* Downers Grove, IL: IVP Books, 2009.

Martin, Dale B. *Sex and the Single Savior: Gender and Sexuality in Biblical Interpretation.* Louisville, KY: Westminster John Knox Press, 2006.

Matheson, David. *Becoming a Whole Man: Principles and Archetypes.* N.p.: CreateSpace, 2013.

May, William B. *Getting the Marriage Conversation Right: A Guide for Effective Dialogue.* Steubenville, OH: Emmaus Road, 2012.

McGrinn, David. *God, Why Was I Born Gay? Biology, the Bible and the Homosexual Debate.* N.p.: Kudu Publishing, 2012.

Michaelson, Jay. *God vs. Gay? The Religious Case for Equality.* Boston: Beacon Press, 2011;

Miner, Jeff and John Tyler Connoley. *The Children Are Free: Reexamining the Biblical Evidence on Same-Sex Relationships.* Indianapolis: Found Pearl Press, 2002.

Mollenkott, Virginia Ramey. *The Divine Feminine: The Biblical Imagery of God as Female.* New York: Crossroad Publishing, 1984.

———. *Sensuous Spirituality: Out From Fundamentalism.* Revised and expanded version. Cleveland, OH: Pilgrim Press, 2008.

Morgan, Patricia M. *Children as Trophies: Examining the Evidence on Same-Sex Parenting.* Newcastle upon Tyne: The Christian Institute, 2002.

Nichols, Jack. *The Gay Agenda: Talking Back to the Fundamentalists.* New York: Prometheus Books, 1996.

Nicolosi, Joseph J. *Shame and Attachment Loss: The Practical Work of Reparative Therapy*. Downers Grove, IL: IVP Academic, 2009.

———. *Healing Homosexuality: Case Stories of Reparative Therapy*. Northvale, NJ: Aronson,1993.

Nicolosi, Joseph J. and Linda Ames Nicolosi. *A Parent's Guide to Preventing Homosexuality*. Downers Grove, IL: InterVarsity Press, 2002.

Nissinen, Marti. *Homoeroticism in the Biblical World: A Historical Perspective*. Eng. trans. Kirsi Stjerna; Minneapolis, MN: Fortress, 1998.

Nordin, John P. *A Biblical Argument for the Acceptance of Homosexuality by the Christian Church*. N.p.: N.p., 2013.

Nyland. A., trans. with notes. *Study New Testament for Lesbians, Gays, Bi, and Transgender. With Extensive Notes on Greek Word Meaning and Context*. N.p.: N.p., 2007.

O'Leary, Dale. *One Man, One Woman: A Catholic's Guide to Defending Marriage*. Manchester, NH: Sophia Institute Press, 2007.

Olyan, Saul and Martha C. Nussbaum, eds. *Sexual Orientation and Human Rights in American Religious Discourse*. New York: Oxford University Press, 1998.

Orr-Ewing, Amy. *Is the Bible Intolerant? Sexist? Oppressive? Homophobic? Outdated? Irrelevant?* Downers Grove, IL: InterVarsity, 2005.

Paris, Kent A. *Means of Grace: A Primer for the Understanding and Care of Souls Affected by Homosexuality*. Joplin, MS: CP Publishing, 2010.

Patterson, Linda J. *Hate Thy Neighbor: How the Bible Is Misused to Condemn Homosexuality*. West Conshohocken, PA: Infinity Publishing, 2009.

Pearce, C. S. *This We Believe: The Christian Case for Gay Civil Rights*. Claremont, CA: Pomona Press, 2012.

Pennington, Sylvia. *Ex-Gays? There Are None! What It Means to Be a New Creature in Christ*. Hawthorne, CA: Lambda Christian Fellowship, 1986.

Piazza, Michael S. *Gay by God: How to be Lesbian or Gay and Christian*. Dallas: Sources of Hope Publishing, 2008. Updated edition of *Holy Homosexuals: The Truth About Being Gay or Lesbian and Christian*.

Pronk, Pim. *Against Nature? Types of Moral Arguments Regarding Homosexuality*. Grand Rapids, MI:Eerdmans, 1993.

Ramer, Andrew. *Queering the Text: Biblical, Medieval, and Modern Jewish Stories*. Brooklyn: White Crane Books, 2010.

Rapoport, Chaim. *Judaism and Homosexuality: An Authentic Orthodox View*. London: Vallentine Mitchell, 2004.

Rauch, Jonathan. *Gay Marriage: Why It Is Good for Gays, Good for Straights, and Good for America*. New York: Henry Holt, 2004.

Reisman, Judith A. *Sexual Sabotage: How One Mad Scientist Unleashed a Plague of Corruption and Contagion on America*. Nashville: WND Books, 2010.

Reynolds, Jim. *The Lepers Among Us: Homosexuality and the Life of the Church*. N.p.: Xulon Press, 2007.

Rhoads, Steven E. *Taking Sex Differences Seriously*. San Francisco: Encounter Books, 2004.

Richards, Renée and John Ames. *No Way Renée: The Second Half of My Notorious Life*. New York: Simon & Schuster, 2007.

Riley, Mona and Brad Sargent. *Unwanted Harvest?* Nashville: Broadman & Homan, 1995.

Roberts, Perri W. *Dying for Love: The Plain Truth About Homosexuality*. Enumclaw, WA: WinePress Publishing, 2003.

Robinson, Gene. *God Believes in Love: Straight Talk About Gay Marriage.* New York: Alfred A. Knopf, 2012.

Rogers, Jack. *Jesus, the Bible, and Homosexuality: Explode the Myths, Heal the Church.* Revised and expanded edition. Louisville, KY: Westminster John Knox, 2009.

Rudy, Kathy. *Sex and the Church: Gender, Homosexuality, and the Transformation of Ethics.* Boston: Beacon Press, 1997.

Saltzman, Russell E., ed. *Christian Sexuality: Normative and Pastoral Principles.* Minneapolis, MN: Kirk House Publishers; and Delhi, NY: ALPB Books, 2003.

Sanchez, Alex. *The God Box.* New York: Simon & Schuster for Young Readers, 2007.

Schmidt, Thomas E. *Straight and Narrow: Compassion and Clarity in the Homosexuality Debate.* Downers Grove, IL: InterVarsity Press, 1995.

Schneider, Yvette. *Leaving Homosexuality: A Practical Guide for Men and Women Looking for a Way Out.* Eugene, OR: Harvest House, 2009.

Scroggs, Robin. *The New Testament and Homosexuality.* Minneapolis, MN: Augsburg Fortress, 1983.

Seow, Choon-Leong. *Homosexuality and Christian Community.* Louisville, KY: Westminster John Knox, 1996.

Shick, Denise and Jerry Gramckow. *My Daddy's Secret.* N.p.: Xulon, 2008.

Shore, John. *UNFAIR: Christians and the LGBT Question.* N.p.: CreatSpace, 2011.

Siker, Jeffrey S., ed. *Homosexuality in the Church: Both Sides of the Debate.* Louisville, KY: Westminster John Knox, 1994.

Soards, Marion L. *Scripture and Homosexuality: Biblical Authority and the Church Today.* Louisville, KY: Westminster John Knox, 1995.

Sphero, M. W. *The Gay Faith: Christ, Scripture, and Sexuality.* New York: Herms Press, 2012.

Stark, Rodney. *The Rise of Christianity: How the Obscure, Marginal Jesus Movement Became the Dominant Religious Force in the Western World in a Few Centuries.* Princeton, NJ: Princeton University Press, 1996.

Stefanowicz, Dawn. *Out From Under: The Impact of Homosexual Parenting.* Enumclaw WA: Annotation Press, 2007.

Stevens, Michael. *Straight Up: The Church's Official Response to the Epidemic of Downlow Living.* Lake Mary, FL: Creation House, 2006.

Stetson, Brad and Joseph G. Conti. *The Truth About Tolerance: Pluralism, Diversity and the Culture Wars.* Downers Grove, IL: InterVarsity, 2005.

Stone, Ken, ed. *Queer Commentary and the Hebrew Bible.* Cleveland, OH: Pilgrim Press, 2001.

Stuart, Elizabeth, et al. *Religion Is a Queer Thing: A Guide to the Faith for Lesbian, Gay, Bisexual, and Transgendered People.* Cleveland, OH: Pilgrim Press, 1997.

Swan, Talbert W., II, ed. *Closing the Closet: Testimonies of Deliverance From Homosexuality.* Indian Orchard, MA: Trumpet in Zion, 2004.

Swartley, Willard M. *Homosexuality: Biblical Interpretation and Moral Discernment.* Scottdale, PA: Herald Press, 2003.

Temple, Gray. *Gay Unions: In the Light of Scripture, Tradition, and Reason.* New York City, NY: Church Publishing, 2004.

Thompson, Chad W. *Loving Homosexuals as Jesus Would: A Fresh Christian Approach.* Grand Rapids, MI: Brazos, 2004.

Thurman, Debbie. *Post-Gay? Post-Christian?: Anatomy of a Cultural and Faith Identity Crisis.* Madison Heights, VA: Cedar House Publishers, 2011.

Tin, Louis-Georges, ed. *The Dictionary of Homophobia: A Global History of Gay and Lesbian Experience*. Eng. trans. Marek Redburn. Vancouver, BC: Arsenal Pulp Press, 2008.

Truscott, Gordon. *Inside Homosexuality: Does My Pain Matter to You?* Singapore: ARMOUR Publishing, 2011.

Turek, Frank. *Correct, Not Politically Correct: How Same-Sex Marriage Hurts Everyone*. Charlotte, NC: CrossExamined, 2008.

Turnbull, Sandra. *God's Gay Agenda*. Bellflower, CA: Glory Publishing, 2012.

Via, Dan O. and Robert A. J. Gagnon. *Homosexuality and the Bible: Two Views*. Minneapolis, MN: Fortress Press, 2003.

Vines, Matthew. *God and the Gay Christian: What the Bible Says—and Doesn't Say—About Homosexuality*. New York: Convergent Books, 2014.

Waiss, John R. *Born to Love: Gay-Lesbian Identity, Relationships, and Marriage; Homosexuality, the Bible, and the Battle for Chaste Love*. N.p.: Outskirts Press, 2011.

Webb, William J. *Slaves, Women and Homosexuals: Exploring the Hermeneutics of Cultural Analysis*. Downers Grove, IL: InterVarsity, 2001.

Weekly, R. D. *Homosexuality: Letting Truth Win the Devastating War Between Scripture, Faith and Sexual Orientation*. N.p.: Judah First Ministries, 2009.

White, James R. and Jeffrey D. Niell. *The Same Sex Controversy*. Minneapolis, MN: Bethany House, 2003.

White, Mel. *Religion Gone Bad: The Hidden Dangers of the Christian Right*. New York: Jeremy P. Tarcher/Penguin, 2006. (Reissued as *Holy Terror: Lies the Christian Right Tells Us to Deny Gay Equality*. New York: Magnus Books, 2012.)

———. *Stranger at the Gate: To Be Gay and Christian in America*. New York: Plume, 1995.

Whitehead, Briar. *Craving for Love: Relationship Addiction, Homosexuality, and the God Who Heals.* Grand Rapids, MI: Monarch Books, 2003.

Williams, Brian Keith. *Ministering Graciously to the Gay and Lesbian Community.* Shippensburg, PA: Destiny Image, 2005.

Wilson, Nancy. *Our Tribe: Queer Folks, God, Jesus and the Bible.* New Mexico: Alamo Square Press, 2000.

Wink, Walter, ed. *Homosexuality and Christian Faith: Questions of Conscience for the Churches.* Minneapolis, MN: Fortress Press, 1999.

Wold, Donald J. *Out of Order: Homosexuality in the Bible and the Ancient Near East.* Grand Rapids, MI: Baker, 1998.

Wolkomir, Michelle. *Be Not Deceived: The Sacred and Sexual Struggles of Gay and Ex-Gay Christian Men.* New Brunswick, NJ: Rutgers University Press, 2006.

Wood, Peter. *Diversity: The Invention of a Concept.* New York: Encounter Books, 2004.

Woog, Dan. *School's Out: The Impact of Gay and Lesbian Issues on America's Schools.* Boston: Alyson Publications, 1995.

Worthen, Frank. *Destiny Bridge: A Journey Out of Homosexuality.* Winnipeg, Canada: Forever Books, 2011.

Wright, Rogers H. and Nicholas A. Cummings, eds. *Destructive Trends in Mental Health: The Well-Intentioned Path to Harm.* New York: Routledge, 2005.

Yarhouse, Mark A. *Homosexuality and the Christian: A Guide for Parents, Pastors, and Friends.* Minneapolis, MN: Bethany House, 2010.

Yuan, Christopher, and Angela Yuan. *Out of a Far Country: A Gay Son's Journey to God. A Broken Mother's Search for Hope.* Colorado Springs, CO: WaterBrook Press, 2011.

NOTES

1. Michael Brown, "Recovering the Lost Letter of Jacob," CharismaNews
   .com, March 11, 2013, http://tinyurl.com/kklvcbp (accessed January 22,
   2014).

1. Justin Lee, *Torn: Rescuing the Gospel From the Gays-vs.-Christians Debate*
   (New York: Jericho Books, 2012).
2. Ibid., 192.
3. Ibid., 205.
4. Ibid.
5. Jackie Calmes and Peter Baker, "Obama Says Same-Sex Marriage Should
   Be Legal," *New York Times*, May 9, 2012, http://tinyurl.com/p8o4z32
   (accessed January 6, 2014). For my critique of Mr. Obama's position, see
   "Equivocating of Evolving, President Obama Is Wrong Either Way," posted
   May 12, 2012, http://tinyurl.com/qgp59x3 (accessed January 6, 2014).
6. Patrick M. Chapman, *"Thou Shalt Not Love": What Evangelicals Really Say
   to Gays* (New York: Haiduk Press, 2008). Used by permission.
7. John Shore, *UNFAIR: Christians and the LGBT Question* (N.p.: CreateSpace Independent Publishing Platform, 2011, 2013), 132, emphasis
   his. Not surprisingly Shore's writings have become increasingly unbib-
   lical, including articles like, "My God Cares About Hearts, Not Crotches,"
   posted October 6, 2010, http://johnshore.com/2010/10/06/about-lgbt
   -folk-ill-listen-to-my-god-thanks/, as if there was no connection between the
   condition of the heart and sexual acts; and "Christian Polyamory?", posted
   April 2, 2013, http://johnshore.com/2013/04/02/christian-polyamory.
8. Ibid., emphasis his.
9. Ibid., emphasis his.
10. Linda J. Patterson, *Hate Thy Neighbor: How the Bible Is Misused to Con-
    demn Homosexuality* (West Conshohocken, PA: Infinity Publishing, 2009).
11. Jay Michaelson, *God vs. Gay? The Religious Case for Equality* (Boston:
    Beacon Press, 2011). Used by permission. Michaelson's academic bio is
    quite impressive; see http://www.jaymichaelson.net.
12. Ibid., 5–14.
13. Ibid., 24–29.

14. Ibid., 28–29; the New Testament scholar he quotes is Yale professor Dale Martin, himself gay. For more on this quote, see chapter 10.

15. Ibid., 29.

16. Gene Robinson, *God Believes in Love: Straight Talk About Gay Marriage* (New York: Alfred A. Knopf, 2012).

17. Judah First Ministries, "About Us," http://www.judahfirst.org/about-us/, and "Publications," http://www.judahfirst.org/publications/ (accessed January 6, 2014).

18. Robinson, *God Believes in Love*, 109–110.

19. William Stacy Johnson, *A Time to Embrace: Same-Gender Relationships in Religion, Law, and Politics* (Grand Rapids, MI: Eerdmans, 2006).

20. Ibid., 227.

21. Jack Rogers, *Jesus, the Bible, and Homosexuality: Explode the Myths, Heal the Church*, revised and expanded (Louisville, KY: Westminster Knox Press, 2009).

22. Ibid., viii.

23. Ibid.

24. Ibid., 101–102.

25. Comment on my article "Gay Rights Activists Can't Put the Church in the Closet," CharismaNews.com, January 28, 2013, http://tinyurl.com/pzxd4z6 (accessed January 6, 2014).

26. C. S. Pearce, *This We Believe: The Christian Case for Gay Civil Rights* (Claremont, CA: Pomona Press, 2012), xvii.

27. Ibid.

28. Ibid., 4.

29. Ibid., 1–2.

30. Ibid., 47.

31. M. W. Sphero, *The Gay Faith: Christ, Scripture, and Sexuality* (New York: Herms Press, 2012; Kindle Edition), Kindle locations 500–505, emphasis his.

32. Ibid., emphasis his.

33. Ibid., Kindle location 134, emphasis his.

34. Ibid., Kindle location 775.

35. Rod Brannum-Harris, *The Pharisees Amongst Us* (N.p.: BookSurge, 2005).

36. Ibid., 112–113.

37. Mel White, *Stranger at the Gate: To Be Gay and Christian in America* (New York: Plume, 1995).

38. Mel White, *Religion Gone Bad: The Hidden Dangers of the Christian Right* (New York: Jeremy P. Tarcher/Penguin, 2006).

39. Mel White, *Holy Terror: Lies the Christian Right Tell Us to Deny Gay Equality* (New York: Magnus Books, 2012).

40. Mel White, "Resist Southern Baptist 'Terrorism,'" *The Blog* (blog), HuffPost Gay Voices, June 26, 2012, http://tinyurl.com/7y78tfr (accessed January 7, 2014).

CHAPTER 2
TO JUDGE OR NOT TO JUDGE?

1. PrayersforBobby.com, "Plot Summary," http://prayersforbobby.com/synopsis.php (accessed January 7, 2014).

2. Ibid.

3. Brian Tashman, "Michael Brown: Gays Use Youth Suicide Victims as 'Pawns,'" RightWingWatch.org, January 27, 2012, http://tinyurl.com/o88mbwb (accessed January 7, 2014).

4. Comment on my article "Sharing God's Goodness Is Never a Failure," guest commentary, *QNotes*, GoQNotes.com, September 27, 2013, http://tinyurl.com/pr54689 (accessed January 7, 2014).

5. Comment on YouTube video "Brown: Ellen DeGeneres Proves That Gay Rights Are Nothing Like Civil Rights," posted by RWW Blog, http://www.youtube.com/watch?v=yR_1VR0u9xo (accessed January 7, 2014). See further my article "Comparing Black Civil Rights to Gay Rights," CharismaNews.com, September 26, 2013, http://tinyurl.com/o3hrne8 (accessed January 7, 2014); for a perspective from the respected Christian philosopher William Lane Craig, see "Inter-Racial Marriage and Same-Sex Marriage," http://tinyurl.com/oanbsos (accessed January 7, 2014).

6. David Kinnaman and Gabe Lyons, *unChristian: What a New Generation Really Thinks About Christianity…and Why It Matters* (Grand Rapids, MI: Baker Books, 2007), 92.

7. Lee, *Torn*, 2.

8. Michael Brown, "Statement to the Gay and Lesbian Community," AskDrBrown.org, May 6, 2006, http://tinyurl.com/og32mzv (accessed January 7, 2014).

9. Ibid.

10. Of course I understand the gospel brings death to the flesh, death to sin, death to self, and lifelong, joyful servitude to Jesus. But all of that equals true life and true freedom, not death and bondage.

11. Benjamin Radford, "Is There a Gay Teen Suicide Epidemic?", LiveScience .com, October 8, 2010, http://www.livescience.com/8734-gay-teen-suicide -epidemic.html (accessed January 7, 2014).

12. Listen to the broadcast of "Dr. Brown and Frank Turek Interact With Gay Activist Mitchell Gold," January 24, 2012, at http://tinyurl.com/ph3cj8x (accessed January 7, 2014). See also my article titled "Is Kirk Cameron an Accomplice to Murder?", Townhall.com, March 7, 2012, http://tinyurl .com/pktg9nq (accessed January 7, 2014).

13. According to KidsHealth.org, "We all feel overwhelmed by difficult emotions or situations sometimes. But most people get through it or can put their problems in perspective and find a way to carry on with determination and hope. So why does one person try suicide when another person in the same tough situation does not? What makes some people more resilient (better able to deal with life's setbacks and difficulties) than others? What makes a person unable to see another way out of a bad situation besides ending his or her life? The answer to those questions lies in the fact that most people who commit suicide have depression." (KidsHealth .org, "Suicide," http://kidshealth.org/teen/your_mind/mental_health/ suicide.html [accessed January 7, 2014].) See also "Youth Suicide Frequently Asked Questions (FAQ)," Youth Suicide Prevention Program, http://www.yspp.org/about_suicide/youth_suicide_FAQ.htm (accessed January 7, 2014).

14. The Line of Fire, "An Interview With Walt Heyer (Who Went From Man to Woman and Back to Man)," August 28, 2013, http://tinyurl.com/ lgv6orn (accessed January 7, 2014).

15. Wikipedia.org, s.v. "comorbidity," http://en.wikipedia.org/wiki/Comor bidity (accessed January 7, 2014). See also "Comorbidity," National Institute of Drug Abuse, http://www.drugabuse.gov/related-topics/comorbidity (accessed January 7, 2014).

16. Paul McHugh, "Surgical Sex," *First Things*, November 2004, http://www .firstthings.com/article/2009/02/surgical-sex--35 (accessed January 7, 2014).

17. Ibid.

18. C. Dhejne, P. Lichtenstein, M. Boman, A. L. Johansson, N. Langstrom, and M. Landen, "Long-Term Follow-Up of Transsexual Persons Undergoing Sex Reassignment Surgery: Cohort Study in Sweden," *PLOS One* 6, no. 2 (February 22, 2011): http://www.ncbi.nlm.nih.gov/ pubmed/21364939 (accessed January 7, 2014).

19. For the question of what to do with a church member (who is also a family member) who claims to be following Jesus and yet is living in open, unrepentant sin, see 1 Corinthians 5.

20. Dan O. Via and Robert A. J. Gagnon, *Homosexuality and the Bible: Two Views* (Minneapolis: Fortress Press, 2003), 98, emphasis his.

21. D. Müller, "Disciple," in Colin Brown, ed., *New International Dictionary of New Testament Theology* (Grand Rapids, MI: Zondervan, 1986), 1:488.

22. C. S. Lewis, *Mere Christianity* (New York: HarperCollins Publishers, 2009), 227.

23. Some of my recent articles on this issue include: "The Contemporary Gospel of Me," CharismaNews.com, October 3, 2013, http://tinyurl.com/ nbvkuzf (accessed January 8, 2014); "Did God Put Us Here to Have Fun?", CharismaNews.com, September 5, 2013, http://tinyurl.com/qfz8mm9 (accessed January 8, 2014); "The Great Sin of Trying to Make the Gospel Palatable," CharismaNews.com, September 6, 2013, http://tinyurl.com/ op3c6vf (accessed January 8, 2014); and "A Compromised Gospel Produces Compromised Fruit," MinistryTodayMag.com, March 12, 2013, http://tinyurl .com/pymxrx9 (accessed January 8, 2014). They are also collected together in Michael L. Brown, *In the Line of Fire: 70 Articles From the Front Lines of the Culture Wars* (Concord, NC: EqualTime Books, 2012).

24. A. W. Tozer, "The Old Cross and the New," viewed at Kjos Ministries, "Excerpts From 'The Old Cross and the New,'" http://www.crossroad.to/ Excerpts/books/faith/Tozer/tozer-cross-long.htm (accessed January 8, 2014).

25. Matt Comer, "A Prayer for Michael Brown," *QNotes*, GoQNotes.com, December 11, 2010, http://goqnotes.com/9424/a-prayer-for-michael -brown/ (accessed January 8, 2014).

26. Michael Brown, "Setting the Record Straight," *QNotes*, GoQNotes.com, December 25, 2010, http://goqnotes.com/9513/setting-the-record-straight/ (accessed January 8, 2014).

27. To combat this, Christopher Doyle, a professional counselor and himself an ex-gay, founded Voice for the Voiceless. See http://www.voiceof thevoiceless.info/ (accessed January 8, 2014).

28. Used by permission.

29. Used by permission.

30. Used by permission.

31. I told the story in the article, "A Gay Struggler Finds Assurance in the Lord," CharismaNews.com, May 7, 2013, http://tinyurl.com/cwrpt4u (accessed January 8, 2014).

32. Used by permission.

33. What I mean is that we are called to abstain from sexual immorality and be conformed to His holy image (see, e.g., Ephesians 5:1–16; 1 Thessalonians 4:1–8) as opposed to being called to be attracted to members of the opposite sex. That being said, holy living often leads to profound and deep changes in our lives—including complete changes in sexual orientation for some, and throughout Scripture, only heterosexual unions are blessed or sanctioned by God. (See chapter 4.)

34. Christopher Yuan, "*Torn*: Justin Lee; Reviewed by Christopher Yuan," The Gospel Coalition, http://thegospelcoalition.org/book-reviews/review/torn (accessed January 8, 2014). For Yuan's own dramatic story in full, see Christopher Yuan and Angela Yuan, *Out of a Far Country: A Gay Son's Journey to God. A Broken Mother's Search for Hope* (Colorado Springs, CO: WaterBrook Press, 2011).

35. Yuan, "*Torn*: Justin Lee; Reviewed by Christopher Yuan."

36. Ibid.

37. This is a theme we will return to repeatedly throughout this book, most fully in chapter 9.

38. Kenda Creasy Dean, *Almost Christian: What the Faith of Our Teenagers Is Telling the American Church* (New York: Oxford University Press, 2010), Kindle locations 204–211, 234–238. Permission requested.

39. Ibid., Kindle locations 240–245, emphasis hers.

40. See Michael Brown, "Is Gay the New Black? Analyzing the Argument That 'I Was Born That Way,'" in *A Queer Thing Happened to America* (Concord, NC: EqualTime Books, 2011), 196–225.

41. As quoted in Kim Campbell, "Gays on Prime Time," *Christian Science Monitor*, April 6, 2001, http://www.csmonitor.com/2001/0406/p13s1.html (accessed January 8, 2014).

42. As quoted in Brown, "Hollywood's Celebration of Queer," *A Queer Thing Happened to America*, 152–195.

43. Marshall Kirk and Hunter Madsen, *After the Ball: How America Will Conquer Its Fear and Hatred of Gays in the 90s* (New York: Penguin, 1989), 153; for the text online, see "The Homosexual Propaganda Campaign in America's Media," http://tinyurl.com/luyabcj (accessed January 8, 2014); for a gay denial that *After the Ball* was actually influential in gay activism,

see Brown, *A Queer Thing Happened to America*, 603, n. 28. See also David Kupelian, *The Marketing of Evil: How Radicals, Elitists, and Pseudo-Experts Sell Us Corruption Disguised as Freedom* (Nashville: WND Books, 2005), especially 17–38.

44. Kirk and Madsen, *After the Ball*, vii, 258. For a more detailed and wide-ranging account, see Kathryn C. Montgomery, *Target: Prime Time: Advocacy Groups and the Struggle Over Entertainment Television* (New York: Oxford University Press, 1989), passim (see the Index under "gay rights); this book also places gay advocacy groups into the larger context of other advocacy groups, thereby making it possible to compare and contrast gay advocacy strategies and techniques with those of other groups.

45. Kirk and Madsen, *After the Ball*. See also their shorter study, which paved the way for the full-length book (note that Madsen used the pseudonym Erastes Pill in this article): Marshall Kirk and Erastes Pill, "The Overhauling of Straight America," http://library.gayhomeland.org/0018/EN/EN_Overhauling_Straight.htm (accessed January 8, 2014).

46. Jeff Jacoby, "Where's the Tolerance Now?", *Boston Globe*, October 23, 1997, as referenced in Abigail Wisse Schachter, "Going After Jeff Jacoby," *The Weekly Standard*, November 17, 1997, http://tinyurl.com/l9a273x (accessed January 8, 2014).

47. Dannika Nash, "An Open Letter to the Church From My Generation," April 7, 2013, DannikaNash.com, http://tinyurl.com/ofdno4d (accessed January 8, 2014). For my response to Dannika's thoughtful blog post, see "A Father's Response to 'An Open Letter to the Church from My Generation,'" CharismaNews.com, April 25, 2013, http://tinyurl.com/bn443u4 (accessed January 8, 2014).

48. Nash, "An Open Letter to the Church From My Generation."

49. Kinnaman and Lyons, *unChristian*, 92–93.

50. See, for example, Gary J. Gates, "How Many People Are Lesbian, Gay, Bisexual and Transgender?", The Williams Institute, April 2011, http://tinyurl.com/87vkgmz (accessed January 8, 2014). In their official brief in the landmark *Lawrence v. Texas* Supreme Court decision, a major coalition of thirty-one gay and pro-gay organizations used the figures of 2.8 percent of the male population and 1.4 percent of the female population as identifying themselves as gay, lesbian, or bisexual (Liberty Counsel, "A Rainbow of Myth," http://www.lc.org/profamily/endoftherainbow.pdf [accessed March 11, 2014]). For a representative discussion of gay population on a gay website and a conservative Christian website, see "Gay Population

Statistics," http://gaylife.about.com/od/comingout/a/population
.htm (accessed January 8, 2014) and "Exposed: 'The Myth That '10% Are
Homosexual,'" http://tinyurl.com/m3m66vq (accessed January 8, 2014).
It is widely recognized today that Alfred Kinsey's (in)famous sex survey,
which provided the basis for the widely quoted "one in ten is gay" myth,
cannot be relied on here. For other, more searing criticisms of Kinsey's
work, including charges of child abuse, see Judith A. Reisman, *Kinsey:
Crimes and Consequences* (Arlington, VA: The Institute for Media Educa-
tion, 1998); Judith A. Reisman, *Sexual Sabotage: How One Mad Scientist
Unleashed a Plague of Corruption and Contagion on America* (Nashville:
WND Books, 2010). For a definitive (937-page) study of Kinsey, see
James H. Jones, *Alfred C. Kinsey: A Public/Private Life* (New York: W. W.
Norton & Co., 1997).

51. Lymari Morales, "U.S. Adults Estimate That 25% of Americans Are Gay
or Lesbian," Gallup.com, May 27, 2011, http://tinyurl.com/3wqmr8o
(accessed January 8, 2014).

52. Lee, *Torn*, 4, emphasis added.

53. For some sobering statistics, all of which represent people's lives, see
chapter 8.

54. William J. Bennett, *The Index of Leading Cultural Indicators: American
Society at the End of the Twentieth Century*, updated and expanded (New
York: Random House, 2011). Viewed online at Google Books.

55. Ibid.

56. Anugrah Kumar, "Nearly Half of All First Births in America Out of Wedlock, Study Says," ChristianPost.com, March 18, 2013, http://tinyurl.com/
l94ox6k (accessed January 8, 2014).

57. Robert Rector, "Marriage: America's Greatest Weapon Against Child Poverty," Heritage Foundation, September 5, 2012, http://tinyurl.com/cydpnsj
(accessed January 8, 2014).

58. Jessica Bennett, "Polyamory: The Next Sexual Revolution?", *Newsweek*,
July 28, 2009, http://www.newsweek.com/polyamory-next-sexual
-revolution-82053 (accessed January 8, 2014).

59. Daily Mail Reporter, "'It's OK for Homosexuals to Do What They Want
at Home, How Is This Different?' Lawyer Defends Columbia Professor
Charged With Incest," *Daily Mail*, October 8, 2012, http://tinyurl.com/
mkkotdk (accessed January 8, 2014).

60. Michael Brown, *A Queer Thing Happened to America* (Concord, NC:
EqualTime Books, 2011).

61. David Hacker/Alliance Defending Freedom, "University Fires Employee for Op-Ed Standing Against Gay Rights as Civil Rights," CharismaNews .com, July 2, 2013, http://tinyurl.com/kusllxs (accessed January 8, 2014). Most recently the Supreme Court refused to hear her appeal: John Jalsevac, "SCOTUS Declines Appeal by Christian University Administrator Fired for Homosexuality Column," LifeSiteNews.com, October 11, 2013, http:// tinyurl.com/mlo269w (accessed January 8, 2014).

62. Maggie Hyde/Religious News Service, "Christian Counselors Claim Discrimination Over Religious Beliefs on Gays," Huff Post Religion, May 25, 2011, http://tinyurl.com/32umf68 (accessed January 8, 2014). For the final, positive outcome of Ward's case, in which a federal district court ruled that "tolerance is a two-way street," see National Organization of Marriage, "Victory: University Settles With Christian Julea Ward," December 11, 2012, http://www.nomblog.com/31559 (accessed January 8, 2014).

63. T. Alan Hurwitz, "Chief Diversity Officer," e-mail sent to campus community from president of Gallaudet, http://www.gallaudet.edu/news/ mccaskill.html (accessed January 8, 2014); Nick Anderson, "Gallaudet Diversity Officer Accuses University of Discrimination in Lawsuit," *Washington Post*, September 30, 2013, http://tinyurl.com/ornzu2o (accessed January 8, 2014). For her reinstatement see, Stephen Tschida, "Angela McCaskill Reinstated After Signing Gay Marriage Petition," WJLA.com, January 8, 2013, http://tinyurl.com/atpztt7 (accessed January 8, 2014).

64. For examples, see the relevant articles compiled in Brown, *In the Line of Fire*. See also the extensive documentation through early 2011 in Brown, *A Queer Thing Happened to America*, 495–546 (with references).

65. Quoted in Eric Metaxas, "Bonhoeffer: Pastor, Martyr, Prophet, Spy," The Blaze.com, April 9, 2013, http://www.theblaze.com/books/bonhoeffer -pastor-martyr-prophet-spy/ (accessed January 8, 2014).

66. California Legislative Information, "SB-777 Discrimination," http:// tinyurl.com/ml4suqh (accessed January 8, 2014).

67. California Legislative Information, "SB-1172: Sexual Orientation Change Efforts," http://tinyurl.com/82atb2x (accessed January 8, 2014).

68. California Legislative Information, "AB-1266: Pupil Rights: Sex -Segregated School Programs and Activities," http://tinyurl.com/ctmhh8m (accessed January 8, 2014).

69. David Crouch, "Toys R Us's Stockholm Superstore Goes Gender Neutral," *The Guardian*, December 23, 2013, http://tinyurl.com/ka7tm5n (accessed January 8, 2014); Alec Torres, "U.K. Toys 'R' Us Going Gender Neutral,"

The Corner (blog), NationalReview.com, http://tinyurl.com/jvtmrqu (accessed January 8, 2014).

70. This is a direct quote from Dr. Barb Burdge, associate professor of social work at Manchester College, in "Lesbian Professor Urges Deconstruction of Gender," http://www.narth.org/docs/deconstruction.html (accessed March 7, 2014); for further details, see Brown, *A Queer Thing Happened to America*, 585; see also pages 570–571.

71. There have actually been a number of such instances in recent months; see, e.g., Wade Rouse, "Transgender Teen Crowned High-School Homecoming Queen," *People*, September 23, 2013, http://tinyurl.com/mc8eh3c (accessed January 8, 2014).

72. Garrance Burke/Associated Press, "Transgender Student Runs for Prom King," *Washington Post*, April 21, 2007, http://tinyurl.com/lclmcvt (accessed January 8, 2014).

73. Sunnivie Brydum, "Trans Six-Year-Old Is Argentina's Youngest to Amend Gender on Birth Certificate," Advocate.com, September 28, 2013, http://tinyurl.com/kp3c5pq (accessed January 8, 2014).

74. Shane L. Windmeyer, *The Advocate College Guide for LGBT Students* (New York: Alyson Books, 2006).

75. Los Angeles Unified School District, Reference Guide, http://tinyurl.com/mrd3gw3 (accessed January 8, 2014). See also Dora J. Dome, "AB 1266: Transgender Students, Privacy and Facilities," California Association of Supervisors of Child Welfare and Attendance, October 18, 2013," http://tinyurl.com/mvgk29g (accessed January 8, 2014).

76. Special thanks to Caleb H. Price for researching and developing this list of terms, which appears in Brown, *A Queer Thing Happened to America*, 592.

77. Taylor Bigler, "'The Notebook' Director on Incest: 'Love Who You Want,'" DailyCaller.com, September 10, 2012, http://tinyurl.com/ly76jzc (accessed January 8, 2014).

78. D. A. Carson, "Matthew," in Tremper Longman III and David E. Garland, eds., *The Expositor's Bible Commentary*, rev. ed. (Grand Rapids, MI: Zondervan, 2010), 9:219.

79. See Michael L. Brown, *Hyper-Grace: Exposing the Dangers of the Modern Grace Message* (Lake Mary, FL: Charisma House, 2013), especially chapter 3.

80. "Augustine of Hippo-Quotes," The European Graduate School," http://www.egs.edu/library/augustine-of-hippo/quotes/ (accessed January 8, 2014).

CHAPTER 3
ARE WE USING THE BIBLE TO SANCTION ANTIHOMOSEXUAL PREJUDICE?

1. "Open Letter From Mel White to Jerry Falwell," June 5, 1999, http://tinyurl.com/nv6wa77 (accessed January 9, 2014).

2. Jerry Falwell, "An Open Letter to Mel White," HolyPop.com, http://tinyurl.com/nzh34vk (accessed January 9, 2014).

3. "Open Letter From Mel White to Jerry Falwell."

4. Ibid.

5. Sarah Pulliam Bailey, "Interview: Desmond Tutu on Gay Rights, the Middle East and Pope Francis," Religion News Service, September 13, 2013, http://tinyurl.com/k4ms4oe (accessed January 9, 2014). Used by permission. The words I omitted from his quote (because they were not directly relevant here) were: "I wish I could keep quiet about the plight of the Palestinians. I can't!"

6. Brian D. McLaren, *A Generous Orthodoxy* (Grand Rapids, MI: Zondervan, 2004), 138.

7. Jay Rogers, "In the Media Spotlight: Furor Over Homosexuality Continues at Harvard," Forerunner.com, April 1, 1992, http://tinyurl.com/kryattx (accessed January 9, 2014). See also, Elaine Woo, "Peter J. Gomes Dies at 68; Harvard's Longtime Spiritual Leader," *Los Angeles Times*, March 6, 2011, http://tinyurl.com/mhmv5xj (accessed January 9, 2014).

8. Peter J. Gomes, *The Good Book: Reading the Bible With Heart and Mind* (San Francisco: HarperSanFrancisco, 1996), 147. The chapter on the "The Bible and Homosexuality" runs from 144–172.

9. Ibid., 146.

10. Bruce Bawer, *Stealing Jesus: How Fundamentalism Betrays Christianity* (New York: Three Rivers, 1997), 143.

11. Comment on "The Fighting Words of Michael Brown" by Dave Rattigan, ExGayWatch.com, January 24, 2008, http://tinyurl.com/otos9gz (accessed January 9, 2014).

12. Ibid.

13. John Corvino, *What's Wrong With Homosexuality?* (New York: Oxford University Press, 2013), 33.

14. Ibid., 35–36.

15. Ibid., 46–47.

16. Willard M. Swartley, *Homosexuality: Biblical Interpretation and Moral Discernment* (Scottdale, PA: Herald Press, 2003), 95–96.

17. Ibid., 96.

18. Luke Timothy Johnson, "Homosexuality and the Church: Scripture and Experience," Commonwealmagazine.org, June 11, 2007, http://tinyurl.com /p3ags3v (accessed January 9, 2014). © 2014 Commonweal Foundation, reprinted with permission. For more information, visit www.commonweal magazine.org. For a candid response to Professor Johnson, see: Dan Phillips, "Who Does Luke Timothy Johnson Think He Is? God?", *Contra Mundum* (blog), March 4, 2008, http://tinyurl.com/njyt84w (accessed January 9, 2014).
19. Johnson, "Homosexuality and the Church: Scripture and Experience."
20. Ibid.
21. Ibid.
22. Ibid.
23. Ibid.
24. Ibid.
25. Ibid.
26. Ibid.
27. Ibid.
28. Ibid.
29. Ibid.
30. The Hebrew word used for "property" in verse 46 is *'aḥuzzah*, which literally means "a possession." This is the only time in the Bible that this word is used with reference to a human being.
31. Ephesians 6:5–8; Colossians 3:22; 1 Timothy 6:1; Titus 2:9–10; 1 Peter 2:18–20.
32. And note how the slave would be sent out in the seventh year: "And when you let him go free from you, you shall not let him go empty-handed. You shall furnish him liberally out of your flock, out of your threshing floor, and out of your winepress. As the LORD your God has blessed you, you shall give to him" (Deut. 15:13–14).
33. See Michael A. Grisanti, "Deuteronomy," in *The Expositor's Bible Commentary*, rev. ed., 2:684-685. According to Duane L. Christensen, *Deuteronomy 21:10–34:12*, Word Biblical Commentary (Dallas: Word, 2002), 549, "This command runs contrary to all known ancient Near Eastern law codes, which forbade the harboring of runaway slaves. In particular, note the words of an Aramaic treaty text known as Sefire III…which expresses the opposite of the words that appear here: 'he shall dwell in your midst, in the place that he will choose in one of your towns, wherever it pleases him.'"

34. Walter C. Kaiser Jr., Peter H. Davids, F. F. Bruce, and Manfred T. Brauch, *Hard Sayings of the Bible* (one-volume edition), (Downers Grove, IL: Inter-Varsity Press, 1996), 149–150. Used by permission of InterVarsity Press, P. O. Box 1400, Downers Grove, IL 60515, USA. www.ivpress.com Note also on page 150, "A female slave who was married to her captor could not be sold again as a slave. If her master, now her husband, grew to hate her, she had to be liberated and was declared a free person (Deut. 21:14)."

35. Ibid., 150. For a nontechnical response to the question of slavery in the Bible, see CompellingTruth.org, "Why Was Slavery Allowed in the Bible?", http://www.compellingtruth.org/slavery-Old-Testament.html (accessed January 9, 2014).

36. Writing on Galatians 3:28 in Deryn Guest, Robert E. Goss, Mona West, and Thomas Bohache, eds. *Queer Bible Commentary* (London: SCM Press, 2006), 626, Patrick S. Cheng explains, "It is not surprising that the promise of radical equality in Galatians 3.28 resonates strongly with queer Christians and our allies. In other words, not only is there no longer Jew or Greek, slave or free, male and female, but *there is no longer straight or queer.*" (Cheng cites other scholars to support this reading.) Of course Dr. Cheng is comparing apples to oranges, since ethnicity, social status, and gender have nothing to do with romantic attractions, sexual desires, or any specific kind of behavior, whereas the heterosexuality and homosexuality divide along these very lines. Paul's point is that in Jesus there is no caste system or class system and that, as he stated in Romans 10:12, "There is no distinction between Jew and Greek; for the same Lord is Lord of all, bestowing his riches on all who call on him."

37. Kaiser, Davids, Bruce, and Brauch, *Hard Sayings of the Bible*, 642–644.

38. Ibid.

39. Ibid., emphasis added; see also comment to 1 Corinthians 7:17, 20 on page 591.

40. Just for the record, although Dr. King had associates such as Bayard Rustin, who was known to be homosexual, he actually made a very clear statement against homosexual practice when replying to some questions that were submitted to him. In "Advice for Living," he directs the young man writing to him to see a psychiatrist and concludes with, "You are already on the right road toward a solution, since you honestly recognize the problem and have a desire to solve it." ("Advice for Living," The Martin Luther King Jr. Papers Project, January 1958, 358–359, http://tinyurl.com /ox7kjb3 [accessed January 9, 2014]).

41. Jody Victor, "Jody Victor Speaks About America's Pastor: Billy Graham," February 14, 2010, http://tinyurl.com/ocyhn7w (accessed January 9, 2014). See also Trevor Freeze, "Remembering Dr. Martin Luther King Jr.," Billy Graham Evangelistic Association, January 12, 2012, http://tinyurl.com/o343c9t (accessed January 9, 2014).

42. An example would be the shameful and totally false claim that the curse of slavery in Genesis 9:25 applied to blacks historically.

43. For the argument that Jonathan and David were involved in a homosexual relationship, see chapter 4.

44. According to Acts 18:26, both Priscilla and Aquila took Apollos "aside and explained to him the way of God more accurately"; also, in four out of the five times their names are mentioned together, her name is put first (Acts 18:18, 26; Romans 16:3; 1 Corinthians 16:19; 2 Timothy 4:19), implying her prominence.

45. Most textual scholars agree that the proper name here is Junia (a woman) rather than Junias (a man); the greater debate is whether she was "outstanding among the apostles" (NIV)—which would mean she herself was an apostle—or "well known to the apostles" (ESV). For a passionate defense of the former view, see New Testament scholar Scot McKnight's short e-book, *Junia Is Not Alone* (Englewood, CO: Patheos Press, 2011).

46. See note 36 above.

47. See, conveniently, Eliezer Segal, "Who Has Not Made Me a Woman," MyJewishLearning.com, http://tinyurl.com/2anyum6 (accessed January 9, 2014).

48. Rodney Stark, *The Rise of Christianity: How the Obscure, Marginal Jesus Movement Became the Dominant Religious Force in the Western World in a Few Centuries* (Princeton, NJ: Princeton University Press, 1996), 95.

49. Ibid., 103.

50. Ibid., 104.

51. Ibid., 97.

52. Ibid., 98–99

53. Ibid., 104.

54. Ibid., 104, 110.

55. Robert A. J. Gagnon, *The Bible and Homosexual Practice: Texts and Hermeneutics* (Nashville: Abingdon, 2001), 328.

56. Craig S. Keener, *The IVP Bible Background Commentary: New Testament* (Downers Grove, IL: InterVarsity Press, 1993), 483.

57. Ibid.

58. First Timothy 2:11–15 presents more difficulties for the egalitarian inter- preters, but even if women should *not* teach men in church settings, Paul does not say that those who do will not inherit the kingdom of God, to give just one difference between this text and his teaching in 1 Corinthians 6:9–11. For egalitarian exegesis of this passage, see, e.g., Craig S. Keener, *Paul, Women, and Wives: Marriage and Women's Ministry in the Letters of Paul* (Grand Rapids, MI: Baker, 1992); Phillip Barton Payne, *Man and Woman, One in Christ: An Exegetical and Theological Study of Paul's Let- ters* (Grand Rapids, MI: Zondervan, 2009). For detailed complementarian exegesis, see, e.g., Andreas Kostenberger and Thomas W. Schreiner, eds., *Women in the Church: An Analysis and Application of 1 Timothy 2:9–15* (Grand Rapids, MI: Baker, 2005).

59. See again the comments of Professor Rodney Stark, cited previously, along with the works cited in notes 34 and 48 of this chapter, above.

60. Hebrews 2:14–18; 4:14–16.

61. Professor Mark Yarhouse speaks of a "three-tier distinction," distin- guishing between same-sex attraction, a homosexual orientation, and a gay identity. See Mark A. Yarhouse, *Homosexuality and the Christian: A Guide for Parents, Pastors, and Friends* (Ada, MI: Bethany House Publishers, 2010).

62. Johnson, "Homosexuality and the Church: Scripture and Experience."

63. In the New Testament alone, see, e.g., Matthew 24:11–14; 1 Corinthians 6:9; 15:33; 2 Corinthians 11:3; Galatians 6:7; Ephesians 5:6; 2 Thessalo- nians 2:3; Jacob (James) 1:16–26; 1 John 2:26; Revelation 12:9.

64. In point of fact, there is no reputable scientific evidence that anyone is born gay; see Brown, *A Queer Thing Happened to America*, 197–225.

65. See ibid., 226–271, and note that many researchers claim that pedo- philia is inborn and immutable, yet who among us would say that makes it acceptable? God forbid! So then, just because something may be innate and immutable, that doesn't make it right for a moment. (I am not equating homosexuality with pedophilia; I'm simply refuting the "born this way" argument as carrying moral force, aside from the fact that there is no reputable scientific evidence that it is true.)

66. For some representative online testimonies, see the People Can Change website, http://www.peoplecanchange.com/stories/index.php (accessed Jan- uary 10, 2014).

67. Richard B. Hays, "The Biblical Witness Concerning Homosexuality," in Maxie D. Dunnam and H. Newton Malony, eds., *Staying the Course:*

Supporting the Church's Position on Homosexuality (Nashville: Abingdon, 2003), 82.

68. William J. Webb, *Slaves, Women and Homosexuals: Exploring the Hermeneutics of Cultural Analysis* (Downers Grove, IL: InterVarsity Press, 2001), 244. Used by permission of InterVarsity Press, P. O. Box 1400, Downers Grove, IL 60515, USA. www.ivpress.com

69. Ibid., 245–246.

70. Ibid., 246.

71. Ibid., 247.

72. Ibid., 248.

73. Ibid., 250–251.

74. Ibid., 252.

75. Willard M. Swartley, *Slavery, Sabbath, War, and Women: Case Issues in Biblical Interpretation* (repr., Scottdale, PA: Herald Press, 2012), from the book's description on Amazon.com, http://tinyurl.com/qebhy2d (accessed January 10, 2014).

76. Swartley, *Homosexuality*, 17–18.

77. Ibid.

CHAPTER 4

THE BIBLE IS A HETEROSEXUAL BOOK

1. See, as one example among countless others, Dr. Mel White, who refers to "those same old clobber passages" (*Religion Gone Bad*, 74). A Google search for "clobber passages" on July 10, 2013, yielded 16,000 hits. For a book just devoted to these passages, see John F. Dwyer, *Those 7 References: A Study of 7 References to Homosexuality in the Bible* (N.p.: BookSurge Publishing, 2007).

2. This illustration was shared with me in private conversation with Larry, who has given me permission to use it in this book. Visit his website at http://www.larrytomczak.com. For his video "Is Gay OK?", watch it at https://www.youtube.com/watch?v=-m88QfCPZX0 (accessed January 14, 2014).

3. Gordon J. Wenham *Genesis 1–15*, Word Biblical Commentary (Dallas: Word, 1998), 70.

4. A. B. Simpson, *The Christ in the Bible Commentary, Book 1* (Camp Hill, PA: Wingspread Publishers, 2009), 25.

5. In a personal e-mail sent April 10, 2013, Robert Gagnon stated: "Reproductive potential is one, but only one, element of a larger array of features

that enables society to differentiate even between infertile heterosexual couples and adoptive homosexual relationships. The structural inability of homosexual relationships to produce offspring is the symptom of the root problem of too much embodied sameness, not enough complementary otherness, between persons of the same sex. It is not the root problem itself. At every level, anatomically, physiologically, and psychologically, it is self-evident that a man is not an appropriate sexual counterpart to another male, nor a woman to another woman; that when two (or more) people of the same sex enter into a sexual relationship they diminish their own sex or gender by treating it as only half intact in relation to their own sex rather than in relation to the other sex that constitutes their sexual other half (2 half-males make a whole male, 2 half-females make a full female, rather than a male and female uniting to integrate a single sexual whole). The extremes of a given sex are ratcheted up in a homosexual union for the transparent reason that the union lacks a true sexual complement to moderate the extremes of a given sex and to fill in the gaps. There is also an infinite difference between [being] erotically attracted to the essence of a sex that is not one's own but complements one's own on the one hand and being erotically attracted by what one already is as a sexual being: males aroused by their own distinctive maleness and females aroused by the essence of the feminine. Nature has made infinitely clear that there are two and only two primary sexes in the sexual spectrum and that these two sexes are structured in ways that complement each other at every level, whereas homosexual unions defy such natural complementarity by seeking sexual otherness in sexual sames and thereby dishonoring the integrity of their own sex or gender in relation to others of the same sex or gender."

6. With all respect to gay pastor R. D. Weekly's attempt to deal honestly with the biblical text, he has obviously missed some of the larger points of the narrative in Genesis 1–2 when he writes that, "Adam and Eve's marriage is *descriptive*, not *prescriptive*. It describes the historical narrative, but does not demonstrate God's intentions for marriage" (R. D. Weekly, *Homosexianity* [N.p.: CreateSpace Independent Publishing Platform, 2009], 78, emphasis his). As we have seen, this argument is patently false, since what is described lays the foundation and becomes the paradigm for the rest of the Bible—including all descriptive rules. Moreover, there is not a descriptive or prescriptive syllable sanctioning or supporting same-sex "marriage" anywhere in the Bible. Weekly is, therefore, quite wrong in the rest of his discussion on the subject of marriage in the Bible (Ibid.,

71–99), in particular in his concluding remarks, "Oh friend, God is love. Reflecting that love is what's important to Him, not the biological sex of those involved. By His own word—rightly interpreted through the lens of love—you'd better believe there's something holy about gay matrimony" (Ibid., 99). Nothing could be further from the truth.

7. For a YouTube response to this chart by Alan Shlemon, see http://www .youtube.com/watch?v=JyjMMbB5KV4.

8. See, e.g., Genesis 4:19; 24:4; 25:1.

9. See, e.g., the extensive warnings in Proverbs 5 and 7, and note the words of Jesus in Matthew 5:27–30.

10. Among many, see Leviticus 19:3; Colossians 3:18–21.

11. Again, among many, see Proverbs 4:1–4; 6:20.

12. Once again, among many, see Jeremiah 33:10–11.

13. See, e.g., Jeremiah 2:1–3; Ephesians 5:22–33.

14. Ephesians 6:1–3, going back to Exodus 20:12; but when Colossians 3:20 refers to parents, the context makes clear as well who is in mind: the father and mother!

15. Robert A. J. Gagnon, "Truncated Love: A Response to Andrew Marin's *Love Is an Orientation*, Part 1," RobGagnon.net, http://tinyurl.com/lzqttz7 (accessed January 10, 2014). Gagnon was rebutting Andrew Marin, *Love Is an Orientation* (Downers Grove, IL: IVP Books, 2009), a book that is good as it is bad. By this I mean, Marin really helps the reader to understand the terrible pain suffered by many gays and lesbians because of their perception that God has rejected them—and the church has often contributed to that pain. At the same time his book contains some of the worst treatment of Scripture in any book I have ever read that was published by a major evangelical publisher, almost glorying in ambiguity and misuse of the biblical text. This is truly unfortunate, since other parts of the book are quite commendable.

16. Michael Brown, "It's an Avalanche, Not a Slippery Slope," CharismaNews .com, http://tinyurl.com/lhxqg2u (accessed January 10, 2014).

17. Equally perverse is Robert Goss's description of John the Baptist as "the hairy bear Baptist" (*Queer Bible Commentary*, 552). Goss, it should be noted, is one of the more influential gay theologians today, because of which he served as an editor of this commentary.

18. As quoted in Ken Stone, ed., *Queer Commentary and the Hebrew Bible* (Cleveland, OH: The Pilgrim Press, 2001), 176–177.

19. Ibid., 177–178.

20. Ibid., 179, emphasis his.

21. Ibid.

22. Ibid., 180. In Koch's "cruising" world, Lydia in Acts 16:11–15 becomes "a shrewd lesbian merchant"; Absalom, David's son, becomes "a very quickly advancing young man" (2 Sam. 16:14–23); Dinah becomes "a raped lesbian sister" (Gen. 34:1–17); while Judges 12:4–6 points to "a huge number of slaughtered lispers" (Ibid., 180, n. 3.). It should be noted that Koch is not dogmatic in his interpretations, but that he can read these texts in these ways at all says more than enough about his twisted interpretive method.

23. These selections have been adapted from the chapter "Queer Theology, a Gay/Lesbian Bible, and a Homoerotic Christ," in Brown, *A Queer Thing Happened to America.*

24. Daniel Helminiak, *What the Bible Really Says About Homosexuality,* updated and expanded edition (New Mexico: Alamo Square Press, 2000), 126.

25. First, the entire context of the Old Testament, along with the specific context of Ruth, makes clear that Ruth and Naomi were involved in heterosexual relationships only; second, it is a figment of the imagination to argue lesbian relationships were common in ancient Israel, to the point of being celebrated in writing. That's just part of the reason for my exclamation of, "Nonsense!"

26. Helminiak, *What the Bible Really Says About Homosexuality,* 127.

27. Ibid.

28. Ibid.

29. The book represents a printed version of material on the GayChristian Survivors.com website and, quite oddly, contains no page numbers. For a more scholarly study, see T. Horner, *Jonathan Loved David: Homosexuality in Biblical Times* (Philadelphia: Westminster, 1978).

30. James D. Cunningham, *Gay Christian Survivors* (N.p.: CreateSpace Independent Publishing Platform, 2013). The book contains no page numbers.

31. Ibid.

32. Ibid.

33. Ibid.

34. Ibid.

35. It is not impossible that this could describe that kind of relationship; the evidence simply goes against it, completely refuting Cunningham's point.

36. V. H. Matthews, M. W. Chavalas, and John H. Walton, *The IVP Bible Background Commentary: Old Testament* (Downers Grove, IL: InterVarsity Press, 2000), 309–310.

37. This was a reference to the Apocryphal book Judith; the verse cited reads, "The sons of maidservants have pierced them through; they were wounded like the children of fugitives, they perished before the army of my Lord" (rsv).

38. Ralph W. Klein, *1 Samuel*, Word Biblical Commentary (Dallas: Word, 1998), 209.

39. R. D. Bergen, *1, 2 Samuel*, The New American Commentary, vol. 7 (Nashville: Broadman and Holman Publishers, 1996), 218.

40. R. L. Omanson and J. Ellington, *A Handbook on the First Book of Samuel*, UBS Handbook Series (New York: United Bible Societies, 2001), 446.

41. Bergen, *1, 2 Samuel*, 218.

42. J. P. Lange, P. Schaff, D. Erdmann, C. H. Toy, and J. A. Broadus, eds., *A Commentary on the Holy Scriptures: 1 & 2 Samuel*, electronic edition (Bellingham, WA: Logos Bible Software, 2008), 266.

43. NET.Bible.org, "NET Notes: 1 Samuel 20:30," https://net.bible.org/#!bible/1+Samuel+20:30 (accessed January 13, 2014).

44. See chapter 5.

45. Cunningham, *Gay Christian Survivors*.

46. Joseph Nicolosi, "Why Gays Cannot Speak for Ex-Gays," Thomas Aquinas Psychological Clinic, http://tinyurl.com/ldwvnyr (accessed January 13, 2014).

47. In brief, see Michael Brown, "The Queen James Bible and 'Homophobic' Interpretations," CharismaNews.com, December 20, 2012, http://tinyurl.com/cz8utoa (accessed January 13, 2014). For the key verses laid out visually, see Matt Slick, "The Queen James Bible, the Gay Bible," Christian Apologetics and Research Ministry, December 20, 2012, http://carm.org/queen-james-bible (accessed January 13, 2014). The major verses in question will be dealt with in the following chapters.

CHAPTER 5

LEVITICAL LAWS AND THE MEANING OF *TO'EVAH* (ABOMINATION)

1. The West Wing, "Open Letter," December 9, 2003, http://westwing.bewarne.com/second/25letter.html (accessed January 13, 2014).

2. For the timing of this letter in conjunction with the TV show *West Wing*, which featured the president raising these same points to a "Dr. Laura" type person, see Brown, *A Queer Thing Happened to America*, 178–182.

3. Patrick Chapman, *Thou Shalt Not Love* (N.p.: Haiduk Press, 2008), 129–130.

4. Ibid., 130.

5. Ibid.

6. He is following the Old Testament scholar Saul M. Olyan here; see his article, "'And With a Man You Shall Not Lie the Lying Down of a Woman': On the Meaning and Significance of Leviticus 18:22 and 20:13," in Gary David Comstock and Susan Henking, eds., *Que(e)rying Religion: A Critical Anthology* (New York: Continuum Press, 1997), 398–414. Not surprisingly, traditional Judaism recognized that this prohibition included all forms of male-male sexual relationships.

7. Michaelson, *God vs. Gay?*, 61–62.

8. Ibid., 62–63. He also states that Kings, Chronicles, and Ezra all use *to'evah* to refer to "acts that other nations committed in the Land of Israel" (ibid., 63). After citing other verses in Deuteronomy and the prophetic books—which really do not help his cause, the truth be told—he claims that the only exception to the cultic, or "taboo," usage of *to'evah* is in Proverbs, where it is used for "ethical failings," claiming, "Aside from Proverbs, though, *toevah* has nothing to do with ethics, and everything to do with cultic behavior, idolatry, and foreign ritual" (ibid., 64). We'll examine the flawed nature of these arguments in further detail shortly.

9. For a concise Orthodox Jewish perspective, see Ezra Schochet, "The Torah: A Moral Compass," Jonah International, June 16, 2008, http://www.jonahweb.org/article.php?secId=317 (accessed January 13, 2014).

10. That does not make me automatically right, of course; it simply means I have invested considerable time, effort, and resources to be able to study the Hebrew Scriptures in their ancient context.

11. Lee, *Torn*, 177.

12. Robert Gagnon, "Does Leviticus Only Condemn Idolatrous Homosexual Practice?—an Open Letter From Robert Gagnon," *Philosophical Fragments* (blog), Patheos.com, March 28, 2013, http://tinyurl.com/lfkldag (accessed January 14, 2014). Permission requested.

13. Justin Lee, "Missing the Forest for the A/Bs," *Crumbs From the Communion Table* (blog), http://tinyurl.com/k538j2r (accessed January 14, 2014).

14. Robert Gagnon, "Is Justin Lee Now Misrepresenting the Fact That He Misrepresented My Views on the Levitical Prohibitions?—an Open Rejoinder to Justin Lee From Robert Gagnon," *Philosophical Fragments* (blog), Patheos.com, April 16, 2013, http://tinyurl.com/mn88uh8 (accessed January 14, 2014). Gagnon rightly noted that "your whole point in this section of your book was to say that *even* 'the foremost authority' among 'the Bible scholars who argue for the traditional view (that gay sex is always a sin)' agrees with the views of 'pro-gay' interpreters that the Levitical prohibitions were 'actually intended to condemn ritual cult prostitution, a form of idolatry in that culture that involved male-male sex.' The views of 'pro-gay' interpreters, you noted, could be dismissed because 'hey, they were arguing in favor of accepting gay relationships, so they might be biased.' Then you immediately add: '*What did the other side say? Pretty much the same thing, it turned out*' (my emphasis; p. 177). Right after saying this you cite me as exhibit A for showing that 'the other side' agrees with the conclusion of 'pro-gay' interpreters."

15. As expressed by Paul, "Food will not commend us to God. We are no worse off if we do not eat, and no better off if we do" (1 Cor. 8:8). He also wrote, with reference to food, "I know and am persuaded in the Lord Jesus that nothing is unclean in itself, but it is unclean for anyone who thinks it unclean" (Rom. 14:14). This builds on the teaching of Jesus, who did not abolish the food laws for Israel but who did make clear that what we eat would not defile us spiritually: "Do you not see that whatever goes into the mouth passes into the stomach and is expelled? But what comes out of the mouth proceeds from the heart, and this defiles a person" (Matt. 15:17–18).

16. For further discussion, see below.

17. The Hebrew word is *zimmah*, which can also mean, "plan, purpose" (in different contexts, obviously), or "wickedness," as here.

18. Again, *to'evah*. For more on the concept of "abomination," see James B. DeYoung, *Homosexuality: Contemporary Claims Examined in Light of the Bible and Other Ancient Literature and Law* (Grand Rapids, MI: Kregel, 2000), 65–68, including discussion of the relevant Greek terms.

19. The Hebrew word is *tevel*, which only occurs here and in Leviticus 20:12; it carries the meaning of "confusion, violation of order."

20. The prominent Leviticus scholar Jacob Milgrom advanced the odd idea that male-male sex was only prohibited *in the land of Israel* (based on this passage from Leviticus), which would lead to the odd idea that homosexual

men in Israel today could have sex outside the land without displeasing God but not inside their homeland! For a serious academic response to this, see Robert A. J. Gagnon, "A Critique of Jacob Milgrom's Views on Leviticus 18:22 and 20:13," http://www.robgagnon.net/articles/homo Milgrom.pdf (accessed January 14, 2014).

21. For these laws for Israel in the Torah, see in particular, "You shall keep my statutes. You shall not let your cattle breed with a different kind. You shall not sow your field with two kinds of seed, nor shall you wear a garment of cloth made of two kinds of material" (Lev. 19:19).

22. For the concept of homosexuality being a violation of divine order according to Leviticus, see Donald J. Wold, *Out of Order: Homosexuality in the Bible and the Ancient Near East* (Grand Rapids, MI: Baker, 1998), 91–100.

23. Of course, adultery remains a serious sin in God's sight, while the ancient Israelite culture of honor—reflected throughout the Bible and still common in some parts of the world—is highly commendable (see, e.g, Leviticus 19:32, "Rise in the presence of the aged, show respect for the elderly and revere your God. I am the LORD" [NIV]). My point is that I'm not advocating the death penalty for adultery or cursing one's parents any more than I'm advocating it for homosexual practice.

24. Remember: God called Israel not to follow *the practices of the nations*. As noted in a rabbinic commentary to Leviticus 18:3: "If you follow the practices of the Egyptians—for what purpose did I bring you out of Egypt?" (*Be'erot Yitzhak*).

25. For more on the attack on gender, see chapters 2 and 9.

26. Ludwig Koehler, Walter Baumgartner, and others (translated and edited under the supervision of M. E. J. Richardson), *Hebrew and Aramaic Lexicon of the Old Testament, Study Edition* (Leiden; Boston; Koln: Brill, 2001), 2:1703, emphasis added.

27. For the larger, negative implications for homosexual practice rightly derived from Genesis 19, see Gagnon, *The Bible and Homosexual Practice*, 71–90; and Wold, *Out of Order*, 77–89.

28. Note that Ezekiel, himself a priest, used priestly language (meaning, language often similar to that found in the book of Leviticus), and the phrase "commit an abomination" (in Hebrew, the verbal root '-s-h and the noun *to'evah*) is used in both Leviticus 20:13 (a text we reviewed earlier, calling male homosexual practice an abomination) and here in Ezekiel 16:50.

29. Lee, *Torn*, 177, citing Gagnon, *The Bible and Homosexual Practice*, 130.

30. Ibid.
31. Gagnon, "Does Leviticus Only Condemn Idolatrous Homosexual Practice?—an Open Letter From Robert Gagnon," emphasis added by Gagnon.
32. Ibid., emphasis added by Gagnon.
33. Ibid., emphasis his.
34. Weekly, *Homosexianity*, 101–102, emphasis his.
35. "Leviticus," in John Sailhammer, Walter C. Kaiser Jr., and Richard Hess, *The Expositor's Bible Commentary* (Grand Rapids, MI: Zondervan, 2008), 742–743.
36. For a different perspective, cf. Robert A. J. Gagnon, "Notes to Gagnon's Essay in the Gagnon-Via *Two Views* Book," note 41, September 2003, http://www.robgagnon.net/2VOnlineNotes.htm (accessed January 14, 2014). Note that "the only 'penalty' mentioned for sex with a menstruating woman is that the man is put into a state of ritual uncleanness for seven days (15:24)."
37. Mel White, "What the Bible Says—and Doesn't Say—About Homosexuality," Soulforce.com, http://tinyurl.com/m28gvy4 (accessed January 14, 2014).
38. Guest, Goss, West, and Bohache, *Queer Bible Commentary*, 83, emphasis his.
39. Gregg Drinkwater, Joshua Lesser, and David Shneer, eds., *Torah Queeries* (New York: New York University Press, 2009), 153.
40. Ibid.
41. Ibid., 153–154.
42. Ibid., 154.
43. Ibid., 153.
44. On a similar note, for the weakness of Rabbi Steven Greenberg's arguments seeking to harmonize traditional Judaism with homosexual practice, compare his book *Wrestling With God and Men: Homosexuality in the Jewish Tradition* (Madison, WI: Univ. of Wisconsin Press, 2004) with the data presented in Arthur Goldberg's *Light in the Closet: Torah, Homosexuality and the Power to Change* (Beverly Hills: Red Heifer Press, 2008); see also Chaim Rapoport, *Judaism and Homosexuality: An Authentic Orthodox View* (London: Vallentine Mitchell, 2004).
45. For documentation, see Brown, *A Queer Thing Happened to America*, 396; see also A. Dean Byrd, Shirley E. Cox, and Jeffrey W. Robinson, "The Innate-Immutable Argument Finds No Basis in Science," National

Association for Research and Therapy of Homosexuality, http://www
.narth.org/docs/innate.html (accessed January 14, 2014).

46. See Brown, *A Queer Thing Happened to America*, 227–271.

47. See in particular chapter 8 for similar observations on "gay Christian"
readings of Paul.

48. See chapter 8 for representative studies.

49. See the documentation in Brown, *A Queer Thing Happened to America*,
483-490, as well as the study cited in note 50, immediately below.

50. See James E. Phelan, Neil Whitehead, and Philip M. Sutton, "What
Research Shows: NARTH's Response to the APA Claims on Homosexuality. A Report of the Scientific Advisory Committee of the National
Association for Research and Therapy of Homosexuality," *Journal for
Human Sexuality* 1 (2009): 5–121, with extensive documentation. Of specific relevance here, see 53–88. It is common in gay activist circles to dismiss NARTH as junk scientists, but that is based on polemics rather than
facts, and this study is carefully researched and presented.

CHAPTER 6
WHAT DID JESUS SAY ABOUT HOMOSEXUALITY?

1. Some good websites to explore include http://www.leestrobel.com/ and
http://www.reasonablefaith.org/.

2. See Michael L. Brown, *The Real Kosher Jesus* (Lake Mary, FL: FrontLine
Books, 2012), with references.

3. As noted by Mary Rose D'Angelo in John J. Collins and Daniel C.
Hartlow, eds., *The Eerdmans Dictionary of Early Judaism* (Grand Rapids,
MI: Eerdmans, 2010), 1223, "Standard treatments of early Judaism tend
to attribute to it an unqualified endorsement of heterosexual marriage and
an implacable hostility to homoeroticism."

4. L. William Countryman, *Dirt, Greed, and Sex: Sexual Ethics in the New
Testament and Their Implications for Today* (Minneapolis, MN: Fortress Press, 2007), cited in Robert A. J. Gagnon, "Prof. Robert Gagnon's
Response to Prof. L. William Countryman's Review in *Anglican Theological Review*: On Careful Scholarship," September 2003, http://robgagnon
.net/RevCountryman.htm (accessed January 14, 2014).

5. For more on this, see chapter 2, with reference to the gay activist elephant
in the room.

6. For more on this, see Michael L. Brown, *Answering Jewish Objections to Jesus: Vol. 4: New Testament Objections* (Grand Rapids, MI: Baker, 2006), 204–236.

7. As we noted in chapter 4, there were certain laws that God gave Israel to keep them separated from the nations but that did not have universal moral application, as opposed to laws He gave Israel that were of universal moral import; the prohibition against homosexual practice falls into the "universal" category.

8. There are two particularly fascinating references to homosexuality from early rabbinic literature, dating to within the first five centuries of this era: "Rabbi Huna said in the name of Rabbi Joseph, 'The generation of the Flood was not wiped out until they wrote marriage documents for the union of a man to a male or to an animal.'" (Genesis Rabbah 26:5; Leviticus Rabbah 23:9) And, "Ula said: Non-Jews [lit., the sons of Noah] accepted upon themselves thirty commandments [Hebrew, *mitzvoth*], but they only abide by three of them: the first one is that they do not write marriage documents for male couples, the second one is that they don't sell dead [human] meat by the pound in stores and the third one is that they respect the Torah" (Babylonian Talmud Chullin 92a–b).

9. According to the gay-affirming biblical scholar Jeffrey Siker, "It is extremely difficult to say much of anything with confidence regarding the attitude of Jesus toward homosexuality. He would have had a different understanding of same-sex relations in his first century Jewish context than is the case in our twenty-first century world. Nor would he have known people of faith who also self-identified as gay or lesbian. At least we have no such evidence." See Jeffrey S. Siker, ed., *Homosexuality in the Church: Both Sides of the Debate* (Louisville, KY: Westminster John Knox, 1994), 138. Really? Such a statement not only strains credulity; it makes current concepts of sexual orientation almost sacrosanct.

10. See SyracuseCulturalWorkers.com, "Postcard—Things You Can Do to Eradicate Gender or Multiply It Exponentially," http://tinyurl.com/ kbro7ro (accessed January 17, 2014). For discussion, see Brown, *A Queer Thing Happened to America*, 93–94.

11. For discussion and documentation, see Brown, *A Queer Thing Happened to America*, 84–119.

12. See ibid., 549–598, for representative quotes.

13. Rick Brentlinger, *Gay Christian 101: Spiritual Self-Defense for Gay Christians—What the Bible Really Says About Homosexuality* (N.p.:

Salient Press, 2007), 229, emphasis his. His treatment of eunuchs (223–257) is filled with false and gratuitous statements, from the chapter title ("Eunuchs in Scripture & History Are Gay Men") to his conclusions ("The term eunuch, in history and scripture, is often a synonym for gay and lesbian.").

14. Sandra Turnbull, *God's Gay Agenda* (Bellflower, CA: Glory Publishing, 2012). This figure is based on my search in Kindle.

15. Sphero, *The Gay Faith*, Kindle locations, 3437–3438.

16. Ibid., Kindle locations 3430–3431.

17. Ibid., Kindle locations 3372–3378.

18. As stated by Professor Leon Morris; see below, note 33.

19. The Hebrew word for "eunuch" is *saris*, which is probably derived from the Akkadian word *ša rēši*, which means "the one at the head" and was used for directors, stewards, and then eunuchs. (Akkadian is the language of the ancient Assyrians and Babylonians.) So it was used to describe high court officials and, because castrated men were often entrusted with these positions (especially overseeing the king's harem), it came to refer to eunuchs as well. The same usage is found in the Bible, and so while it is very clear that the text is referring to castrated men (as in Isaiah 56:3–4), in other cases it is unclear whether *saris* in Hebrew or *eunochos* in Greek refers to a castrated man or to a high court official. This would be the case with Ebed Melech, called a *saris* in Jeremiah 38:7; was he "a eunuch who was in the king's house" (ESV)—thus a castrated man who served in the royal palace— or simply "a court official in the royal palace" (NET)? The same question arises with the Ethiopian eunuch whom Philip led to Jesus in Acts 8. Was he specifically a castrated man serving in the queen's court (the most likely interpretation) or simply a high court official? To be sure, the Greek word *eunuchos* refers to a castrated man, but there is a linguistic phenomenon called "calque" in which concepts from one language (in this case, Hebrew) can be borrowed into other language.

20. See in particular here Sphero and Brentlinger; for a more serious discussion (but still with wrong conclusions), see Faris Malik's website "Born Eunuchs," http://www.well.com/user/aquarius/ (accessed January 17, 2014).

21. For representative and aggressive examples, see immediately above, note 20.

22. Michaelson, *God vs. Gay?*, 76–77.

23. For a useful Internet discussion, see "Is the Word 'Eunuch' Really the Bible's Way of Saying Homosexuals?", http://www.fredsbibletalk.com/eunuchs.html (accessed January 17, 2014).

24. See, e.g., Sphero, *The Gay Faith*, who argues for civil unions for homo-
    sexuals based on this passage, stating, "It becomes even clearer that the
    first category *did* in fact refer directly to those who are attracted to the
    same sex (i.e., gays and lesbians, as his listeners would have understood
    it to mean as per the inclusive definition of the word at the time), and are
    thus *not* meant to marry in the same manner that he previously described
    in verse 19:4 in regards to male and female marriage" (Kindle locations
    976-980). So Jesus is allegedly saying that gay men *can* be sexually united,
    not just in conventional marriage. When I read these "gay Christian"
    attempts to rewrite what Jesus actually said, I feel only sadness for those
    who are wrestling to unite active homosexuality and Christian faith, and I
    encourage others who find their claims outlandish to pray for them rather
    than be upset with them.

25. See, e.g., Brentlinger, *Gay Christian 101*, 236–242.

26. B. M. Newman and P. C. Stine, *A Handbook on the Gospel of Matthew*,
    UBS Handbook Series (New York: United Bible Societies, 1988), 596,
    emphasis theirs.

27. W. Arndt, F. W. Danker, F. Wilbur Gingrich, and Walter Bauer, *A Greek-
    English Lexicon of the New Testament and Other Early Christian Literature*,
    3rd ed. (Chicago: University of Chicago Press, 2000), 409.

28. H. R. Balz and G. Schneider, eds., *Exegetical Dictionary of the New Testa-
    ment*, Eng. tr. (Grand Rapids, MI: Eerdmans, 1990–1993), 2:81.

29. Donald A. Hagner, *Matthew 14–28*, Word Biblical Commentary (Dallas:
    Word, 1998), 550–551.

30. Craig Blomberg, *Matthew*, The New American Commentary (Nashville:
    Broadman & Holman Publishers, 1992), 294.

31. W. D. Davies and D. C. Allison, *Matthew* (in the International Critical
    Commentary series), 3:23, cited in the NET translation note to Matthew
    19:14.

32. Cited here from the one-volume abridgement, Gerhard Kittel and Gerhard
    Friedrich, eds., *Theological Dictionary of the New Testament*, tr. G. W. Bro-
    miley (Grand Rapids, MI: Eerdmans, 1985), 277.

33. Leon Morris, *The Gospel According to Matthew*, The Pillar New Testament
    Commentary (Grand Rapids, MI: Eerdmans, 1992), 485–486. Used by
    permission.

34. According to M. A. Powell, ed., *The HarperCollins Bible Dictionary*, third
    edition (New York: HarperCollins, 2011), 265, *eunuch* referred to "a male

who lacks testicles, either because he was born that way or because he has been castrated (cf. Matt. 19:12)."

35. Again, I encourage you to believe the stories of those who have been changed and who have lived above reproach for many years, just as I believe the stories of those who tell me they tried to change and could not. For discussion of the wider issues involved, see Joe Dallas and Nancy Heche, *The Complete Christian Guide to Understanding Homosexuality: A Biblical and Compassionate Response to Same-Sex Attraction* (Eugene, OR: Harvest House, 2010).

36. Sam Allberry, *Is God Anti-Gay? And Other Questions About homosexuality, the Bible and Same-Sex Attraction* (N.p.: The Good Book Company, 2013), 9.

37. Ibid., 10.

38. Michael L. Brown, *It's Time to Rock the Boat: A Call to God's People to Rise Up and Preach a Confrontational Gospel* (Shippensburg, PA: Destiny Image, 1993), 81.

39. Ibid.

40. In point of fact, many Christian ministries with emphasis on healthy families and marriages have brought attention to this problem for decades, but in light of the significance of the scandal of rampant evangelical divorce, especially divorces without any possible biblical support, there has been a relative silence on the issue.

CHAPTER 7
THE HEALING OF THE CENTURION'S SERVANT

1. See Frank Heinz, "Church's Billboards Affirm Gay Love," NBCDFW .com, September 9, 2009, http://tinyurl.com/mt6sefq (accessed January 17, 2014); see also "Would Jesus Discriminate?", WhyWouldWe.org, http:// www.whywouldwe.net/site/ (accessed January 17, 2014).

2. Michaelson, *God vs. Gay?*, 72; in support of this he cites Jack Clark Robinson, "Jesus, the Centurion, and His Lover," *Gay and Lesbian Review* 14, no. 6 (2007): 70–72; Theodore W. Jennings Jr., *The Man Jesus Loved* (Cleveland, OH: Pilgrim Press, 2009), 131–144; Brentlinger, *Gay Christian 101*, 193–221; and Jeff Miner and John Tyler Connoley, *The Children Are Free: Reexamining the Biblical Evidence on Same-Sex Relationships* (Indianapolis: Found Pearl Press, 2002), 46–51.

3. Miner and Connoley, *The Children Are Free*, 47. The section is headed, "When Jesus meets a gay person."

4. Ibid., 49.

5. Ibid.

6. See, e.g., the reviews and articles listed here: "People With a History: An Online Guide to Lesbian, Gay, Bisexual and Trans History: John Boswell Page," Fordham University, http://www.fordham.edu/halsall/pwh/index -bos.asp (accessed January 17, 2014). Note in particular Marian Therese Horvat, "Rewriting History to Serve the Gay Agenda," Traditionin Action.org, http://www.traditioninaction.org/bkreviews/A_002br_ SameSex.htm (accessed January 17, 2014); for critical reviews of Boswell by *gay scholars*, see "Warren Johansson, Wayne R. Dynes, and John Lauritsen, "Homosexuality, Intolerance, and Christianity: A Critical Examination of John Boswell's Work," http://pinktriangle.org.uk/lib/hic/index.html (accessed January 17, 2014); and Camille Paglia, "Boswell Reviews," *Washington Post*, July 17, 1994, as posted on Fordham.edu, http://www.fordham .edu/halsall/pwh/bosrev-paglia.asp (accessed January 17, 2014).

7. These Greek lexicons (and theological encyclopedias), which, for the most part, are *not* the product of conservative Christian scholarship and therefore cannot be subject to the charge that they are biased against homosexuals (which, from a scholastic viewpoint, would still be a baseless charge), include: H. G. Liddell and R. Scott, *A Greek-English Lexicon*, ninth edition with a revised supplement (Oxford: Clarendon Press, 1996); Walter Bauer, Frederick Danker, et al., *A Greek-English Lexicon of the New Testament and Other Early Christian Literature* (Chicago: University of Chicago Press, 2001); Joseph Thayer, *Thayer's Greek-English Lexicon of the New Testament* (repr., Peabody, MA: Hendrickson, 1996); Gerhard Kittel and Gerhard Friedrich, eds., *Theological Dictionary of the New Testament*, 10 vols., trans. G. W. Bromiley (Grand Rapids, MI: Eerdmans, 1977); Horst Balz and Gerhard Schneider, eds., *The Exegetical Dictionary of the New Testament*, 3 vols. (Grand Rapids, MI: Eerdmans, 1990); Colin Brown, ed., *The New International Dictionary of New Testament Theology*, 4 vols. (Grand Rapids, MI: Zondervan, 1986). See also Johannes P. Louw and Eugene A. Nida, *Greek-English Lexicon of the New Testament Based on Semantic Domains*, 2 vols., second edition (New York: United Bible Societies, 1989). Note that these lexicons are also consistent in their rendering of key Greek terms identified with homosexuality in important New Testament (or related ancient Greek) contexts.

8. Brentlinger, *Gay Christian 101*, 199.

9. Michaelson, *God vs. Gay?*, 75.

10. While by no means universally accepted in "gay Christian" circles, especially the most conservative ones, it is becoming increasingly accepted, as evidenced by the billboard campaign mentioned at the onset of this chapter, which was hardly protested or repudiated by "gay Christians" nationally. The widespread acceptance of this bizarre rewriting of the biblical text is also indicated by the fact that gay scholars are presenting it in more and more dogmatic terms.

11. WhyWouldWe.org, "Jesus Affirmed a Gay Couple," emphasis added, http://www.whywouldwe.net/site/jesus-affirmed-a-gay-couple (accessed January 20, 2014).

12. Brentlinger, *Gay Christian 101*, 197, emphasis added.

13. Michaelson, *God vs. Gay?*, 75, emphasis added.

14. Brentlinger, *Gay Christian 101*, 199, emphasis added.

15. Michaelson, *God vs. Gay?*, 75.

16. For questions as to the original textual placement of John 8:1–11, see, e.g., Craig S. Keener, *The Gospel of John: A Commentary* (Peabody, MA: Hendrickson, 2004).

17. Miner and Connoley, *The Children Are Free*, 50. One of the "proofs" offered by the authors that the slave, also described as such (using the Greek word *doulos*), was the centurion's male lover was that, according to Luke 7:2, this slave was "valued highly" by his master—and so he *must* have been his master's male lover. After all, why else would a slave be highly esteemed by his master?

18. Brentlinger, *Gay Christian 101*, 194.

19. A more serious attempt to put forth these arguments was made by Theodore W. Jennings Jr. and Tat-Siong Benny Liew, "Mistaken Identities but Model Faith: Rereading the Centurion, the Chap, and the Christ in Matthew 8:5–13," in *Journal of Biblical Literature* 123 (2004): 467–494; for a short but clear exposé of some of the errors in their article, see D. B. Saddington, "The Centurion in Matthew 8:5–13: Consideration of the Proposal of Theodore W. Jennings Jr., and Tat-Siong Benny Liew," *Journal of Biblical Literature* 125 (2006): 140–142. See further Robert A. J. Gagnon, "Did Jesus Approve of a Homosexual Couple in the Story of the Centurion at Capernaum?," April 24, 2007, http://robgagnon.net/articles/homosex CenturionStory.pdf (accessed January 20, 2014). In sum, Gagnon rightly states, "There are six main arguments against the assumption that Jesus was endorsing homosexual relations in his encounter with the centurion

at Capernaum. Individually, they are strong arguments. Collectively they make an airtight case against a pro-homosex reading."

20. *Study New Testament for Lesbians, Gays, Bi, and Transgender. With Extensive Notes on Greek Word Meaning and Context*, translated with notes by A. Nyland (n.p.: n.p., 2007). Nyland was a scholar in classics and ancient history, specializing in Greek and Hittite lexicography.

21. Elizabeth Stuart, ed., *Religion Is a Queer Thing: A Guide to the Christian Faith for Lesbian, Gay, Bisexual and Transgendered People* (Cleveland, OH: Pilgrim Press, 1997), 128, emphasis in the original. Dr. Gorsline is the former pastor of the Metropolitan Community Church in Richmond, Virginia.

22. Gagnon, "Did Jesus Approve of a Homosexual Couple in the Story of the Centurion at Capernaum?," emphasis his.

23. I. Howard Marshall, *The Gospel of Luke: A Commentary on the Greek Text*, New International Greek Testament Commentary (Grand Rapids, MI: Eerdmans, 1978), 279.

24. Gagnon, "Did Jesus Approve of a Homosexual Couple in the Story of the Centurion at Capernaum?"

25. Ibid., his emphasis. He notes further that, *"Jesus' fraternization with tax collectors and sexual sinners does not suggest support for their behavior.* The fact that Jesus healed the centurion's 'boy' (*pais*) in Matt 8:5–13 and Luke 7:1–10 communicates nothing in the way of approval of any potential sexual intercourse that the centurion may have been engaging in, whether with his 'boy' or anyone else. Jesus also reached out to tax collectors. Yet he certainly was not commending their well-deserved reputation for collecting more taxes from their own people than they had a right to collect. Jesus reached out to sexual sinners yet, given his clear statements on divorce/remarriage, he certainly was not condoning their sexual activity. Why should we conclude that Jesus' silence about the centurion's sexual life communicates approval?"

26. Ibid., emphasis his. Regarding the objection that for Jesus to heal the centurion's servant would have been to condone slavery, first, as noted in chapter 3, Jesus did not attempt to overthrow the system of slavery in His lifetime; in contrast, as seen here in this chapter, He clearly opposed homosexual practice; second, it is certainly possible that a highly valued servant would be treated well by his master, and Jesus, with perfect discernment and recognizing the centurion's concern for this servant, would have known that to be the case; third, Jesus was moved with compassion to

heal (see, e.g., Matthew 14:14), and we can safely assume that the servant would rather be alive than dead, otherwise he could have easily taken his life on his own.

27. For the possible connection between this account and the one under discussion here, see again Gagnon, "Did Jesus Approve of a Homosexual Couple in the Story of the Centurion at Capernaum?"

28. Brentlinger, *Gay Christian 101*, 205–208, attempts to soften this based on alleged ages of sexual activity back then.

CHAPTER 8

PAUL AND HOMOSEXUALITY

1. Robin Scroggs, *The New Testament and Homosexuality* (Philadelphia: Fortress, 1983), 127, emphasis his. And quite obviously Paul wrote more than "one sentence" in Romans 1 regarding homosexual practice. See also chapter 4, "The Bible Is a Heterosexual Book."

2. This was pointed out by Professor N. T. Wright, one of the world's foremost New Testament scholars; for his video discussion, see "N. T. Wright Debate About Homosexuality 4," http://tinyurl.com/y8eze9u (accessed January 20, 2014); for a written discussion, see John L. Allen Jr., "Interview With Anglican Bishop N. T. Wright of Durham, England," *National Catholic Reporter*, May 21, 2004, http://tinyurl.com/6nezu5 (accessed January 20, 2014); for a rather weak attempt to rebut this, see Richard Fellows, "N. T. Wright's Blunder on Homosexuality," *Paul and Co-Workers* (blog), November 29, 2011, http://tinyurl.com/lvklsjw (accessed January 20, 2014). I say the attempt to rebut Wright is rather weak because: (1) it assumes that Paul would have been totally ignorant of the classical Greek literature, (2) it assumes that because Wright is not an expert on homosexuality that his use of the historical sources as a first-class ancient historian is to be rejected, and (3) it assumes that there were no committed same-sex relationships that Paul would have observed in Rome or Corinth (actually, he wrote Romans prior to having gone to Rome as an apostle), which means there was no such thing as homosexuality back then. (Do gay activists want to argue this?) To quote Professor Wright directly, "As a classicist, I have to say that when I read Plato's *Symposium*, or when I read the accounts from the early Roman empire of the practice of homosexuality, then it seems to me they knew just as much about it as we do. In particular, a point which is often missed, they knew a great deal about what people

today would regard as longer-term, reasonably stable relations between two people of the same gender.

"This is not a modern invention, it's already there in Plato. The idea that in Paul's today it was always a matter of exploitation of younger men by older men or whatever...of course there was plenty of that then, as there is today, but it was by no means the only thing. They knew about the whole range of options there.

"Indeed, in the modern world that isn't an invention of the 20th century either. If you read the recent literature, for example Graham Robb's book *Strangers*, which is an account of homosexual love in the 19th century, it offers an interesting account of all kinds of different expressions and awarenesses and phenomena. I think we have been conned by Michel Foucault into thinking that this is all a new phenomena."

3. In particular, Boswell's book *Same-Sex Unions in Premodern Europe* (New York: Vintage, 1995), which was widely panned after its initial enthusiastic reception.

4. For relevant reviews, see chapter 7, note 6 above.

5. Pim Pronk, *Against Nature? Types of Moral Arguments Regarding Homosexuality* (Grand Rapids, MI: Eerdmans, 1993), 279. Pronk, however, rejects the plain verdict of the Scriptures based on "hermeneutics." For a critical review of Pronk's book by Gene B. Chase of Messiah College, see http://home.messiah.edu/~chase/talk2/pronk.htm (accessed January 20, 2014).

6. Bernadette Brooten, *Love Between Women: Early Christian Reponses to Female Homoeroticism* (Chicago: University of Chicago Press, 1996), 244.

7. "Louis Crompton (1925-2009)," *Scarlet*, June 27, 2009, http://scarlet.unl .edu/?p=2230 (accessed January 20, 2014).

8. Louis Crompton, *Homosexuality and Civilization* (Cambridge, MA: Harvard University Press, 2003), 114.

9. Walter Wink, "To Hell With Gays?" *Christian Century Review* 119, no. 13 (June 5, 2002), 33.

10. Via and Gagnon, *Homosexuality and the Bible: Two Views*, 93.

11. Eugene Rice, in *GLBTQ*, s.v. "St. Paul (d. *ca* 66 C.E.)," http://tinyurl.com/ k22uspy (accessed January 20, 2014).

12. Ibid.

13. Ibid.

14. Ibid.

15. Ibid.

16. With regard to Romans 1, she claimed that what Paul wrote there was based on an attempt to "maintain a gender asymmetry based on female subordination. I hope that churches today, being apprised of the history that I have presented, will no longer teach Rom. 1:26f. as authoritative." (*Love Between Women*, 302.)

17. Rice, in *GLBTQ*, s.v. "St. Paul (d. *ca* 66 C.E.)."

18. Ibid. This would also suggest that anal intercourse between heterosexual couples would be wrong, although not as plainly proscribed as male homosexuality.

19. See *Study New Testament for Lesbians, Gays, Bi, and Transgender*, 262–264.

20. Ibid., 262.

21. Ibid., 263.

22. For a serious "gay Christian" attempt to challenge the traditional understanding of these two Greek words, see Brentlinger, *Gay Christian 101*, 306–356; from a gay scholar, see Dale B. Martin, *Sex and the Single Savior: Gender and Sexuality in Biblical Interpretation* (Louisville, KY: Westminster John Knox Press, 2006), 37–50; for Robert Gagnon's refutation of Martin, see *The Bible and Homosexual Practice*, 498 (index), and note 323: "Given the attested occurrences, Martin's unwillingness to admit that *arsenokoitēs* is limited to homosexual behavior is surprising." For Gagnon's detailed discussion of these Greek words, see ibid., 306–339 (with discussion of *arsenokoitēs* in 1 Timothy 1:10 as well); for extensive, scholarly debate, see Robert A. J. Gagnon, "'The Dogs Bark but the Caravan Moves On': My Response to Jean-Fabrice Nardelli's Critique of *The Bible and Homosexual Practice*," July 26, 2012, http://tinyurl.com/kn6n6yt (accessed January 20, 2014); and Jean-Fabrice Nardelli, "Rejoinder to Gagnon's 'The Dogs Bark but the Caravan Moves On, Part 1,'" http://tinyurl.com/ktxtqy3 (accessed January 20, 2014). According to New Testament scholar Anthony C. Thiselton, "We remain on speculative ground *until we consider the two terms in relation to each other*..." (*The First Epistle to the Corinthians: A Commentary on the Greek Text*, New International Commentary on the Greek New Testament [Grand Rapids, MI: Eerdmans, 2000], 449, emphasis his.

23. See *Study New Testament for Lesbians, Gays, Bi, and Transgender*, 262.

24. Guest, Goss, West, and Bohache, *Queer Bible Commentary*, 614.

25. Paul uses the word *arsenokoitēs* again in 1 Timothy 1:10, where he writes, "Now we know that the law is good, if one uses it lawfully, understanding this, that the law is not laid down for the just but for the lawless and

disobedient, for the ungodly and sinners, for the unholy and profane, for those who strike their fathers and mothers, for murderers, the sexually immoral, men who practice homosexuality [*arsenokoitēs*], enslavers, liars, perjurers, and whatever else is contrary to sound doctrine, in accordance with the gospel of the glory of the blessed God with which I have been entrusted" (1 Tim. 1:8–11). As Gagnon notes in *The Bible and Homosexual Practice*, 334–335, "the order of the last half of the list of vices corresponds to the order of the Decalogue. 'Killers of fathers and killers of mothers' corresponds to the fifth commandment to honor one's parents; 'murderers' corresponds to the sixth commandment; 'the sexually immoral, males who take others males to bed' corresponds to the seventh commandment against adultery; 'kidnappers' corresponds to the eighth commandment against stealing [interpreted in the ancient world to include kidnapping]; and 'liars' and 'perjurers' corresponds to the ninth commandment against bearing false witness."

26. Thiselton, *The First Epistle to the Corinthians*, 452.

27. Ibid.

28. Amy Orr-Ewing, *Is the Bible Intolerant? Sexist? Oppressive? Homophobic? Outdated? Irrelevant?* (Downers Grove, IL: InterVarsity, 2005), 118–119, emphasis added. According to Professor Jeffrey Siker, "What Paul said about same-sex relations and why he said it is relatively clear, especially given his first-century Jewish values. What Paul would have made of modern expressions of homosexuality, and particularly of notions of naturally occurring sexual orientations, is merely speculation." (Jeffrey S. Siker, ed., *Homosexuality and Religion: An Encyclopedia* [N.p.: Greenwood, 2006], 173.) To the contrary, everything we have seen in this chapter indicates that we would know exactly what Paul would have to say about homosexuality today.

29. Eva Cantarella, *Bisexuality in the Ancient World*, second ed. (New Haven: Yale University Press, 2002), 211.

30. Ibid., 217, but also pointing out some contrasts with Greek sexuality. Note also that although the Stoics were known for their opposition to homosexuality based on the principles of nature, it has been claimed that the "Stoic founder Zeno…was known to chase his [male] students and encourage androgynous dress" (Diana M. Swancutt, cited in Guest, Goss, West, and Bohache, *Queer Bible Commentary*, 597).

31. Timothy Bradshaw, ed., *The Way Forward? Christian Voices on Homosexuality and the Church* (Grand Rapids, MI: Eerdmans, 2004), 156.

32. Ibid., 167–168. Bradshaw's book was even endorsed by the openly gay Harvard professor and minister Peter J. Gomes, which indicates the gracious nature of the book's tone. Professor Gagnon has some very incisive criticism for those who attempt to limit the meaning of *arsenokoitai*: "There is no chance that the very same Paul who was concerned about blurring the distinctions between the sexes even over such relatively minor matters as hair coverings in 1 Cor 11:2–16 could have limited the meaning of *arsenokoitai* in the same letter to only specific types of same-sex intercourse.

"If in Paul's view inappropriate hairstyles and head coverings were a source of shame because they compromised the sexual differences between men and women, how much more would a man taking another male to bed be a shameful act (Rom 1:27), laying with another male 'as though lying with a woman'? Paul did not make head coverings an issue vital for inclusion in God's kingdom, but he did put same-sex intercourse on that level. Suppose the Corinthians had written back then:

"'Paul, we have a brother in our church who is having sex with another man. But that other man does not put on makeup or heavy perfume, wear women's clothing, braid his hair, or otherwise try to look like a woman. And the other male is an adult. The two men really do love each other and are committed to spending the rest of their lives together. Neither is involved in idolatrous cults of prostitution. When you mentioned that *arsenokoitai* would be excluded from the coming kingdom of God, you were not including somebody like this man, were you?'

"Given the context of 1 Cor 5–6 and 11, can anyone seriously propose that Paul would have said, 'That's right, such a man would not be an *arsenokoitēs*'"? (Gagnon, *The Bible and Homosexual Practice*, 328–329.) See also Peet H. Botha, *The Empty Testament: Four Arguments Against Gay Theology* (Victoria, BC, Canada: Trafford Publishing, 2008), 174–188.

33. Matthew Vines, "The Gay Debate: The Bible and Homosexuality," http://www.matthewvines.com/transcript (accessed January 20, 2014).

34. Again, this is the most common explanation among gay theologians.

35. To be clear, there are godly people who are sick, but sickness, in and of itself, is never viewed as a positive condition in the Bible.

36. James D. G. Dunn, *Romans 1–8*, Word Biblical Commentary (Dallas: Word, 1998), 64.

37. See note 2 for this chapter. And, contrary to gay talking points, no one is born gay.

38. Dunn, *Romans 1–8*, 64.
39. CoalitionofConscience.org, "A Christian Response to Homosexuality: Knox/Brown Debate," http://tinyurl.com/og7xvr3 (accessed January 20, 2014).
40. Ibid.
41. If you say, "What about a heterosexual couple who can't have a baby?", you actually illustrate my point, since this is not something to be celebrated. Rather, this means that something is wrong, that something in either the husband or the wife is not functioning properly, and therefore extraordinary measures might need to be taken for the couple to have a baby. In contrast, gays and lesbians insist there is nothing wrong with them, that God made them this way, and that their homosexuality is something to be celebrated.
42. For refutation of the idea that Galatians 3:28 can somehow also mean "there is no homosexual or heterosexual," see chapter 3, note 36.
43. For example, he uses the common word for "man, husband" *anēr, andros*, fifty-nine times in his letters in contrast with *arsen*, male, which he uses just *four times*, three in Romans 1:27 and once in Galatians 3:28, as noted. This is highly significant.
44. Colin Brown, ed., *New International Dictionary of New Testament Theology* (Grand Rapids, MI: Zondervan, 1986), 3:660; again, the point is not that this only happened in the context of idolatry. Rather, the point is that these are consequences of human sin against God. For more on *para physin* in Romans 11 and 1 Corinthians 11, see Gagnon, *The Bible and Homosexual Practice*, 254–270.
45. Gagnon, *The Bible and Homosexual Practice*, 290–291.
46. Vines, in "The Gay Debate: The Bible and Homosexuality," referring to the Greek word *arsenokoitēs* in 1 Corinthians 6:9, claims that, "There is no contextual support for linking this term to loving, faithful relationships." But, as noted, even if true (which could easily be disputed; who is to say that Paul did *not* include "loving, faithful relationships" here?), it is completely irrelevant, since any sexual acts between men are proscribed by God, here through Paul.
47. Cited in Dunn, *Romans 1–8*, 64.
48. Wolfhart Pannenberg, "Should We Support Gay Marriage? NO," http://tinyurl.com/lwbyrhv (accessed January 20, 2014). One "gay Christian" went so far as to claim that Paul actually sanctioned same-sex marriage in 1 Corinthians 7, a claim so ludicrous that he would have done

better arguing that Paul sanctioned marriage between humans and aliens. Remarkably—really, outrageously—he bases his ideas on 1 Corinthians 7. Go ahead and read it ten times through in the Greek or in any translation, and you will never find what this "gay Christian" is arguing for in the text. That's why I only address this in an endnote, and even at that, it's giving the idea too much credit.

49. See the studies cited below, note 64; cf. also note 59, below.

50. Brown, *A Queer Thing Happened to America*, 380–381.

51. Cf., Steven E. Rhoads, *Taking Sex Differences Seriously* (San Francisco: Encounter Books, 2004), especially 45–78 (the chapter is titled "Men Don't Get Headaches"). As noted by Lisa M. Diamond, *Sexual Fluidity: Understanding Women's Love and Desire* (Cambridge, MA: Harvard University Press, 2009), 45, "both gay and heterosexual men place more emphasis on sex in relationships than do lesbian and heterosexual women (who, comparatively, place more emphasis on emotional intimacy)," with reference to L. A. Peplau and L. R. Spalding, "The Close Relationships of Lesbians, Gay Men, and Bisexuals," in C. Hendrick and S. S. Hendrick, eds., *Close Relationships: A Sourcebook* (Thousand Oaks, CA: Sage, 2000), 111–123.

52. See again Rhoads, *Taking Sex Differences Seriously*, 45–78.

53. This is part of his point that marriage "*Civilizes men* and focuses them on productive pursuits. Unmarried men cause society much more trouble than married men." See Frank Turek, *Correct, Not Politically Correct: How Same-Sex Marriage Hurts Everyone* (Charlotte, NC: Cross Examined, 2008), 18, emphasis his.

54. See Jesse Monteagudo, "Much Ado About Dan Savage," *Gay Today*, http://tinyurl.com/lmwa5wz (accessed January 20, 2014).

55. Michael Bronski, *The Pleasure Principle: Sex, Backlash, and the Struggle for Gay Freedom* (New York: St. Martins Press, 1998), 9. One colleague who reviewed the manuscript of the book added here: "Many would also argue that female and male sexuality differ in such profound ways that they each have a tempering effect on the other. And so, in broad terms, since males tend to be more physically based in terms of their sexuality while females tend to be more emotionally based, two males together would more likely be hyper-sexual while two females would more likely be hyper-emotional. Males and females, however, gel in such a way as to create a sexual balance between the partners. Of course, it isn't always perfect, nor does it always

work out like that, but generally speaking, male-female couples achieve this balance to a workable degree."

56. Cited in Jeffrey Satinover, *Homosexuality and the Politics of Truth* (Grand Rapids, MI: Baker, 1996), 55.

57. Paul Van de Ven, Pamela Rodden, June Crawford, and Susan Kippax, "A Comparative Demographic and Sexual Profile of Older Homosexually Active Men," *Journal of Sex Research* 34, no. 4 (1997): 349–360, as referenced in Robert Gagnon, "Immoralism, Homosexual Unhealth, and Scripture. A Response to Peterson and Hedlund's 'Heterosexism, Homosexual Health, and the Church'; Part II: Science: Causation and Psychopathology, Promiscuity, Pedophilia, and Sexually Transmitted Disease," http://tinyurl.com/n82m8a3 (accessed January 20, 2014).

58. See Robert T. Michael, John H. Gagnon, Edward O. Laumann, and Gina Kolata, *Sex in America: A Definitive Survey* (Boston: Little, Brown & Company, 1994).

59. Satinover, *Homosexuality and the Politics of Truth*, 55. For a critique of the use of this study (and other, older studies) by a gay watchdog group, see Jim Burroway, "The FRC's Briefs Are Showing," December 4, 2006, http://tinyurl.com/nah3z8t (accessed January 20, 2014). After treating several hundred homosexual clients, and with reference to this same McWhirter and Mattison study, Dutch psychologist Dr. Gerard van den Aardweg opined that: "Homosexual restlessness cannot be appeased, much less so by having one partner, because these persons are propelled by an insatiable opining for the unattainable fantasy figure. Essentially, the homosexual is a yearning child, not a satisfied one.

"The term *neurotic* describes such relationships well. It suggests the ego-centeredness of the relationship; the attention seeking, the continuous tensions, generally stemming from the recurrent complaint, 'You don't love me'; the jealousy, which so often suspects, 'He (she) is more interested in someone else.' *Neurotic*, in short, suggests all kinds of dramas and childish conflicts as well as the basic disinterestedness in the partner, notwithstanding the shallow pretensions of 'love.' Nowhere is there more self-deception in the homosexual than in his representation of himself as a lover. One partner is important to the other only insofar as he satisfies that other's needs. Real, unselfish love for a desired partner would, in fact, end up destroying homosexual 'love'! Homosexual 'unions' are clinging relationships of two essentially self-absorbed 'poor me's.'" See Gerard J. M. van den Aardweg, *The Battle for Normality: A Guide for (Self) Therapy for Homosexuality* (San Francisco: Ignatius Press, 1997), 62–63.

I'm aware, of course, that some will affirm these comments as accurate while others will read them with outrage, as representing the height of offensiveness. I am simply citing the perspective of one psychologist, just as I cited the perspectives of many gay-affirming psychologists throughout *A Queer Thing Happened to America*, from which this material has been adapted. Of related interest is the comment of Kenneth Lewes in the *Archives of Sexual Behavior* 31 (2002): 380–383, reviewing Dr. Jack Drescher's volume *Psychoanalytic Therapy and the Gay Man* (New York: Routledge, 2001), in which Lewes notes that Drescher does not address issues such as gay clients' "amazing search for sexual variety and frequency, the importance to them of fantasy and sado-masochistic scenarios, the abuse of drugs to heighten sexual experience, their apparently adolescent narcissistic physical display.... Therapists working with gay men hear about these behaviors frequently" (383), cited in Linda Ames Nicolosi, "Sexual Variety and Frequency, S&M Are Part of What Makes Gay Orientation 'Distinctive and Valuable,' Says Psychologist," NARTH.org, http://www.narth.org/docs/promiscuity.html (accessed January 20, 2014). Note that both Lewes and Drescher are openly gay as well as advocates for gay issues.

60. Cf. Gagnon, *The Bible and Homosexual Practice*, 453-460, and see subsequent endnotes in this chapter.

61. Ryan Lee, "Gay Couples Likely to Try Non-Monogamy, Study Shows: Separate Research Shows Lack of 'Gay-Boy Talk' Hampers Safe-Sex," *Washington Blade*, August 22, 2003, http://tinyurl.com/paywrzr (accessed January 20, 2014). Note the comments from a man named Paul who e-mailed our organization on May 6, 2009: "I live in the UK and became aware of Dr. Brown's ministry through the Internet. I lived a 'gay lifestyle' for years. I was an evangelical Christian who left the church and gave in to my desires and pursued a life of wild sexual abandon and with multiple failed relationships. Sadly liberal Christians encouraged me to 'accept myself,' which further encouraged me to sin....*I have never met a monogomous [sic] homosexual couple who have been together beyond the 'first stages of romantic and sexual attraction.' The relationships that last have accommodations that include promiscuity of some sort*" (emphasis added).

62. As related by gay psychotherapist Joe Kort, "Monogamous Ever After?", JoeKort.com, 2004, http://www.joekort.com/articles33.htm (accessed January 20, 2014). Kort seeks to apply the same principles of redefined

monogamy to both homosexual and heterosexual couples. For a comparison of studies confirming this trend with studies claiming greater sexual faithfulness among gay couples, see Harold Miller, "Making Sense (Trying to!) of Varying Statistics on Gay Monogamy," http://tinyurl.com/n4mb8eq (accessed January 20, 2014).

63. Mark Oppenheimer, "Married, With Infidelities," *New York Times Magazine*, June 30, 2011, http://tinyurl.com/dy8wdso (accessed January 20, 2014); and Dan Savage, "Watch: Dan Savage Explains the Pros and Cons of a 'Monogamish' Relationship," Queerty.com, http://tinyurl.com/p3uneeb (accessed January 20, 2014).

64. C. H. Mercer, G. J. Hart, A. M. Johnson, and J. A. Cassell, "Behaviourally Bisexual Men as a Bridge Population for HIV and Sexually Transmitted Infections? Evidence From a National Probability Study," *International Journal of STD and AIDS* 20, no. 2 (February 2009): 87–94, as referenced in James E. Phelan, Neil Whitehead, and Philip M. Sutton, "What Research Shows: NARTH's Response to the APA Claims on Homosexuality," *Journal of Human Sexuality*, vol. 1 (2009): http://tinyurl.com/kfpcgaa (accessed January 20, 2014). Whitehead's simplified summary statement is that, "Both gays and lesbians have 3–4 times as many partners as heterosexuals (comparison of medians)" (N. E. Whitehead, "Common Misconceptions About Homosexuality," http://tinyurl.com/m7hzwjp (accessed January 20, 2014). Cf. D. P. Schmitt, "Sexual Strategies Across Sexual Orientations: How Personality Traits and Culture Relate to Sociosexuality Among Gays, Lesbians, Bisexuals, and Heterosexuals," *Journal of Psychology and Human Sexuality* 18 (2007), 183–214, (with "sociosexuality" being a code-word for promiscuity). More broadly, see A. Dean Byrd, "Sexual Addiction: A Psycho-Physiological Model for Addressing Obsessive-Compulsive Behaviors," http://www.narth.org/docs/coll-byrd.html (accessed January 20, 2014).

65. Centers for Disease Control and Prevention, "HIV Surveillance in Adolescents and Young Adults," http://tinyurl.com/kkszo2s (accessed January 20, 2014); and Peter LaBarbera, "CDC: 94 to 95 Percent of HIV Cases Among Boys and Young Men Linked to Homosexual Sex," Americans for Truth About Homosexuality, http://tinyurl.com/mpqm7rb (accessed January 20, 2014).

66. And from a design perspective, it is equally clear that God didn't design women to be with women.

67. For just one example, note that there is a potential decrease in breast cancer for women who had babies and nursed them; see "Health Benefits of Pregnancy and Motherhood," slide 3, WhattoExpect.com, http://tinyurl.com/kx95vcv (accessed January 20, 2014).

68. Michael S. Piazza, *Holy Homosexuals: The Truth About Being Gay or Lesbian and Christian* (Dallas: Sources of Hope Publishing, 1997).

69. Joe Dallas, *The Gay Gospel* (Eugene, OR: Harvest House Publishers, 2007), explains how terrified the homosexual community was when AIDS broke out, lamenting the fact that, rather than reaching out with mercy to AIDS sufferers, many Christians pointed to the epidemic as evidence of divine judgment. While it is true that immoral behavior has a natural consequence of various health risks, in this case leading to AIDS, that is different from pronouncing it a divinely sent gay plague.

70. See, e.g., "HIV & AIDS in Uganda," Avert.org, http://www.avert.org/hiv-aids-uganda.htm (accessed January 20, 2014). Note: this is *not* written from a conservative Christian perspective.

71. Notice how Dr. David Reuben, in the days before political correctness took over some scientific discussion, described anal sex in his 1969 book, *Everything You Wanted to Know About Sex but Were Afraid to Ask* (New York: David McKay, 1969), 164–169.

72. Dave Barnhart, a United Methodist church planter, offered what he called "A Scandalous Rhetorical Reading of Romans 1 and 2," and while he makes some good points about judgmentalism (see chapter 2), the only thing scandalous about his paraphrase is how deeply it misconstrues Paul's words in Romans 1:26–27. See Dave Barnhart, "A Scandalous Rhetorical Reading of Romans 1 and 2," *RMNBlog* (blog), July 20, 2013, http://tinyurl.com/kq7f66s (accessed January 20, 2014).

73. See Michael Brown, "The Gospel of Martyrdom vs. the Gospel of Success," CharismaNews.com, October 21, 2013, http://tinyurl.com/kunpr96 (accessed January 20, 2014).

74. Thiselton, *The First Epistle to the Corinthians*, 452. He continues, "As writers as different from each other in stance as Kenneth Bailey [a conservative Christian scholar] and Dale Martin [a gay New Testament scholar] agree, 1 Corinthians strongly affirms that *the body* and its practices occupies a place of paramount importance for those who are united with Christ."

CHAPTER 9
EVERYTHING REPRODUCES AFTER ITS OWN KIND

1. See Galatians 6:7–8.
2. See Job 4:8; Proverbs 11:18; 22:8; Hosea 8:7; 10:12–13; Matthew 13:24–30, 37–39; Jacob (James) 3:18.
3. Brown, *A Queer Thing Happened to America*, 343.
4. Ibid., 346.
5. See ibid., 343–347.
6. See ibid., 404–407 for references.
7. *Creating Change: The National Conference on LGBT Equality 2010* program, http://www.thetaskforce.org/downloads/creating_change/cc10/cc10_program_book.pdf, 1 (accessed September, 19, 2010). This link is no longer available online.
8. I refer to the 2010 conference because I downloaded the program while working on *A Queer Thing Happened to America* and had the data at hand. But the program was in no way atypical for these conferences.
9. *Creating Change: The National Conference on LGBT Equality 2010* program, 9.
10. Ibid., 17.
11. Ibid.
12. Ibid., 28.
13. Ibid., 47.
14. Ibid., 88. The 2009 Leather Leadership Award was given to Graylin Thornton who, according to Americans for Truth About Homosexuality, was a purveyor of gay porn videos. See Peter LaBarbera, "National Gay and Lesbian Task Force Talks of 'Moral Leadership' while Honoring Homosexual S&M Pornographer," Americans for Truth About Homosexuality, http://tinyurl.com/odxj44c (accessed January 20, 2014).
15. *Creating Change: The National Conference on LGBT Equality 2010* program, 25.
16. According to psychologist Gerard J. M. van den Aardweg, "The life of most committed homosexuals revolves around one thing: homosexuality. In their self-centeredness they are often unaware of the suffering they inflict on their environment." See his review of Dawn Stefanowicz's *Out from Under* in the *Empirical Journal of Same-Sex Sexual Behavior*, 1 (2007): 3.
17. Guest, Goss, West, and Bohache, *The Queer Bible Commentary*, 528.
18. Drinkwater, Lesser, and Shneer, *Torah Queeries*, 137. Dr. Tamar Kamionkowski cites the first-century Jewish philosopher Philo in support of both

the priests being naked and their being taken up by God's passionate fire, adding, however, "Philo's reading can be expanded through a queer reading lens" (ibid., 136–137), which is necessary of course, since there was not the slightest hint of anything homoerotic in Philo's reading of the text. In fact, such an interpretation would have been utterly unthinkable to him.

19. See *A Queer Thing Happened to America*, 368–371.

20. "Patrick S. Cheng," http://www.patrickcheng.net/index.html (accessed January 20, 2014).

21. Sharon Groves, "From Sin to Amazing Grace," *HRC Blog* (blog), August 1, 2012, http://tinyurl.com/qdjqq9l (accessed January 20, 2014).

22. Ibid; Patrick S. Cheng, *From Sin to Amazing Grace: Discovering the Queer Christ* (New York: Seabury Books, 2012).

23. "Radical Love," http://www.patrickcheng.net/radical-love.html (accessed January 20, 2014).

24. Patrick S. Cheng, *Radical Love: An Introduction to Queer Theology* (New York: Seabury Books, 2011). Used by permission.

25. Ibid., 84.

26. Ibid., 102.

27. Ibid., 108.

28. Ibid.

29. Ibid., 109.

30. Praise from other religious scholars and theologians is even more effusive than the praise for his previous volume.

31. Cheng, *From Sin to Amazing Grace*, Kindle locations 1882–1888.

32. Ibid., Kindle locations 1888–1893.

33. Ibid., Kindle locations 1896–1900. Cheng continues (Kindle locations 1900–1903), "In sum, LGBT theologians have written about the Erotic Christ in terms of both power-as-relation as well as sexual desire. This arises out of the fact that Jesus Christ, as the Word made flesh, is the incarnational expression of God's deepest desires for us, particularly in a Christ-centered model of sin and grace."

34. Ibid., Kindle locations 2605–2606.

35. Ibid., Kindle locations 2825–2826.

36. See Jennings, *The Man Jesus Loved*, and also chapter 4 of this book.

37. See, e.g., Luke 21:8; 1 Corinthians 6:9; 15:33; Jacob (James) 1:22.

38. For more examples, see Brown, *A Queer Thing Happened to America*, 338–371.

39. Justin Tanis, "Freedom, Glorious Freedom?" http://tinyurl.com/n77wzky (accessed November 24, 2013).

40. "Sceneprofiles: Interview With Justin Tanis," http://tinyurl.com/ld82b7e (accessed November 24, 2013).

41. Ibid.

42. See Brown, *A Queer Thing Happened to America*, 293–296, also citing San Francisco Mayor Gavin Newsom's welcome to the Folsom Street Fair as an expression of the city's "diversity."

43. In Yuan, "*Torn*: Justin Lee; Reviewed by Christopher Yuan," an insightful review of Justin Lee's book *Torn*, cited in chapter 2, note 34, Christopher Yuan, himself formerly a practicing homosexual, writes, "*Torn* is an honest memoir of a Christian wrestling through issues of sexuality, but Lee's conclusions for how to live appear to be more anthropocentric than Christocentric." Of his own experience of becoming a follower of Jesus, Yuan writes, "I eventually realized I'd put great emphasis on 'being gay.' Now I needed to place my primary identity in Christ."

CHAPTER 10
BALANCING GRACE AND TRUTH

1. Michaelson, *God vs. Gay?*, 28.

2. Martin, *Sex and the Single Savior*, 49–50; used by permission. To see where Martin's position ultimately takes him, see "Gay Religion Professor Tells Audience to "Abandon the Bible," Gay Christian Movement Watch, http://tinyurl.com/lkf2odd (accessed January 21, 2014).

3. Comment posted on my Facebook page, August 24, 2013, http://tinyurl .com/otxggg7 (accessed January 21, 2014). See also the firsthand testimony of ex-gay leader Joe Dallas, himself a former "gay Christian," in *The Gay Gospel: How Pro-Gay Advocates Misread the Bible* (Eugene, OR: Harvest House, 2007).

4. Comment on my article "The Most Selfish Thing in the World," CharismaNews.com, July 23, 2013, http://tinyurl.com/p6dxdxj (accessed January 21, 2014).

5. "Adam," in communication with the author. Used with permission. "Adam" recommended the following articles in conjunction with his statements: Michael Hannon, "Against Heterosexuality," http://www.firstthings.com/ article/2014/03/against-heterosexuality-1 (accessed March 11, 2014); David Benkof, "The Phantom Gay Past," http://playfulwalrus.blogspot

.com.au/2013/03/david-benkof-on-phantom-gay-past.html (accessed March 11, 2014).

6. For some important reflections on the question of "gay identity," see Michael W. Hannon, "Sexual Disorientation: The Trouble With Talking About 'Gayness,'" FirstThings.com, http://tinyurl.com/p7et3jb (accessed January 21, 2014); Andrew M. Haines, "Understanding Gays: What's Fiction?", EthikaPolitika.org, October 15, 2013, http://tinyurl.com/psh9ofm (accessed January 21, 2014); and Andrew M. Haines, "Coming Out as X-Ray," EthikaPolitika.org, October 11, 2013, http://tinyurl.com/ppm bzgn (accessed January 21, 2014).

7. "Adam," in communication with the author.

8. NARTH.org, "Canadian Transgender Activists Urge Legal Protection for Gender Fluidity," September 19, 2005, http://www.narth.org/docs/fluidity .html (accessed January 21, 2014).

9. As related in Denise, "Life in the T Zone," *Life, Law, Gender* (blog), April 6, 2006, http://tinyurl.com/qfuda77 (accessed January 21, 2014).

10. Comment on Timothy Kincaid, "Youth in the Ex-Gay Crosshairs," *Ex-Gay Watch*, March 2, 2006, http://tinyurl.com/qypn87z (accessed January 21, 2014).

11. Some experience bisexuality over periods of time, meaning they are attracted to one sex at one time and another sex at another time, while for others it is both attractions at the same time, which is the particular point I was making. Why must all desires be satisfied? If one has homosexual and heterosexual attractions, why not say no to the homosexual attractions? Others have noted (especially women) that they fall in love with a person, not a gender, which again underscores that there are things we can say no to, regardless of our desires.

12. Martin, *Sex and the Single Savior*, 50.

13. According to the Genetic Sexual Attraction website (http://www.genetic sexualattraction.org/), GSA refers to "a phenomenon of familial bonding, that has been delayed until adulthood" (accessed January 21, 2014).

14. Falwell, "An Open Letter to Mel White."

15. Ibid., emphasis added.

16. White, *Religion Gone Bad*, 1, note *.

17. "Adam," in communication with the author.

18. Kris Vallotton Ministries Facebook page, https://www.facebook.com/ kvministries/posts/10151688318143741; the pastor, Kris Vallotton, is a

personal friend of mine, although we certainly have some theological differences. Used by permission.

19. Some have even accused them of putting *too much* emphasis on God's goodness to the exclusion of repentance and holiness. As one of their websites states, "God is in a good mood. He loves me all the time" ("Offering of Thanks #4," http://www.ibethel.org/offering-readings [accessed January 21, 2014]). For questions on this perspective, see Brown, *Hyper-Grace* (Lake Mary, FL: Charisma House, 2014), chapter 10.

20. Kris Vallotton Ministries Facebook page, emphasis added.

21. One of the best known of the twentieth-century would be the Catholic leader Henri J. M. Nouwen. For a representative work, see *The Wounded Healer: Ministry in Contemporary Society* (New York: Doubleday, 1979).

22. For recent books advocating "gay Christianity," see the bibliography.

23. Comment on my article "Sharing God's Goodness Is Never a Failure." I'm not sure why he referred to Andrew Marin as my friend, since we've never met nor had any personal interaction (although I have reached out to him to join me on my radio show or engage in dialogue, thus far without response); for my assessment of Marin's book, *Love Is an Orientation*, see chapter 4, note 15.

24. Troy D. Perry, *Don't Be Afraid Anymore: The Story of Reverend Troy Perry and the Metropolitan Community Churches* (New York: St. Martins Press, 1992), 2.

25. As I read Rev. Perry's book, I was also saddened to read about the sexual abuse he suffered at the hands of his stepfather's "brother," but, of course, he speaks of that in negative terms, since it was, in fact, abusive and forced. On the other hand, there's not the slightest hint offered that this could have played into his ongoing sexual development.

26. Perry, *Don't Be Afraid Anymore*, 14.

27. Ibid., 14–15.

28. Ibid., 20.

29. Ibid., 24–25. For Rabbi Steve Greenberg's journey into "gay Orthodox Judaism," see his book *Wrestling With God and Men*, and note how he simply describes his own coming out as a very religious, young Jewish man without any hint of the wrongness of his sexual acts (both outside of wedlock and with a man) on page 8 of his book. This was simply part of his journey of self-discovery. See also chapter 5, note 44.

30. As one of my colleagues rightly noted, "To think that philosophers and thinkers throughout the ages have, and still do, think long and hard,

writing pages and pages, tomes and whatnot, to answer this very question, and yet Troy Perry and the gay community have discovered it so easily, is ludicrous." Comment used with permission.

31. When I prepared myself to watch the 2011 DVD *Call Me Troy*, directed by Scott Bloom and celebrating Perry's life as a champion of gay rights, I expected to be moved emotionally by his courage and the nature of his struggle, despite my profound disagreements. Instead, as the story unfolded, especially of his sexual activity with gay men while married to his wife and the consequent shaping of his "theology," I said to myself, "This is a theology and denomination built on sexual desire."

32. See "Leatherfolk With Rev. Troy Perry," Gay Books Review, PFOX.org, http://pfox.org/Rev_Troy_Perry_leather_queen.html (accessed January 21, 2014). See also chapter 9 of this book.

33. IMDB.com, "Chariots of Fire (1981) Quotes," http://www.imdb.com/title/tt0082158/quotes (accessed January 21, 2014).

34. J. P. Moreland, "Why Happiness Isn't a Feeling," Boundless.org, December 16, 2004, http://tinyurl.com/mwca55m (accessed January 21, 2014).

35. Ibid.

36. Ibid.

37. Frank Houghton, *Amy Carmichael of Dohnavur: The Story of a Lover and Her Beloved* (Fort Washington, PA: Christian Literature Crusade, 1980). Viewed online at Google Books.

38. Sarah J. Rhea, *Life of Henry Martyn, Missionary to India and Persia, 1781 to 1812*, http://tinyurl.com/pndxqg5 (accessed January 21, 2014).